# the AMAZING SPIDER-MAN

## SHATTERED WEB

WRITER **NICK SPENCER**

**AMAZING SPIDER-MAN #56-57 & #60**

PENCILER **MARK BAGLEY**

INKERS **ANDREW HENNESSY** & **JOHN DELL** WITH **ANDY OWENS** (#57)

COLOR ARTIST **RACHELLE ROSENBERG** (#56-57 & #60) & **EDGAR DELGADO** (#56-57)

**AMAZING SPIDER-MAN #58-59**

PENCILER **MARCELO FERREIRA**

INKERS **WAYNE FAUCHER**

COLOR ARTIST **MORRY HOLLOWELL** WITH **ANDREW CROSSLEY** (#59)

LETTERER **VC's JOE CARAMAGNA**

COVER ART **MARK BAGELY** & **JOHN DELL** WITH **EDGAR DELGADO** (#56, #58), **MORRY HOLLOWELL** (#57) & **NATHAN FAIRBAIRN** (#59-60)

ASSISTANT EDITORS **LINDSEY COHICK**
EDITOR **NICK LOWE**

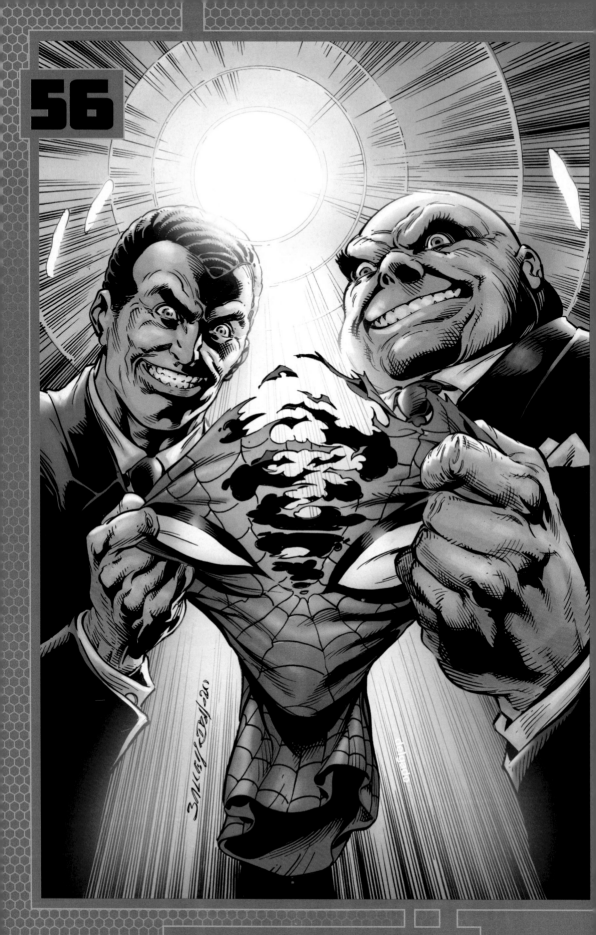

56

LAST REMAINS: POST-MORTEM PART 1

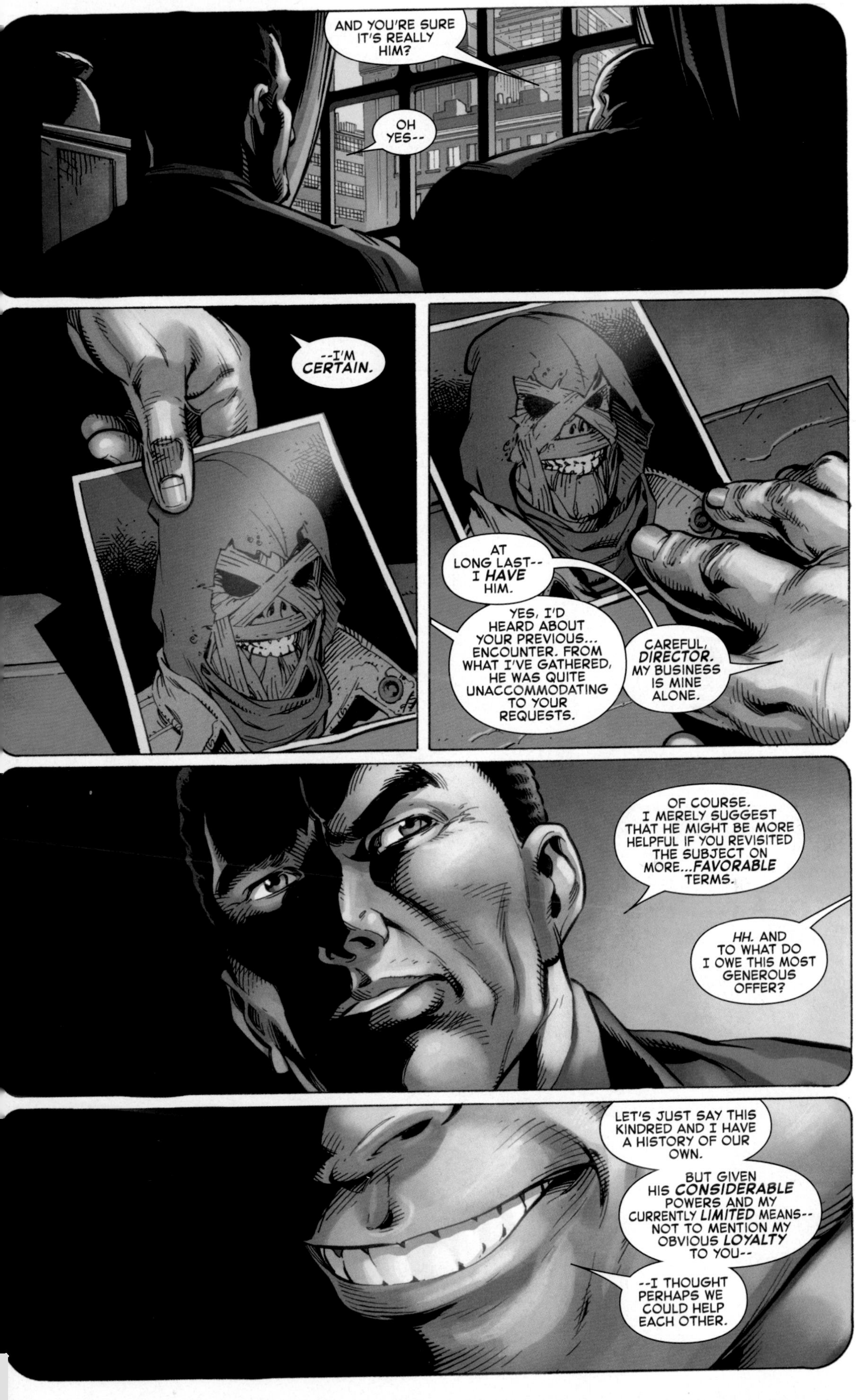
AND YOU'RE SURE IT'S REALLY HIM?
OH YES--
--I'M CERTAIN.
AT LONG LAST-- I HAVE HIM.
YES, I'D HEARD ABOUT YOUR PREVIOUS... ENCOUNTER. FROM WHAT I'VE GATHERED, HE WAS QUITE UNACCOMMODATING TO YOUR REQUESTS.
CAREFUL, DIRECTOR. MY BUSINESS IS MINE ALONE.
OF COURSE. I MERELY SUGGEST THAT HE MIGHT BE MORE HELPFUL IF YOU REVISITED THE SUBJECT ON MORE...FAVORABLE TERMS.
HH. AND TO WHAT DO I OWE THIS MOST GENEROUS OFFER?
LET'S JUST SAY THIS KINDRED AND I HAVE A HISTORY OF OUR OWN.
BUT GIVEN HIS CONSIDERABLE POWERS AND MY CURRENTLY LIMITED MEANS-- NOT TO MENTION MY OBVIOUS LOYALTY TO YOU--
--I THOUGHT PERHAPS WE COULD HELP EACH OTHER.

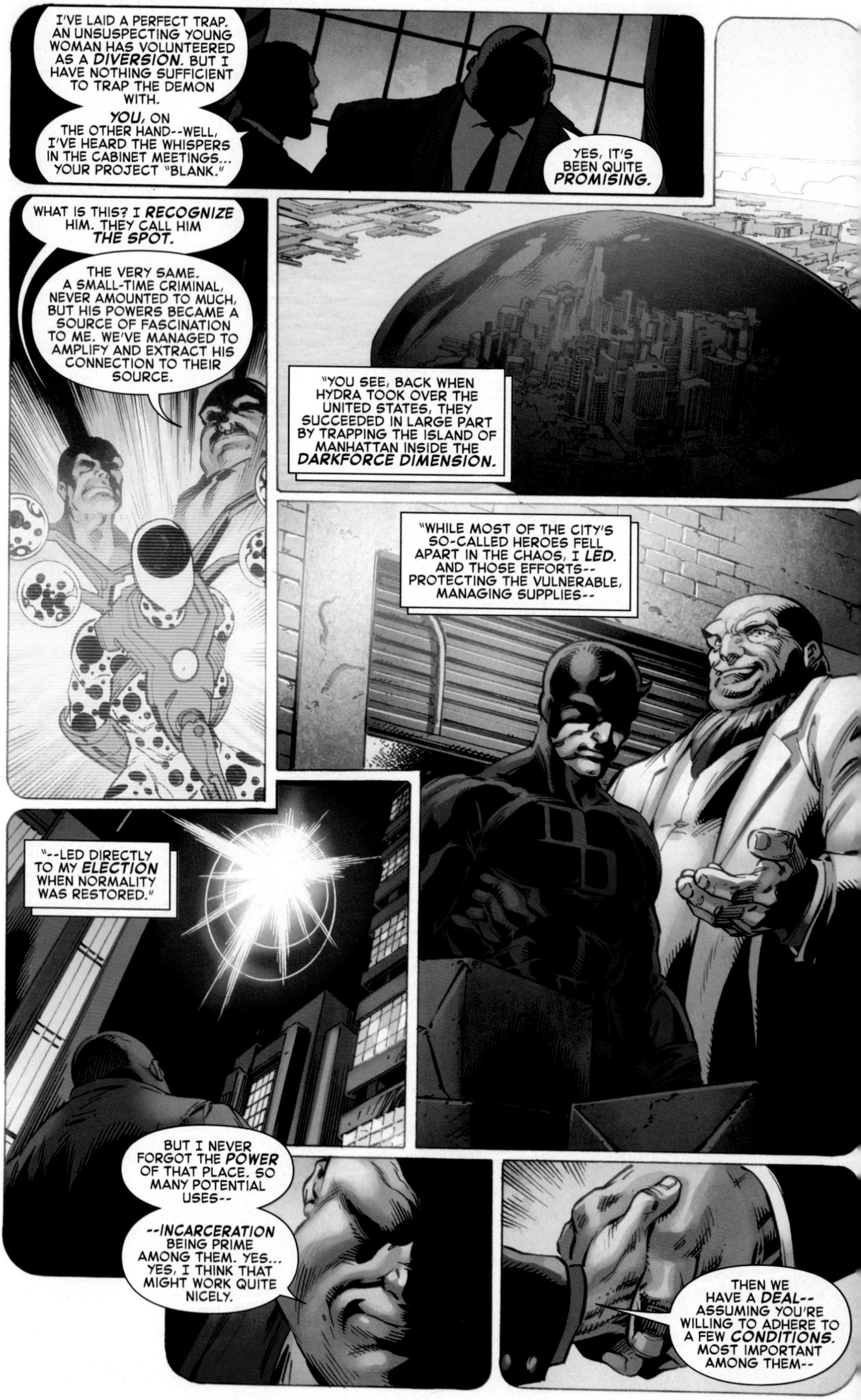

I'VE LAID A PERFECT TRAP. AN UNSUSPECTING YOUNG WOMAN HAS VOLUNTEERED AS A *DIVERSION.* BUT I HAVE NOTHING SUFFICIENT TO TRAP THE DEMON WITH.
*YOU,* ON THE OTHER HAND--WELL, I'VE HEARD THE WHISPERS IN THE CABINET MEETINGS... YOUR PROJECT "BLANK."
YES, IT'S BEEN QUITE *PROMISING.*
WHAT IS THIS? I *RECOGNIZE* HIM. THEY CALL HIM *THE SPOT.*
THE VERY SAME. A SMALL-TIME CRIMINAL, NEVER AMOUNTED TO MUCH, BUT HIS POWERS BECAME A SOURCE OF FASCINATION TO ME. WE'VE MANAGED TO AMPLIFY AND EXTRACT HIS CONNECTION TO THEIR SOURCE.
"YOU SEE, BACK WHEN HYDRA TOOK OVER THE UNITED STATES, THEY SUCCEEDED IN LARGE PART BY TRAPPING THE ISLAND OF MANHATTAN INSIDE THE *DARKFORCE DIMENSION.*
"WHILE MOST OF THE CITY'S SO-CALLED HEROES FELL APART IN THE CHAOS, I *LED.* AND THOSE EFFORTS--PROTECTING THE VULNERABLE, MANAGING SUPPLIES--
"--LED DIRECTLY TO MY *ELECTION* WHEN NORMALITY WAS RESTORED."
BUT I NEVER FORGOT THE *POWER* OF THAT PLACE. SO MANY POTENTIAL USES--
--*INCARCERATION* BEING PRIME AMONG THEM. YES... YES, I THINK THAT MIGHT WORK QUITE NICELY.
THEN WE HAVE A *DEAL*--ASSUMING YOU'RE WILLING TO ADHERE TO A FEW *CONDITIONS.* MOST IMPORTANT AMONG THEM--

"--I GET HIM *FIRST*."

NOW, FISK-- *NOW!*

BEGIN.

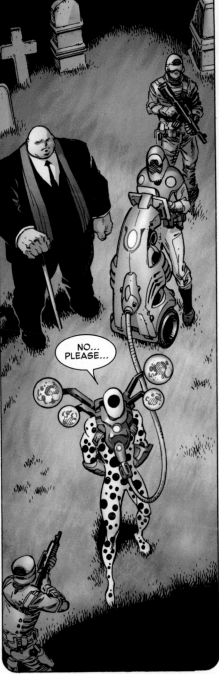

NO... PLEASE...

PLEASE... I DON'T WANT TO DO THIS!

ACTIVATE

ACTIVATING.

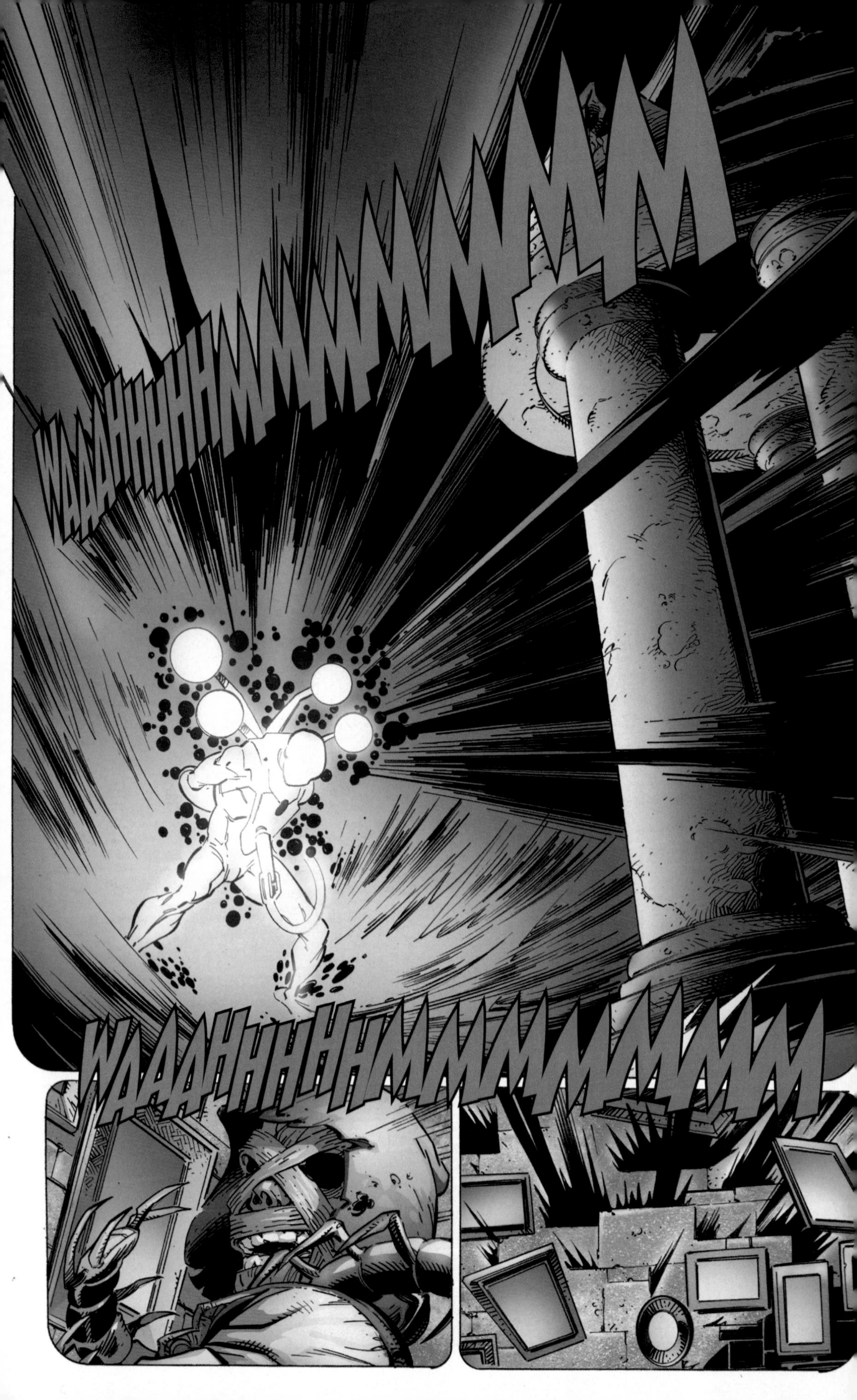
WAAAHHHHHMMMMMMMMMMM
WAAAHHHHHHMMMMMMMMMMM

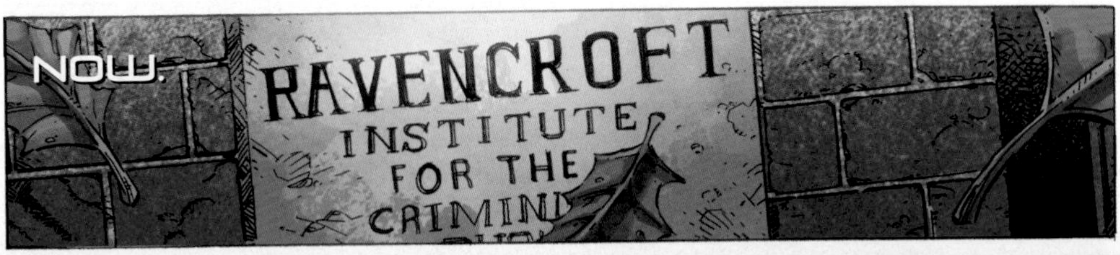
NOW.
RAVENCROFT
INSTITUTE
FOR THE
CRIMIN

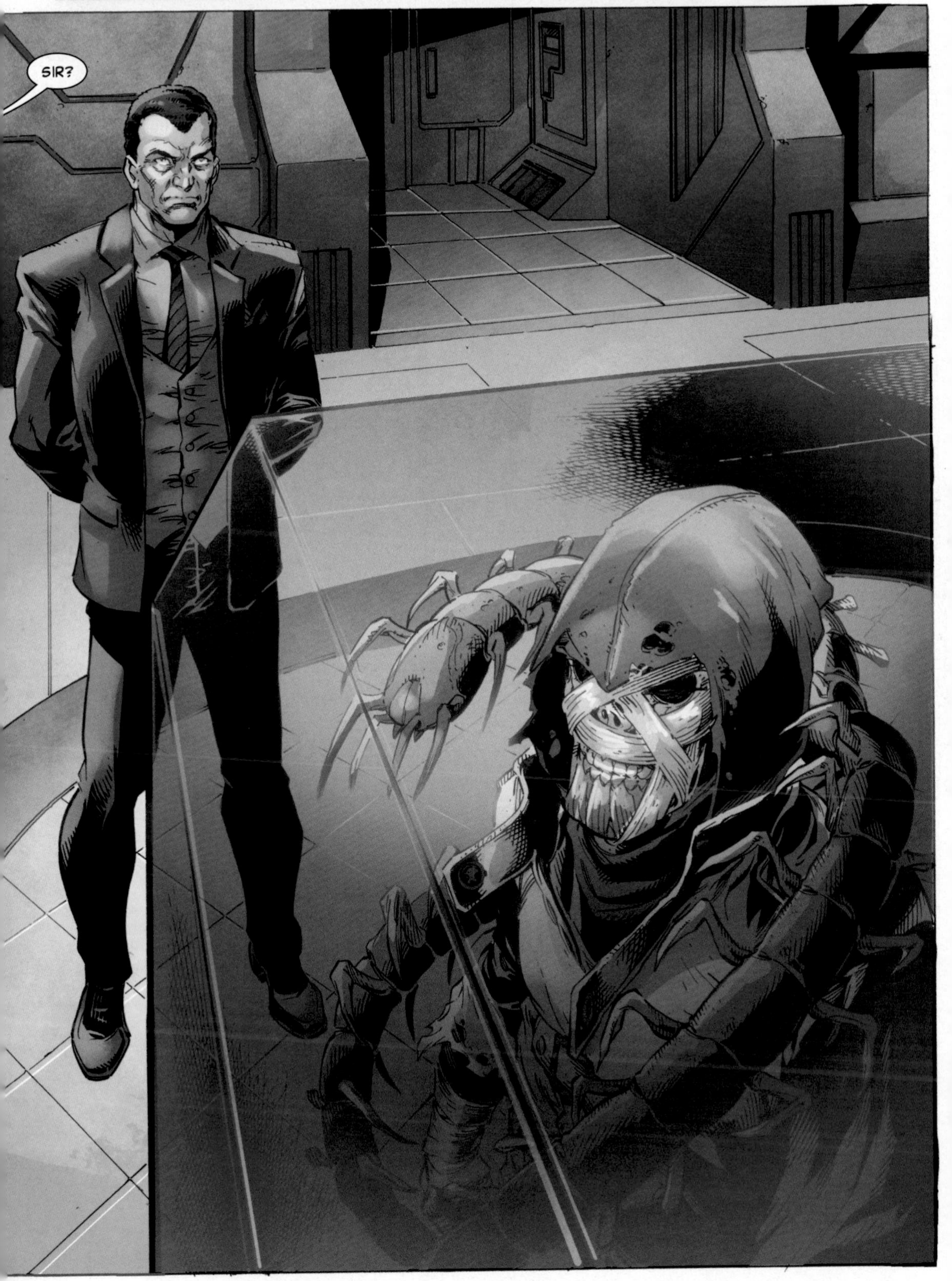
SIR?

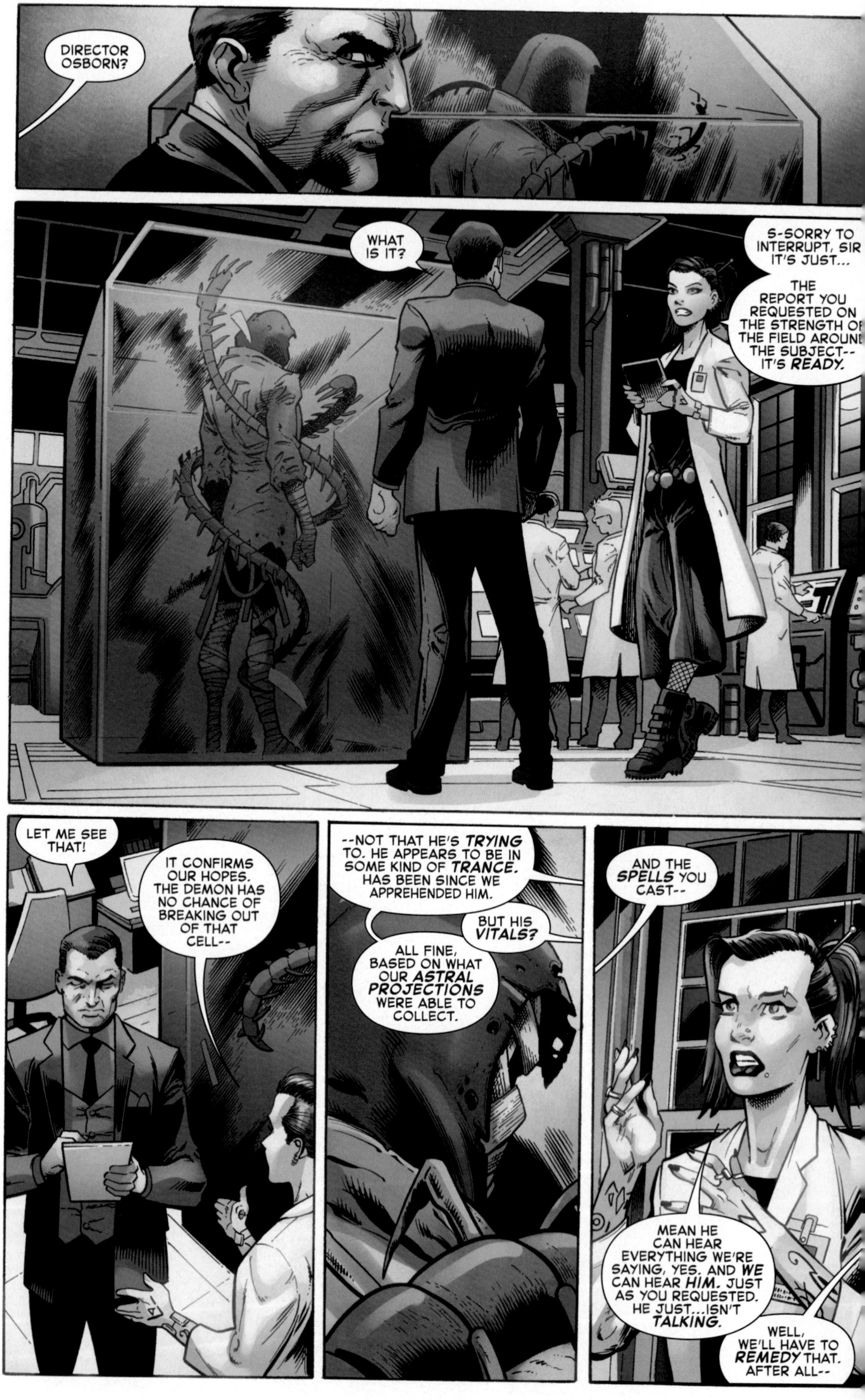
DIRECTOR OSBORN?
WHAT IS IT?
S-SORRY TO INTERRUPT, SIR IT'S JUST...
THE REPORT YOU REQUESTED ON THE STRENGTH OF THE FIELD AROUND THE SUBJECT-- IT'S READY.
LET ME SEE THAT!
IT CONFIRMS OUR HOPES. THE DEMON HAS NO CHANCE OF BREAKING OUT OF THAT CELL--
--NOT THAT HE'S TRYING TO. HE APPEARS TO BE IN SOME KIND OF TRANCE. HAS BEEN SINCE WE APPREHENDED HIM.
BUT HIS VITALS?
ALL FINE, BASED ON WHAT OUR ASTRAL PROJECTIONS WERE ABLE TO COLLECT.
AND THE SPELLS YOU CAST--
MEAN HE CAN HEAR EVERYTHING WE'RE SAYING, YES. AND WE CAN HEAR HIM. JUST AS YOU REQUESTED. HE JUST...ISN'T TALKING.
WELL, WE'LL HAVE TO REMEDY THAT. AFTER ALL--

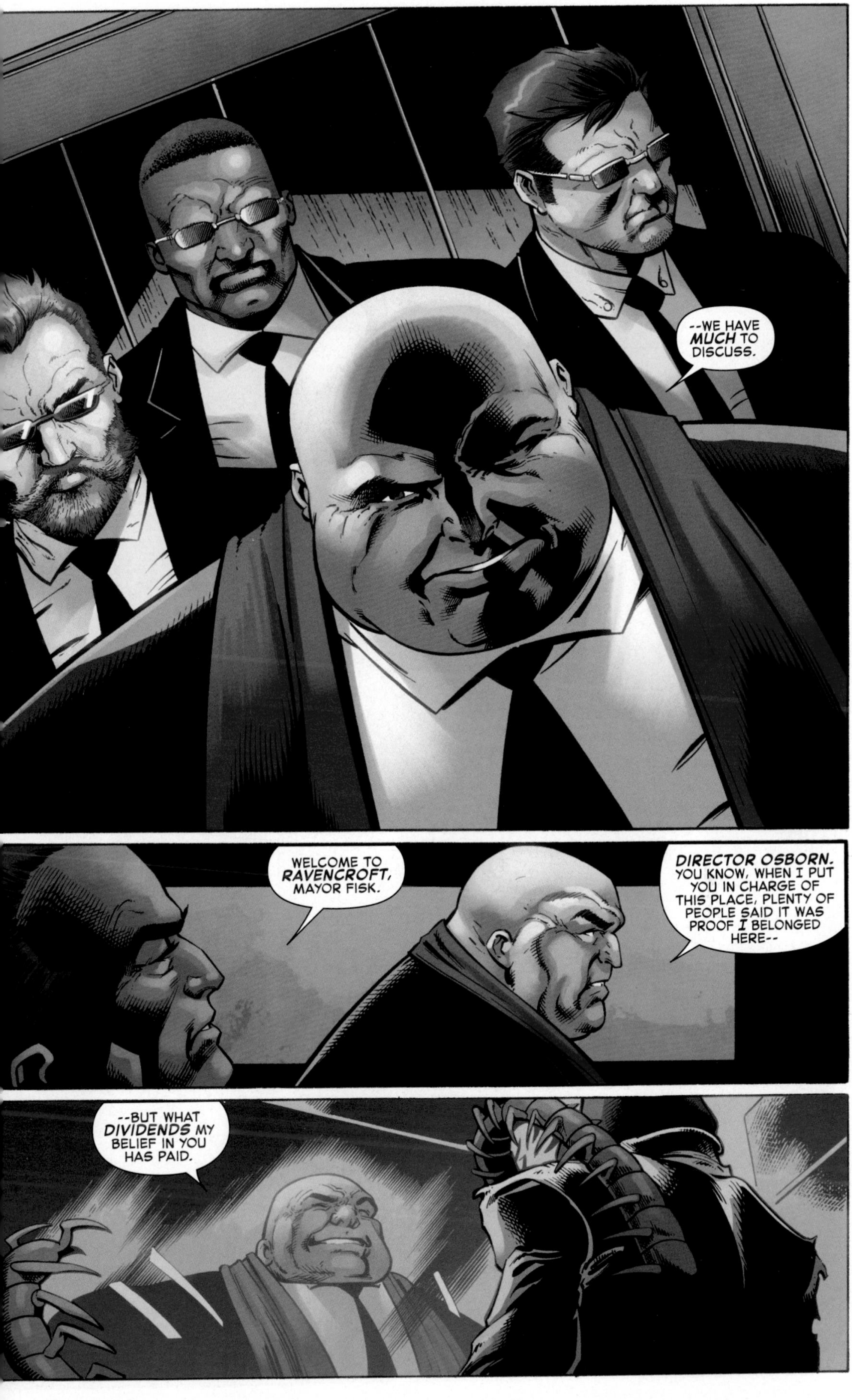
--WE HAVE MUCH TO DISCUSS.
WELCOME TO RAVENCROFT, MAYOR FISK.
DIRECTOR OSBORN. YOU KNOW, WHEN I PUT YOU IN CHARGE OF THIS PLACE, PLENTY OF PEOPLE SAID IT WAS PROOF I BELONGED HERE--
--BUT WHAT DIVIDENDS MY BELIEF IN YOU HAS PAID.

REMEMBER ME, DEMON?

ONCE, I CAME TO YOU WITH A *REQUEST*--THE THING I YEARNED FOR MOST IN THIS LIFE-- ON BENDED KNEE. YOU *REFUSED* ME THEN--

--SO NOW I COME TO YOU WITH THE *FIST*.

LET'S SEE HOW ACCOMMODATING YOU CAN BE *THIS* TIME. PREPARE THE RESTRAINTS IT'S TIME TO BEGIN THE INTERROGATION.

*NO!*

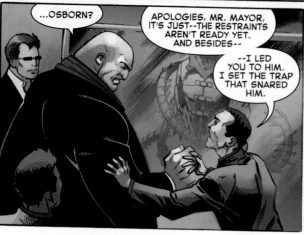

...OSBORN?

APOLOGIES, MR. MAYOR, IT'S JUST--THE RESTRAINTS AREN'T READY YET. AND BESIDES--

--I LED YOU TO HIM. I SET THE TRAP THAT SNARED HIM.

WE HAD A *DEAL*.

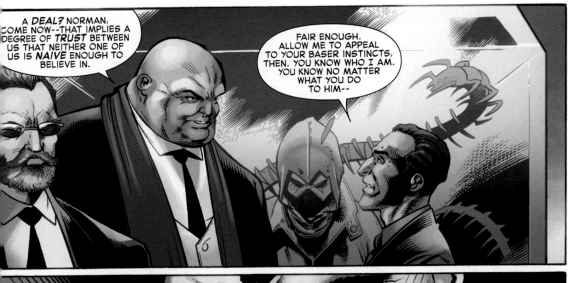

A **DEAL?** NORMAN, COME NOW--THAT IMPLIES A DEGREE OF **TRUST** BETWEEN US THAT NEITHER ONE OF US IS **NAIVE** ENOUGH TO BELIEVE IN.

FAIR ENOUGH. ALLOW ME TO APPEAL TO YOUR BASER INSTINCTS, THEN. YOU KNOW WHO I AM. YOU KNOW NO MATTER WHAT YOU DO TO HIM--

--YOU CAN'T **HURT** HIM LIKE **I** CAN.

LET ME HAVE MY FUN. AND WHEN I'M FINISHED, HE'LL BE A BROKEN MESS.

MORE THAN WILLING TO GIVE YOU WHAT YOU WANT.

HH...

YOU'RE MY KIND OF **MONSTER**, NORMAN. BUT DON'T TRY MY PATIENCE--

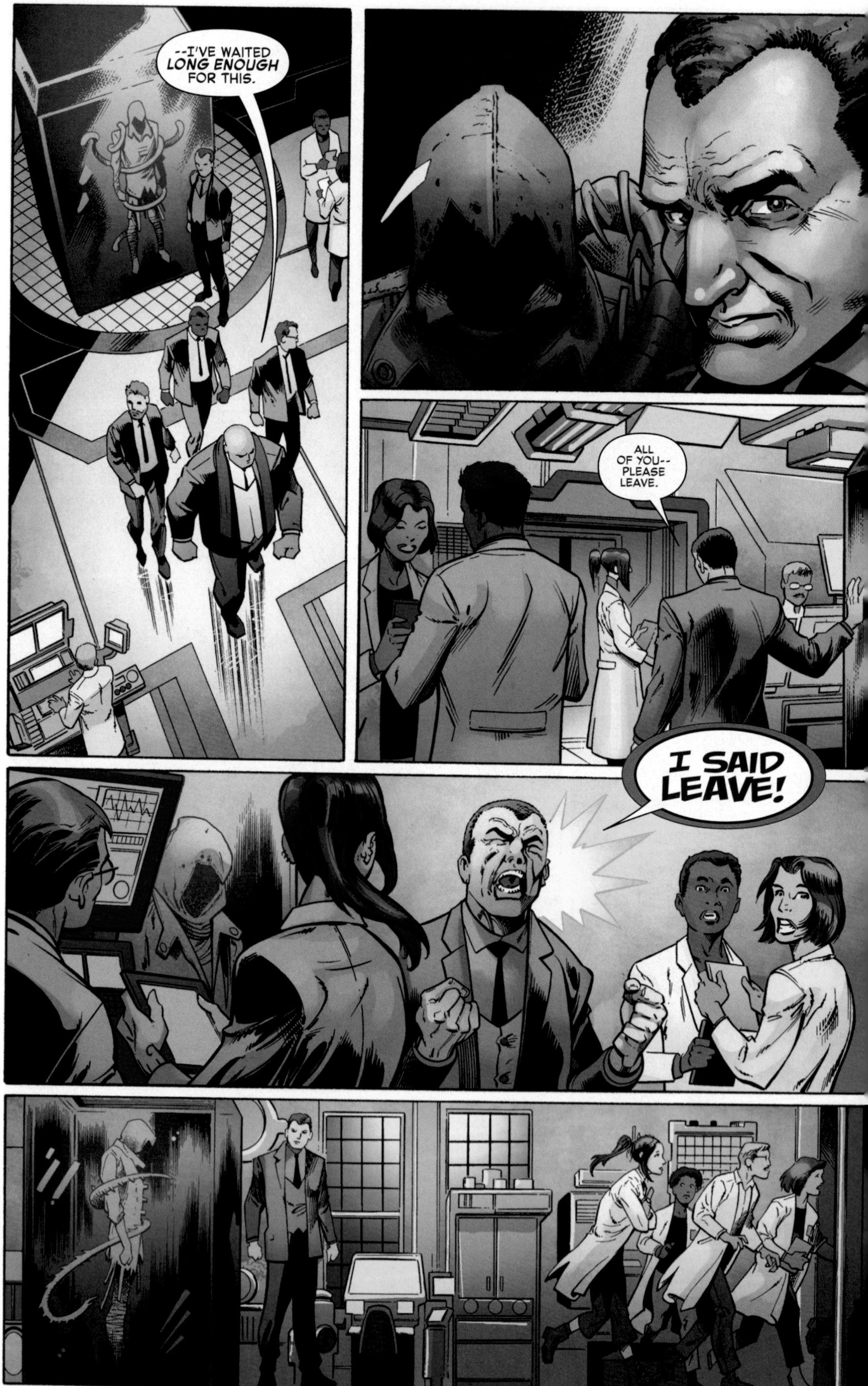
--I'VE WAITED LONG ENOUGH FOR THIS.
ALL OF YOU-- PLEASE LEAVE.
I SAID LEAVE!

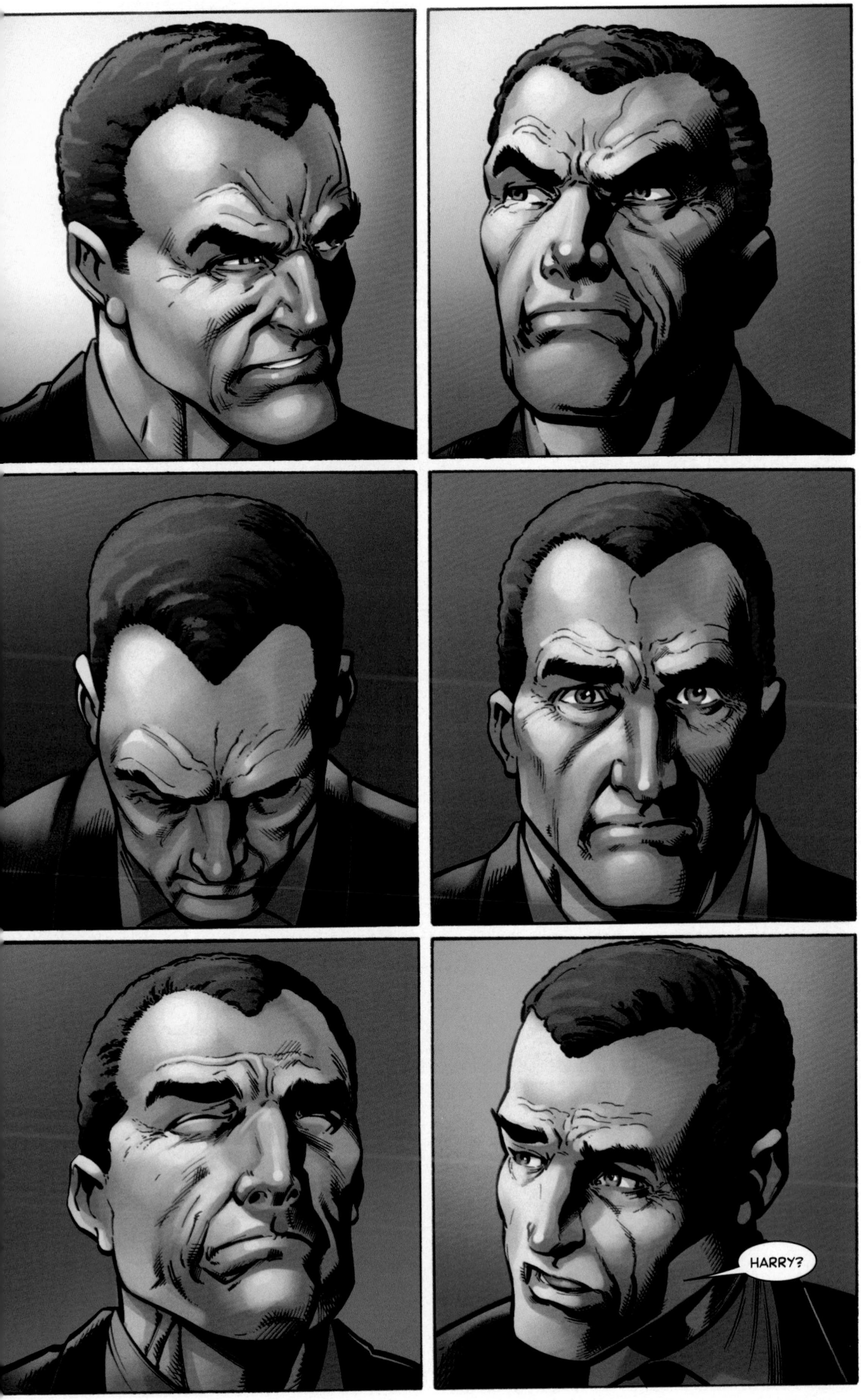
HARRY?

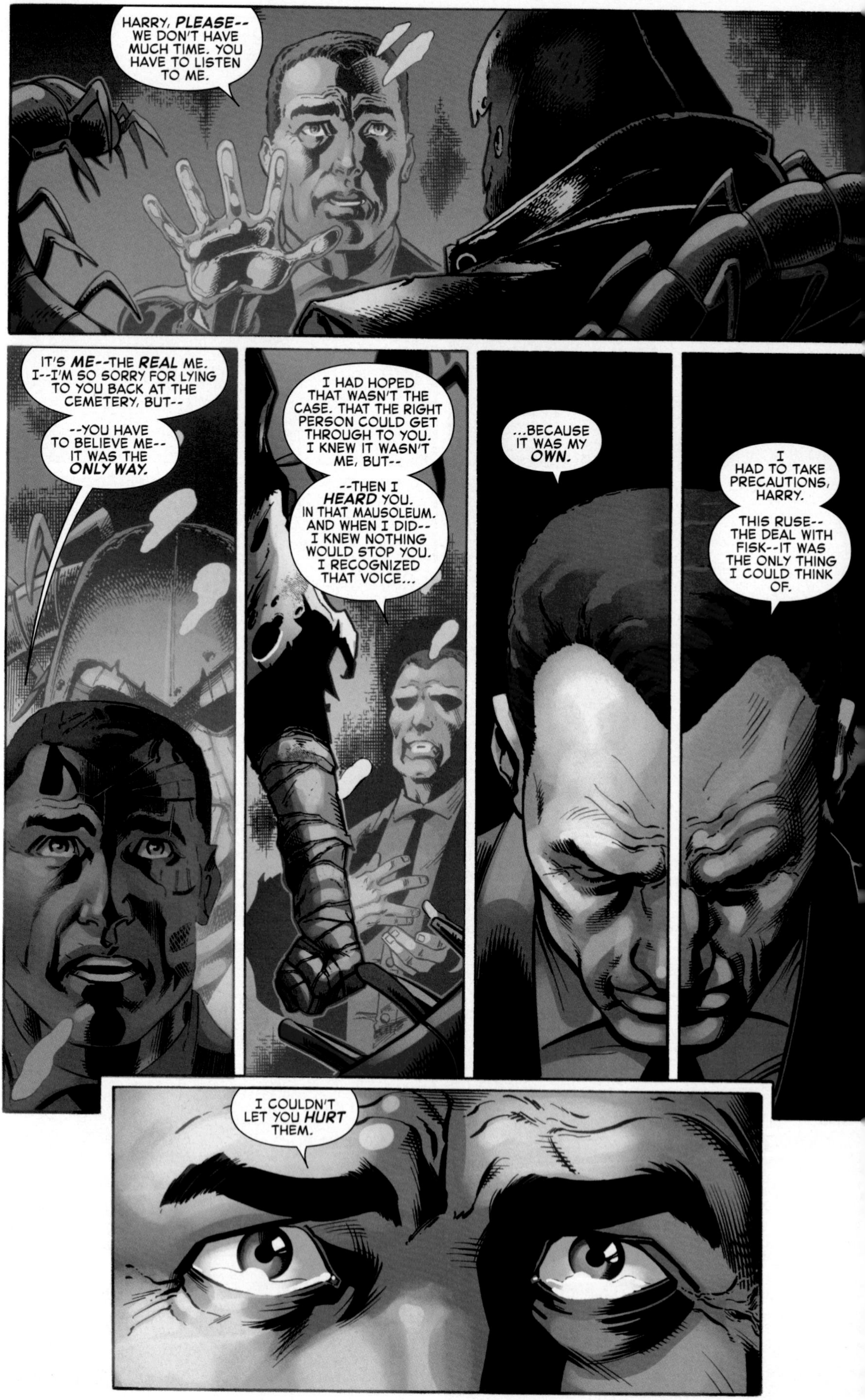
HARRY, PLEASE-- WE DON'T HAVE MUCH TIME. YOU HAVE TO LISTEN TO ME.
IT'S ME--THE REAL ME. I--I'M SO SORRY FOR LYING TO YOU BACK AT THE CEMETERY, BUT--
--YOU HAVE TO BELIEVE ME-- IT WAS THE ONLY WAY.
I HAD HOPED THAT WASN'T THE CASE. THAT THE RIGHT PERSON COULD GET THROUGH TO YOU. I KNEW IT WASN'T ME, BUT--
--THEN I HEARD YOU. IN THAT MAUSOLEUM. AND WHEN I DID-- I KNEW NOTHING WOULD STOP YOU. I RECOGNIZED THAT VOICE...
...BECAUSE IT WAS MY OWN.
I HAD TO TAKE PRECAUTIONS, HARRY.
THIS RUSE-- THE DEAL WITH FISK--IT WAS THE ONLY THING I COULD THINK OF.
I COULDN'T LET YOU HURT THEM.

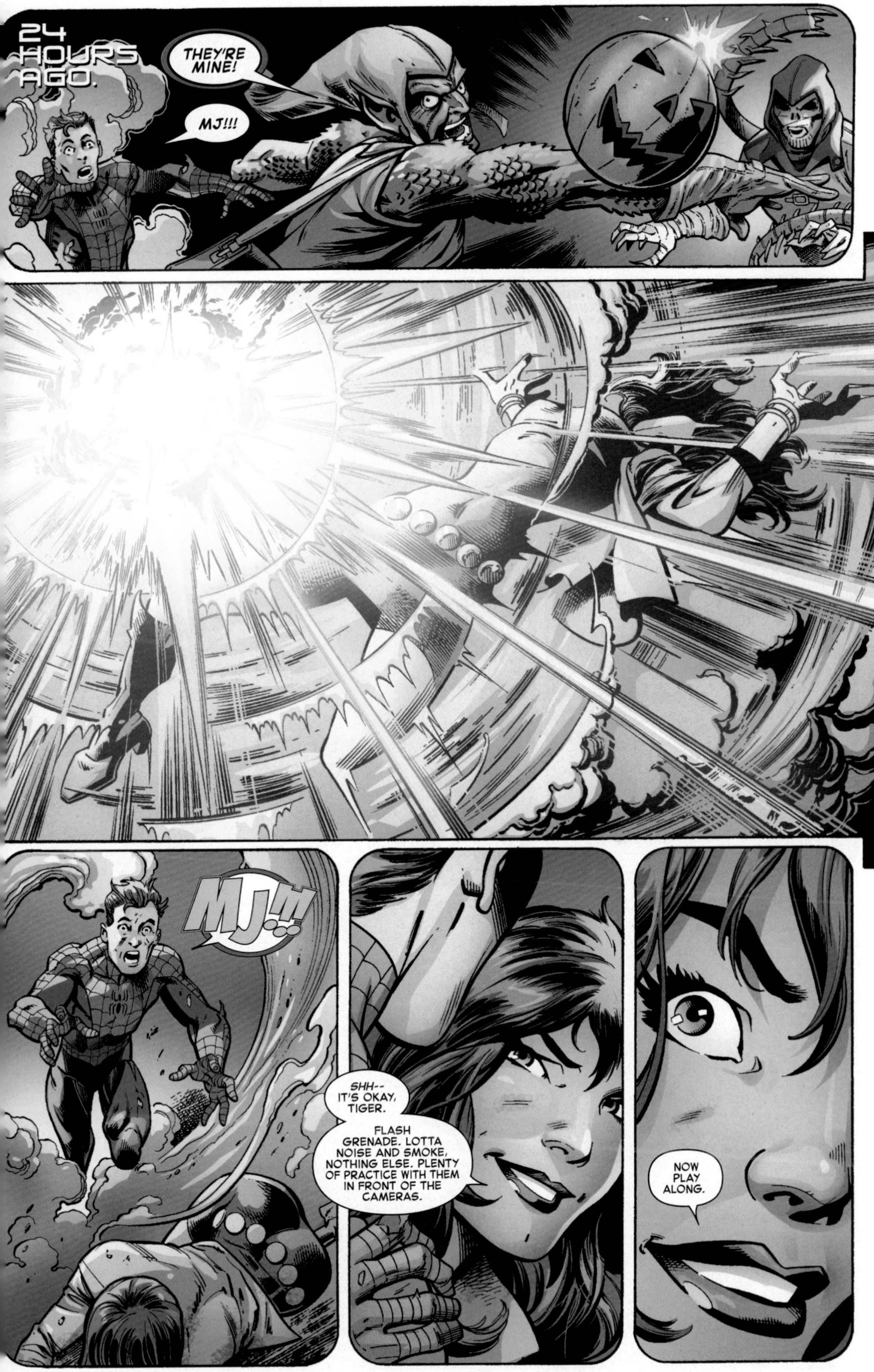
24 HOURS AGO.
THEY'RE MINE!
MJ!!!
MJ!!!
SHH-- IT'S OKAY, TIGER.
FLASH GRENADE. LOTTA NOISE AND SMOKE, NOTHING ELSE. PLENTY OF PRACTICE WITH THEM IN FRONT OF THE CAMERAS.
NOW PLAY ALONG.

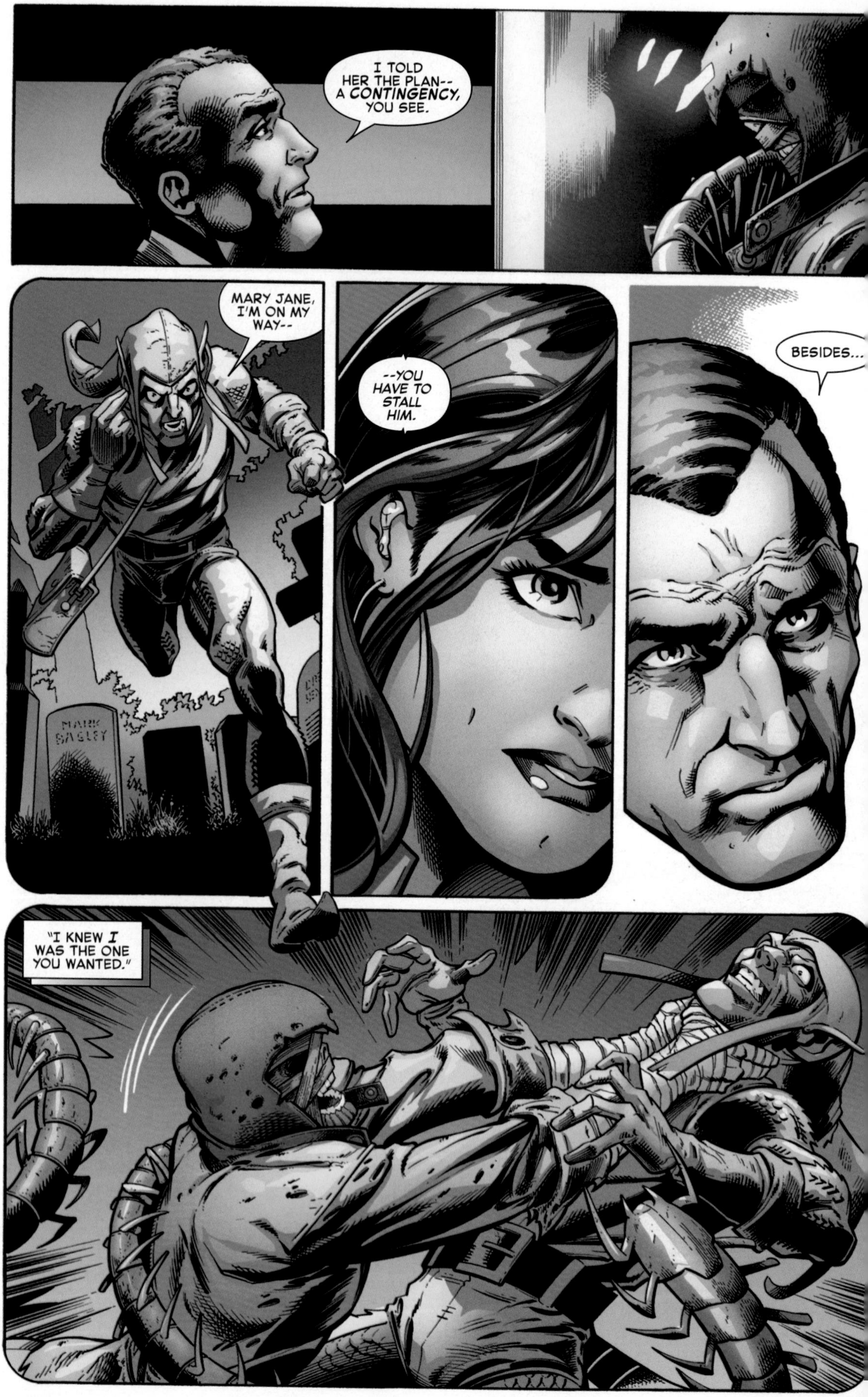

I TOLD HER THE PLAN-- A CONTINGENCY, YOU SEE.
MARY JANE, I'M ON MY WAY--
MARK BAGLEY
--YOU HAVE TO STALL HIM.
BESIDES...
"I KNEW I WAS THE ONE YOU WANTED."

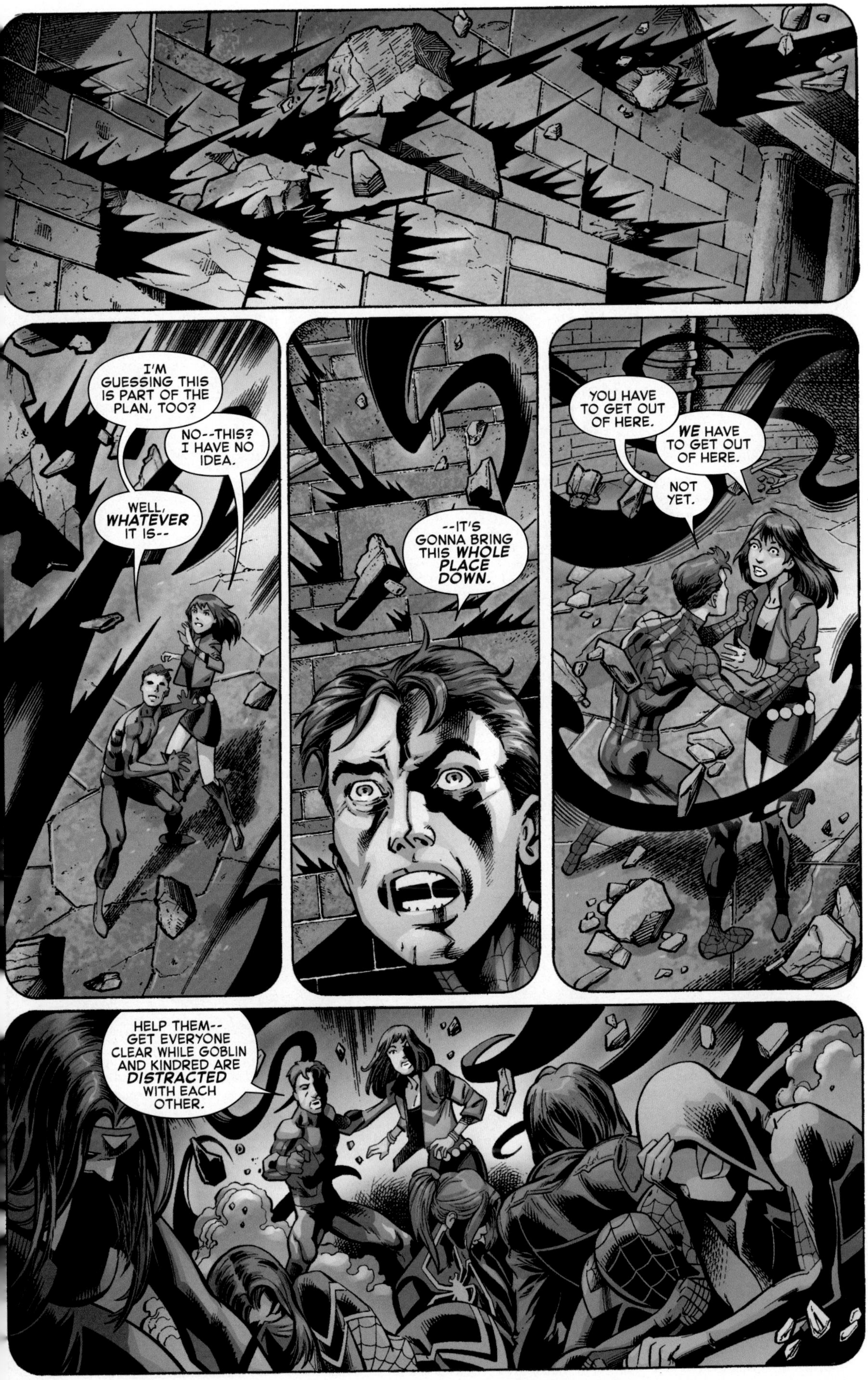
I'M GUESSING THIS IS PART OF THE PLAN, TOO?
NO--THIS? I HAVE NO IDEA.
WELL, WHATEVER IT IS--
--IT'S GONNA BRING THIS WHOLE PLACE DOWN.
YOU HAVE TO GET OUT OF HERE.
WE HAVE TO GET OUT OF HERE.
NOT YET.
HELP THEM--GET EVERYONE CLEAR WHILE GOBLIN AND KINDRED ARE DISTRACTED WITH EACH OTHER.

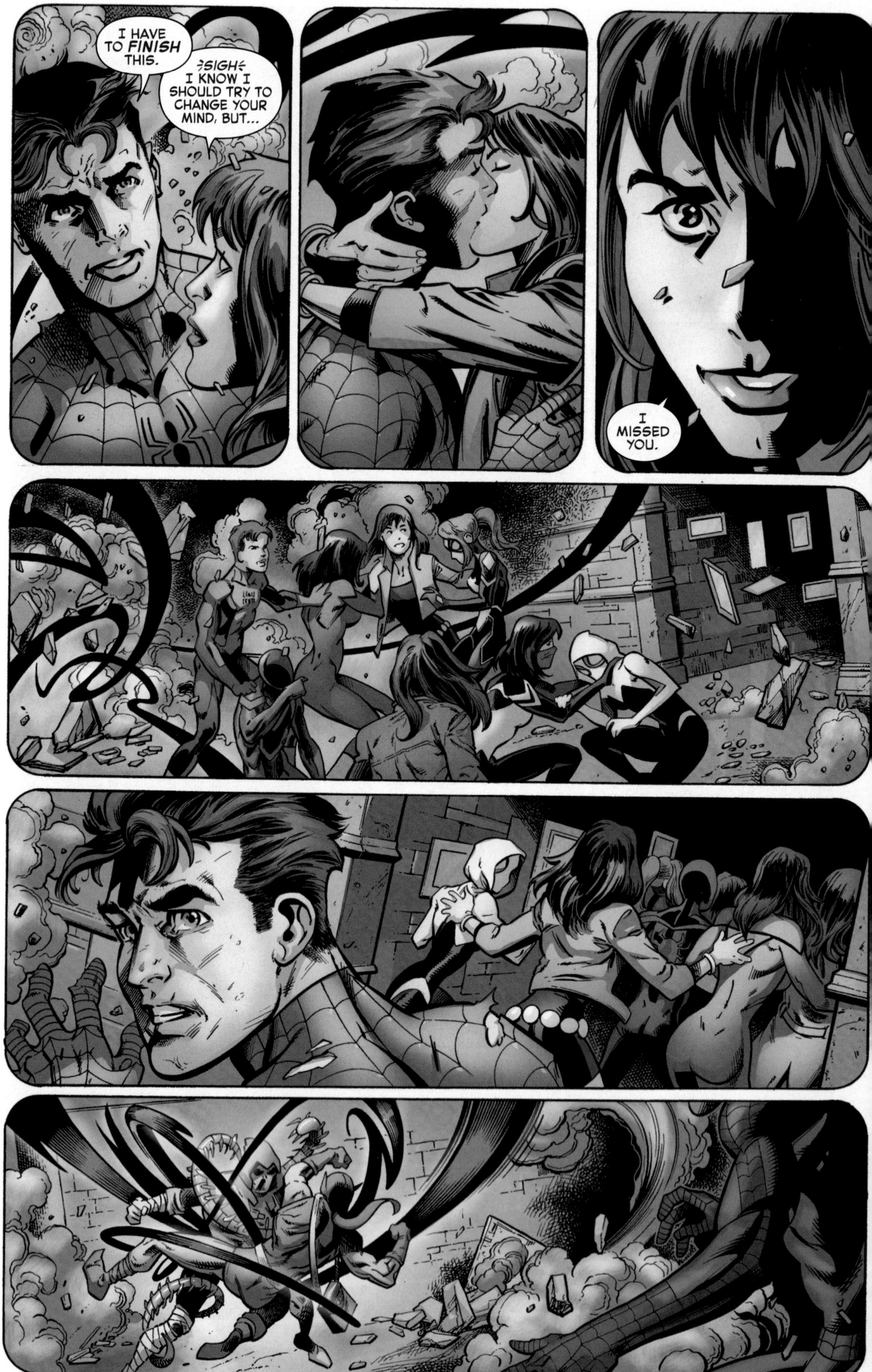
I HAVE TO FINISH THIS.
≶SIGH≷ I KNOW I SHOULD TRY TO CHANGE YOUR MIND, BUT...
I MISSED YOU.

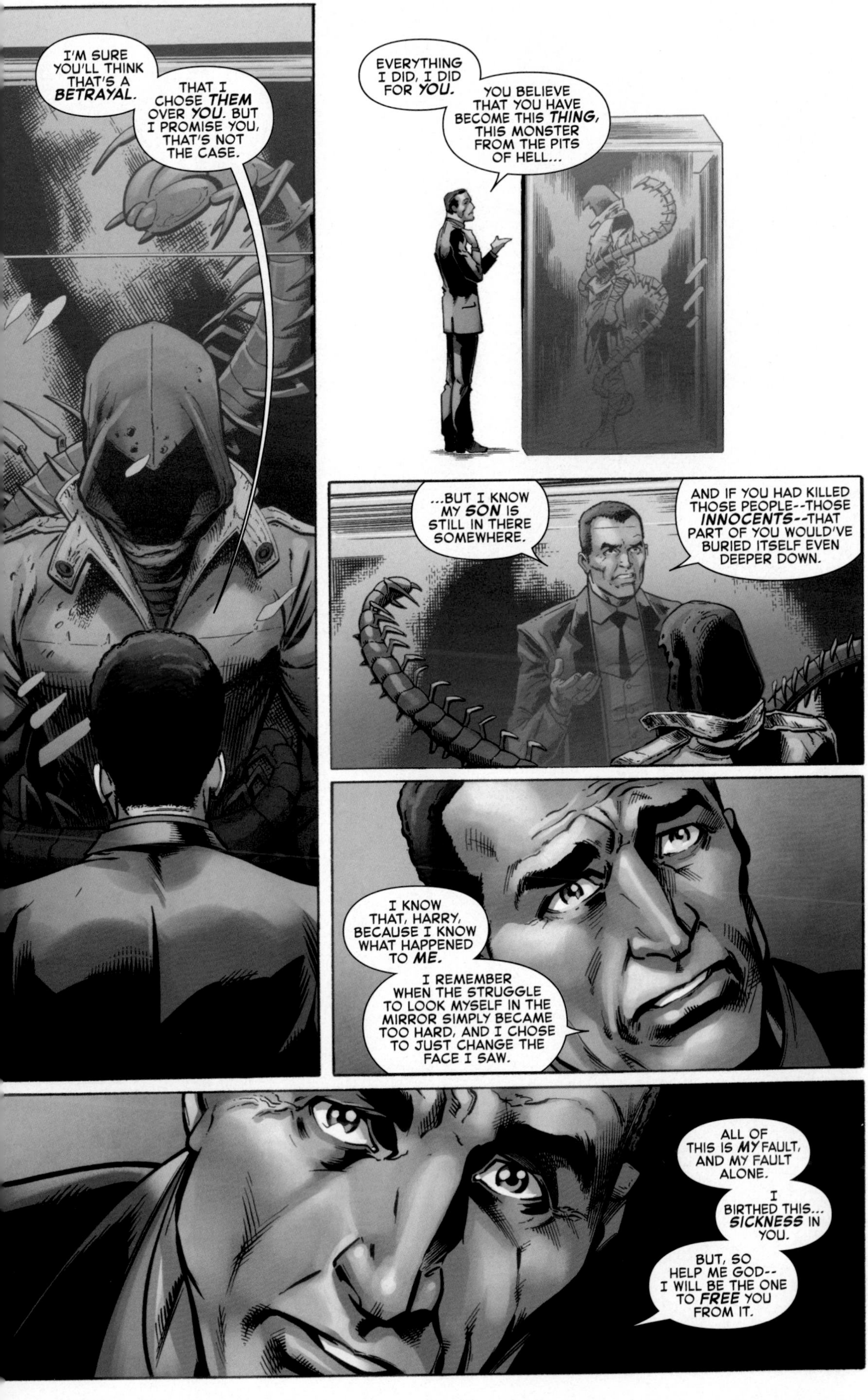
I'M SURE YOU'LL THINK THAT'S A **BETRAYAL.**
THAT I CHOSE **THEM** OVER **YOU.** BUT I PROMISE YOU, THAT'S NOT THE CASE.
EVERYTHING I DID, I DID FOR **YOU.**
YOU BELIEVE THAT YOU HAVE BECOME THIS **THING,** THIS MONSTER FROM THE PITS OF HELL...
...BUT I KNOW MY **SON** IS STILL IN THERE SOMEWHERE.
AND IF YOU HAD KILLED THOSE PEOPLE--THOSE **INNOCENTS**--THAT PART OF YOU WOULD'VE BURIED ITSELF EVEN DEEPER DOWN.
I KNOW THAT, HARRY, BECAUSE I KNOW WHAT HAPPENED TO **ME.**
I REMEMBER WHEN THE STRUGGLE TO LOOK MYSELF IN THE MIRROR SIMPLY BECAME TOO HARD, AND I CHOSE TO JUST CHANGE THE FACE I SAW.
ALL OF THIS IS **MY** FAULT, AND MY FAULT ALONE.
I BIRTHED THIS... **SICKNESS** IN YOU.
BUT, SO HELP ME GOD-- I WILL BE THE ONE TO **FREE** YOU FROM IT.

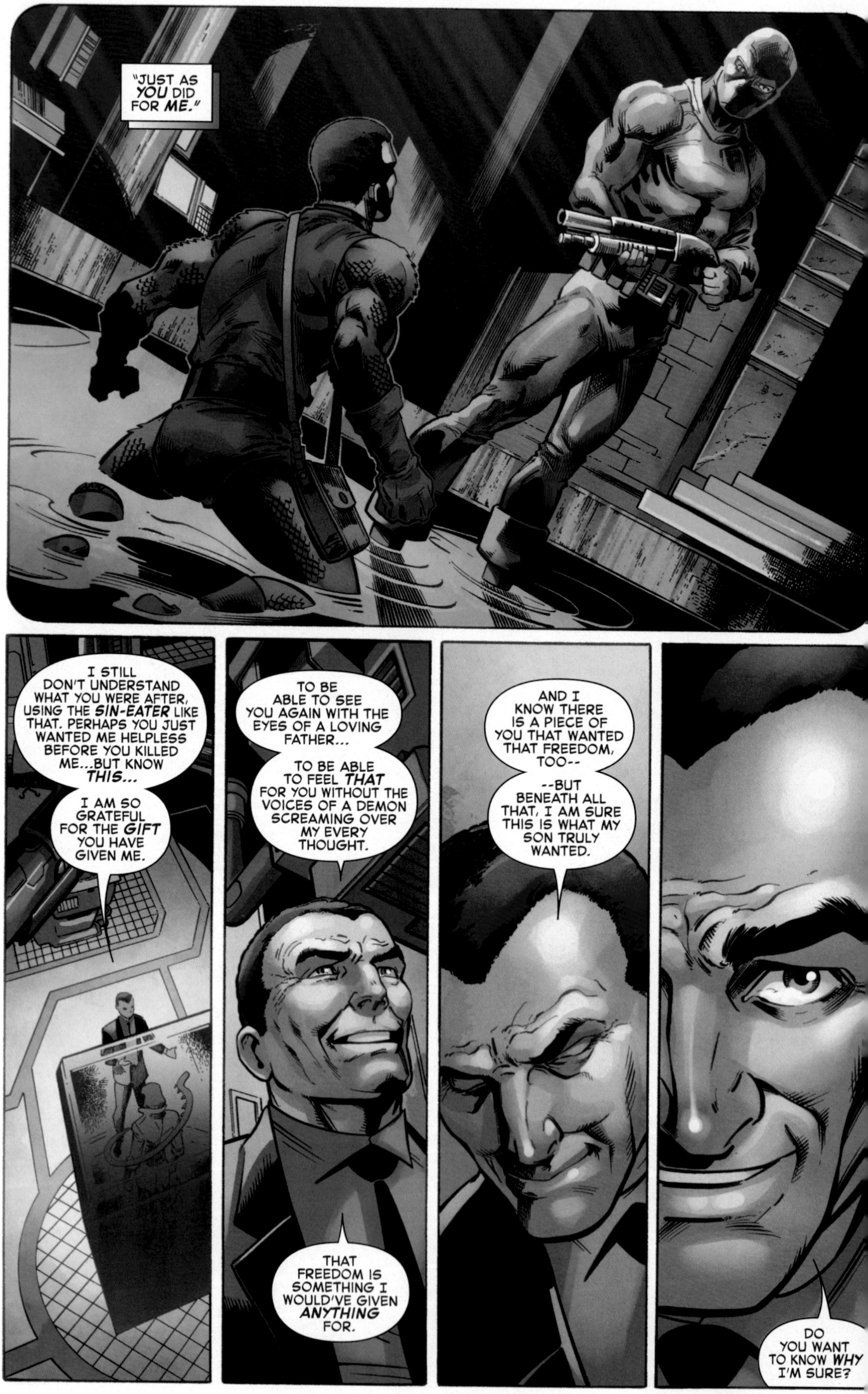
"JUST AS YOU DID FOR ME."
I STILL DON'T UNDERSTAND WHAT YOU WERE AFTER, USING THE SIN-EATER LIKE THAT. PERHAPS YOU JUST WANTED ME HELPLESS BEFORE YOU KILLED ME...BUT KNOW THIS...
I AM SO GRATEFUL FOR THE GIFT YOU HAVE GIVEN ME.
TO BE ABLE TO SEE YOU AGAIN WITH THE EYES OF A LOVING FATHER...
TO BE ABLE TO FEEL THAT FOR YOU WITHOUT THE VOICES OF A DEMON SCREAMING OVER MY EVERY THOUGHT.
THAT FREEDOM IS SOMETHING I WOULD'VE GIVEN ANYTHING FOR.
AND I KNOW THERE IS A PIECE OF YOU THAT WANTED THAT FREEDOM, TOO--
--BUT BENEATH ALL THAT, I AM SURE THIS IS WHAT MY SON TRULY WANTED.
DO YOU WANT TO KNOW WHY I'M SURE?

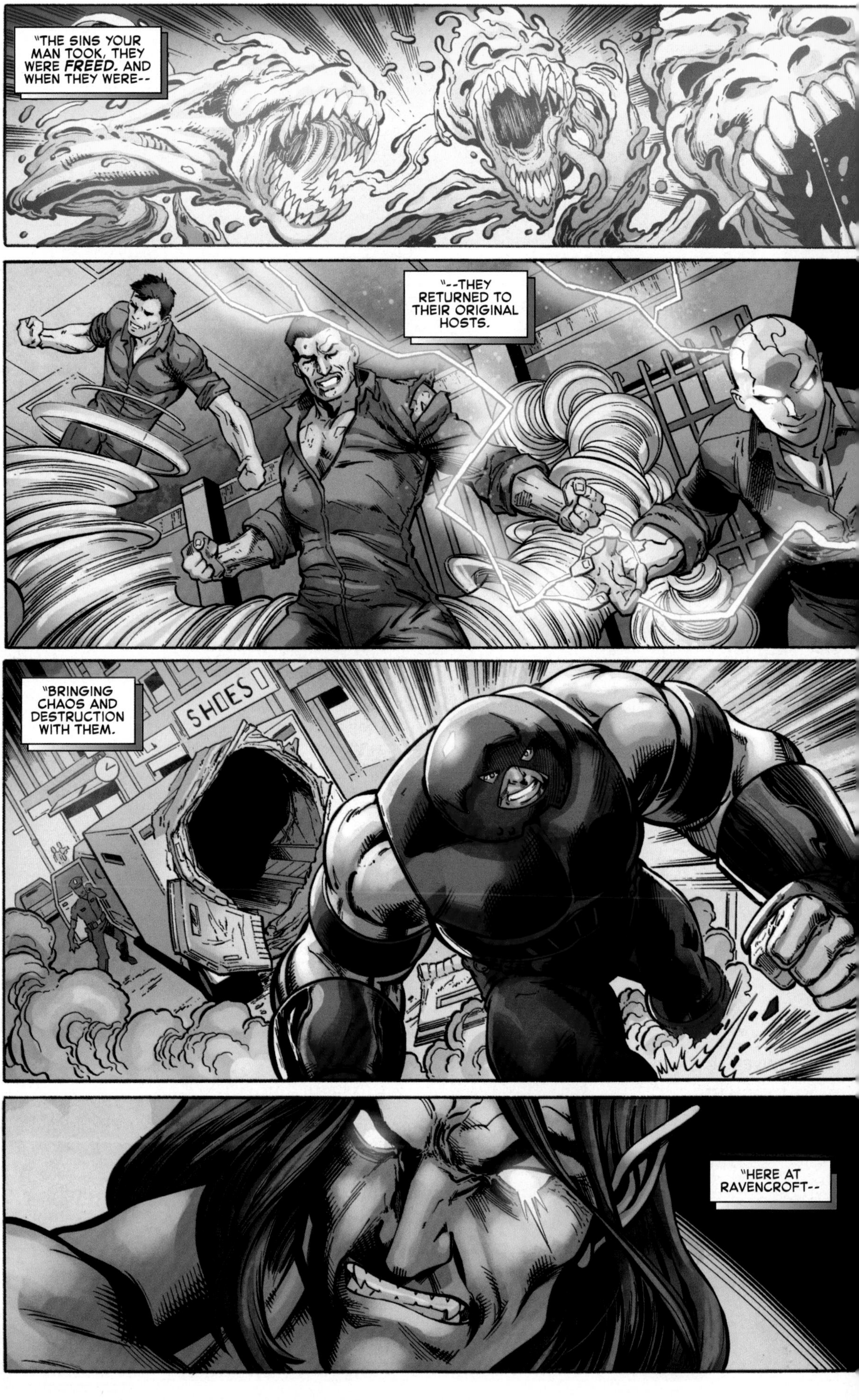
"THE SINS YOUR MAN TOOK, THEY WERE FREED. AND WHEN THEY WERE--
"--THEY RETURNED TO THEIR ORIGINAL HOSTS.
"BRINGING CHAOS AND DESTRUCTION WITH THEM.
SHOES
"HERE AT RAVENCROFT--

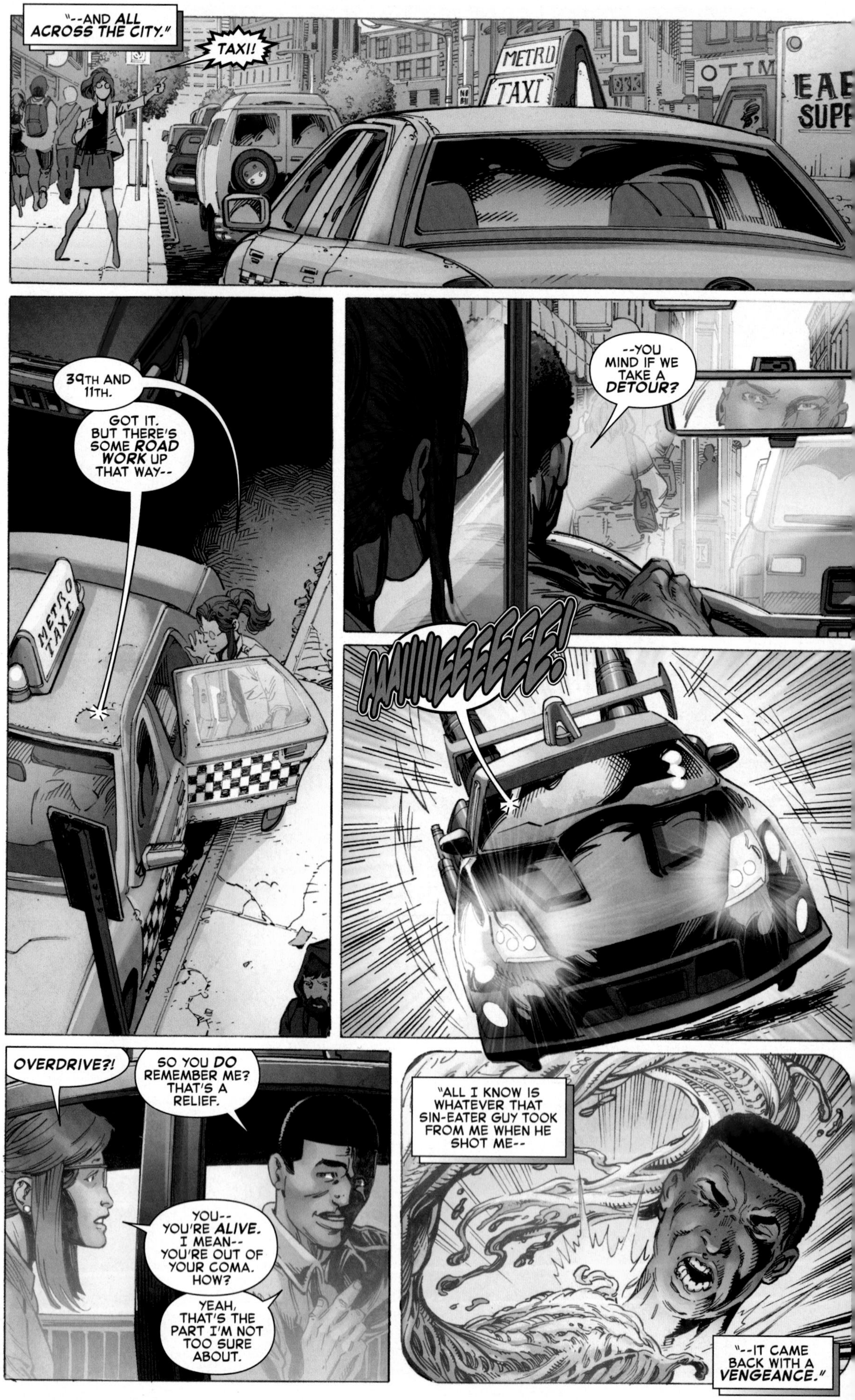
"--AND ALL ACROSS THE CITY."
TAXI!
METRO TAXI
39TH AND 11TH.
GOT IT. BUT THERE'S SOME ROAD WORK UP THAT WAY--
METRO TAXI
--YOU MIND IF WE TAKE A DETOUR?
AAAIIIIEEEEEEE!
OVERDRIVE?!
SO YOU DO REMEMBER ME? THAT'S A RELIEF.
YOU-- YOU'RE ALIVE. I MEAN-- YOU'RE OUT OF YOUR COMA. HOW?
YEAH, THAT'S THE PART I'M NOT TOO SURE ABOUT.
"ALL I KNOW IS WHATEVER THAT SIN-EATER GUY TOOK FROM ME WHEN HE SHOT ME--
"--IT CAME BACK WITH A VENGEANCE."

AND THEN...YOU ESCAPED POLICE CUSTODY, I'M GUESSING?

WHAT'S THE LINE--"I RELEASED MYSELF ON MY OWN RECOGNIZANCE."

YOU GONNA TURN ME IN, OFFICER COOPER?

OKAY, THEN, WHAT'S THE PLAN? JUST KEEP RUNNING?

I WAS ACTUALLY THINKING ABOUT TAKING YOU TO DINNER.

DINNER?

YEAH.

ARE YOU-- ARE YOU OUT OF YOUR MIND?!

WHY NOT?

YOU'RE A SUPER VILLAIN, FOR GOD'S SAKE!!!

RIGHT. ABOUT THAT...

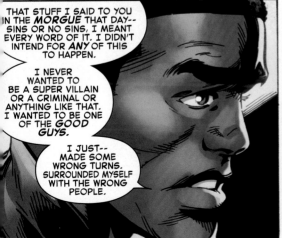

THAT STUFF I SAID TO YOU IN THE MORGUE THAT DAY-- SINS OR NO SINS, I MEANT EVERY WORD OF IT. I DIDN'T INTEND FOR ANY OF THIS TO HAPPEN.

I NEVER WANTED TO BE A SUPER VILLAIN OR A CRIMINAL OR ANYTHING LIKE THAT. I WANTED TO BE ONE OF THE GOOD GUYS.

I JUST-- MADE SOME WRONG TURNS. SURROUNDED MYSELF WITH THE WRONG PEOPLE.

AND THEN I MET YOU.

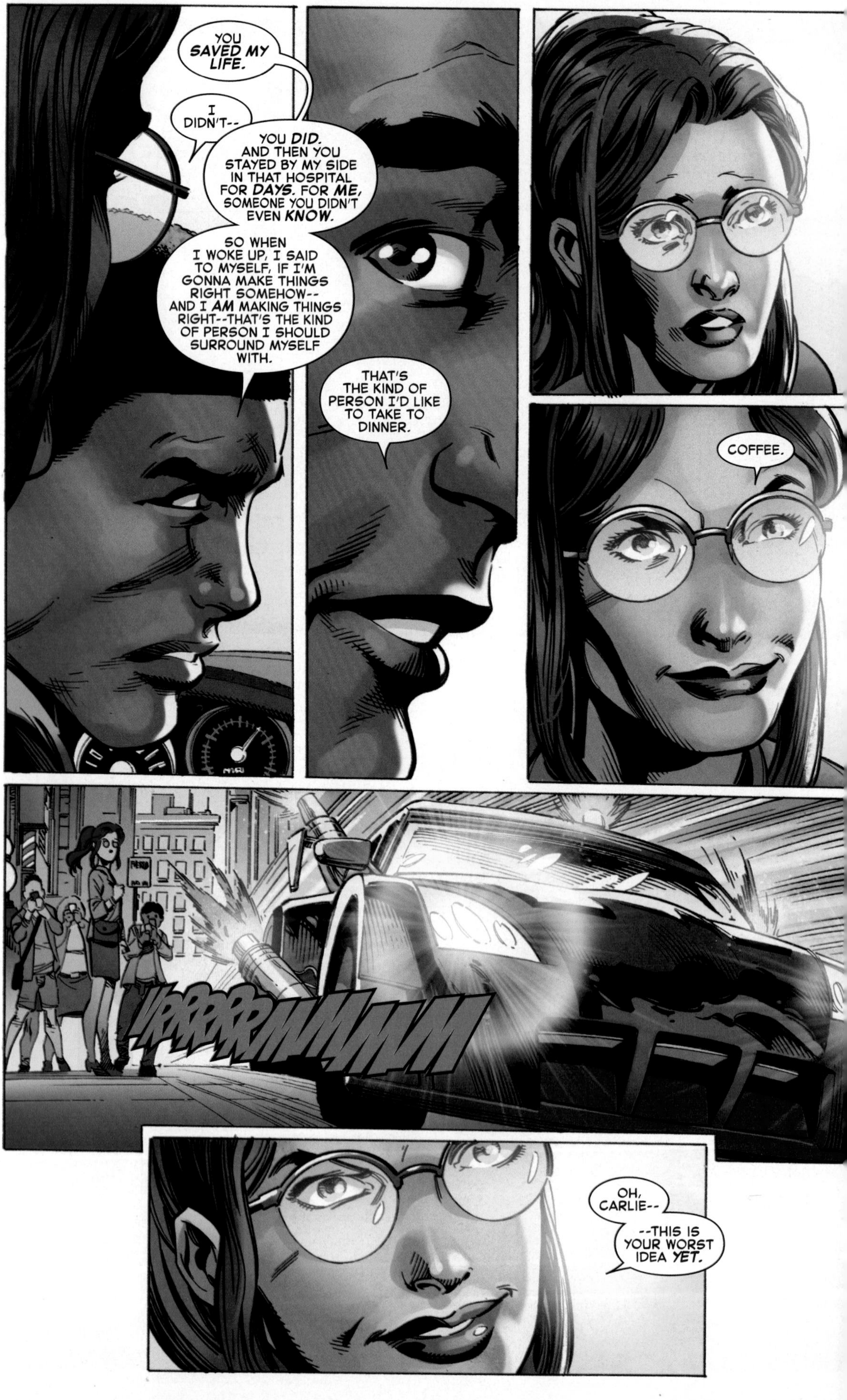
YOU SAVED MY LIFE.
I DIDN'T--
YOU DID. AND THEN YOU STAYED BY MY SIDE IN THAT HOSPITAL FOR DAYS. FOR ME, SOMEONE YOU DIDN'T EVEN KNOW.
SO WHEN I WOKE UP, I SAID TO MYSELF, IF I'M GONNA MAKE THINGS RIGHT SOMEHOW-- AND I AM MAKING THINGS RIGHT--THAT'S THE KIND OF PERSON I SHOULD SURROUND MYSELF WITH.
THAT'S THE KIND OF PERSON I'D LIKE TO TAKE TO DINNER.
COFFEE.
VRRRRRMMMMMM
OH, CARLIE--
--THIS IS YOUR WORST IDEA YET.

THE THREE OF US COULD GET *BRUNCH!*

AUNT MAY, I TOLD YOU--ME AND THAT GIRL, WE'RE NOT EVEN *TOGETHER* ANYMORE.

I THINK.

WELL, ALL THESE DELIVERIES FROM YOUR *MYSTERY SWEETHEART* BEG TO DIFFER.

IF ENOUGH ORGANIC CANNED GOODS TO KEEP THE F.E.A.S.T. CENTER STOCKED FOR A YEAR DON'T SAY "I LOVE YOU," I DON'T KNOW WHAT DOES.

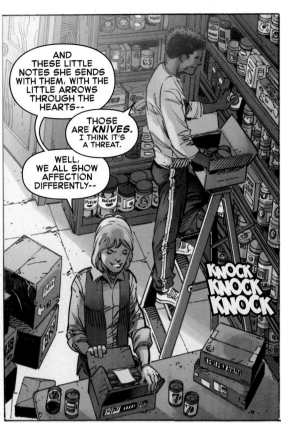

AND THESE LITTLE NOTES SHE SENDS WITH THEM, WITH THE LITTLE ARROWS THROUGH THE HEARTS--

THOSE ARE *KNIVES.* I THINK IT'S A THREAT.

WELL, WE ALL SHOW AFFECTION DIFFERENTLY--

KNOCK KNOCK KNOCK

OH MY, ANOTHER? *JUST A MINUTE!*

KNOCK KNOCK

≥SIGH≤ CAN *YOU* GET THIS ONE? THE LAST DELIVERY GUYS, SHE MADE 'EM TRY TO *SING* TO ME.

AND IT WAS *DELIGHTFUL.* I LOVE THAT "KISS FROM A ROSE" SONG.

HI THERE, IF IT'S MORE THAN A FEW BOXES, WOULD YOU MIND BRINGING THEM AROUND TO THE--

--BACK.

PLEASE--

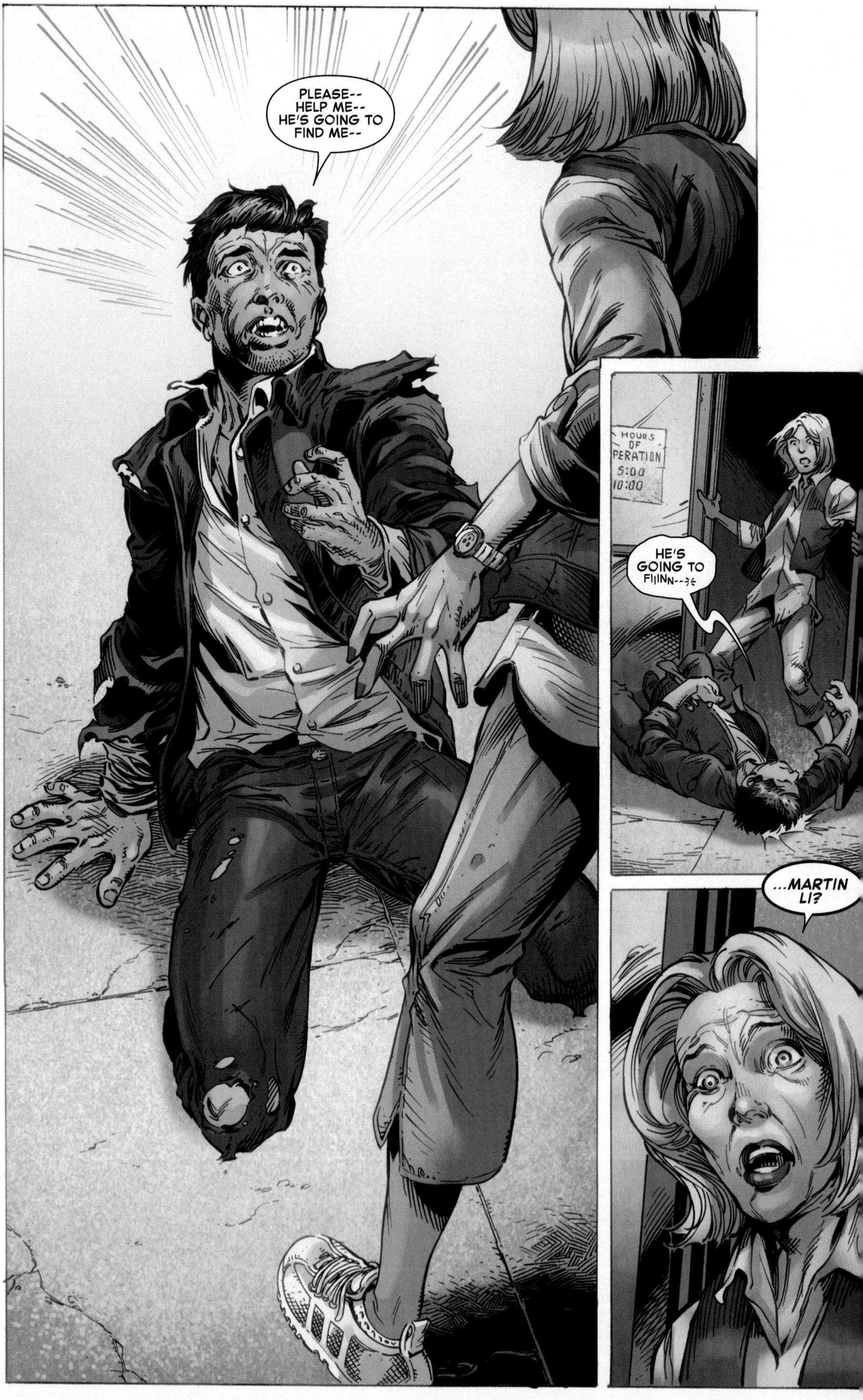
PLEASE-- HELP ME-- HE'S GOING TO FIND ME--
HOURS OF OPERATION 5:00 10:00
HE'S GOING TO FIIINN--
...MARTIN LI?

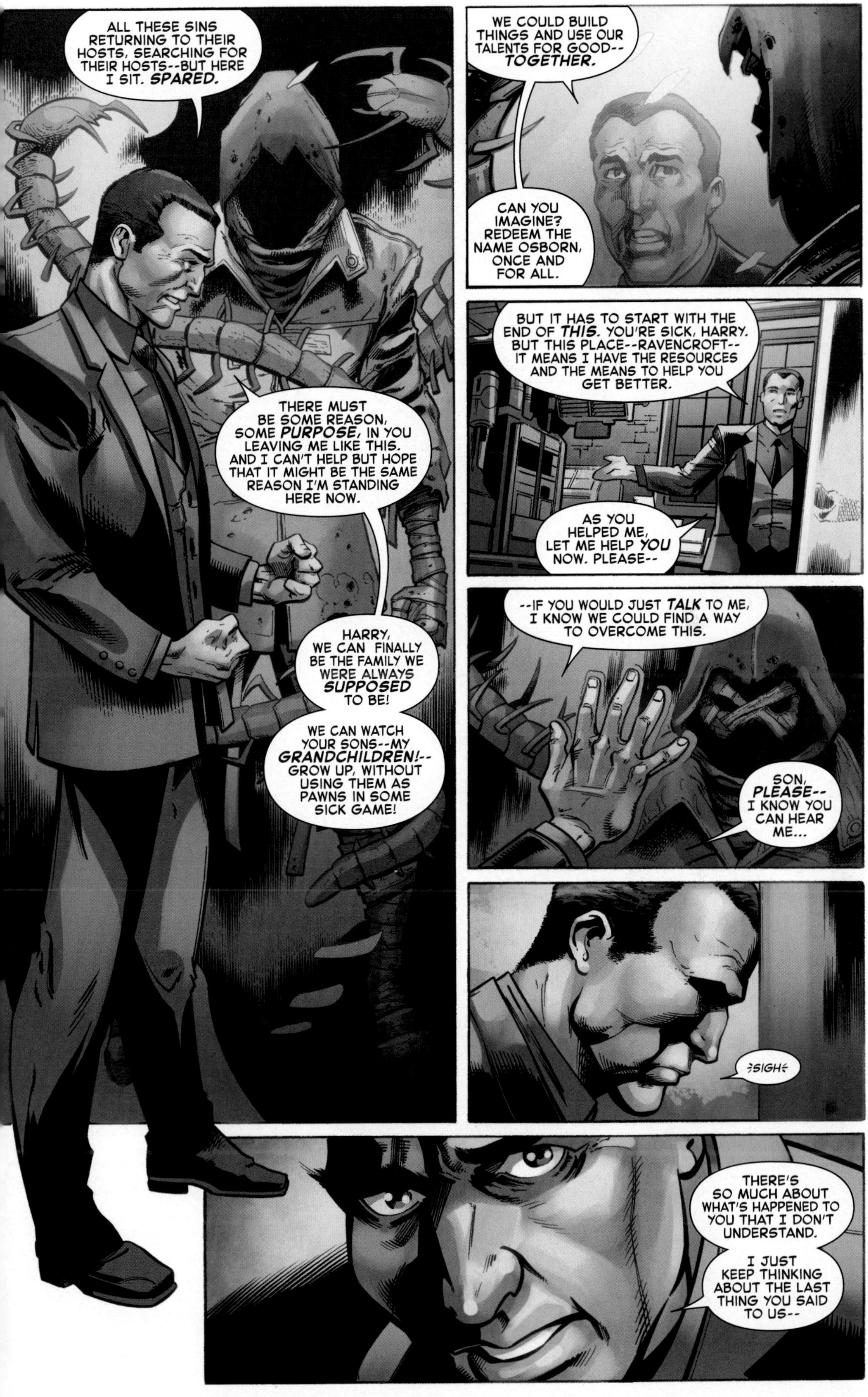
ALL THESE SINS RETURNING TO THEIR HOSTS, SEARCHING FOR THEIR HOSTS--BUT HERE I SIT. SPARED.
THERE MUST BE SOME REASON, SOME PURPOSE, IN YOU LEAVING ME LIKE THIS. AND I CAN'T HELP BUT HOPE THAT IT MIGHT BE THE SAME REASON I'M STANDING HERE NOW.
HARRY, WE CAN FINALLY BE THE FAMILY WE WERE ALWAYS SUPPOSED TO BE!
WE CAN WATCH YOUR SONS--MY GRANDCHILDREN!--GROW UP, WITHOUT USING THEM AS PAWNS IN SOME SICK GAME!
WE COULD BUILD THINGS AND USE OUR TALENTS FOR GOOD--TOGETHER.
CAN YOU IMAGINE? REDEEM THE NAME OSBORN, ONCE AND FOR ALL.
BUT IT HAS TO START WITH THE END OF THIS. YOU'RE SICK, HARRY. BUT THIS PLACE--RAVENCROFT--IT MEANS I HAVE THE RESOURCES AND THE MEANS TO HELP YOU GET BETTER.
AS YOU HELPED ME, LET ME HELP YOU NOW. PLEASE--
--IF YOU WOULD JUST TALK TO ME, I KNOW WE COULD FIND A WAY TO OVERCOME THIS.
SON, PLEASE--I KNOW YOU CAN HEAR ME...
SIGH
THERE'S SO MUCH ABOUT WHAT'S HAPPENED TO YOU THAT I DON'T UNDERSTAND.
I JUST KEEP THINKING ABOUT THE LAST THING YOU SAID TO US--

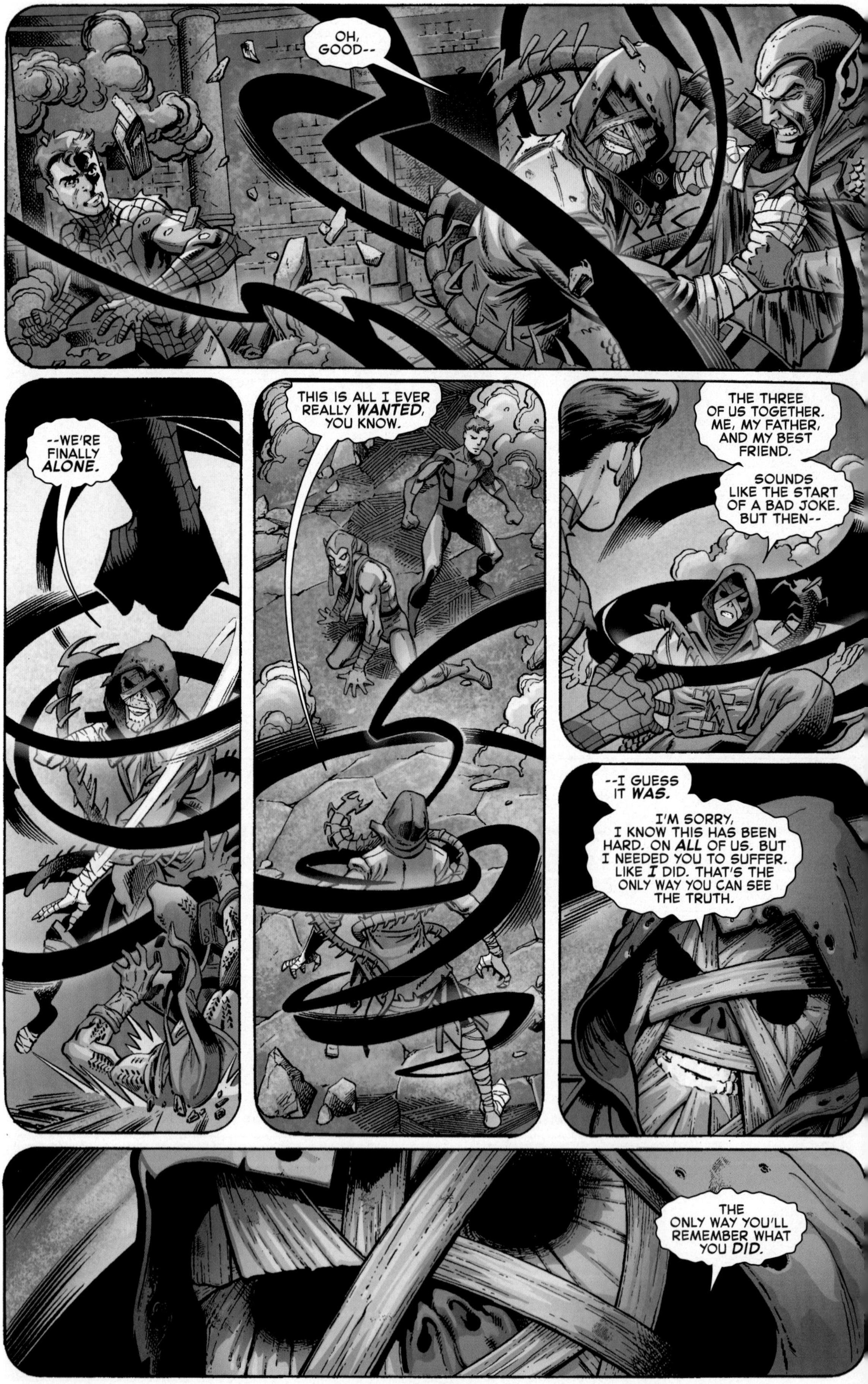
OH, GOOD--
--WE'RE FINALLY ALONE.
THIS IS ALL I EVER REALLY WANTED, YOU KNOW.
THE THREE OF US TOGETHER. ME, MY FATHER, AND MY BEST FRIEND.
SOUNDS LIKE THE START OF A BAD JOKE. BUT THEN--
--I GUESS IT WAS.
I'M SORRY, I KNOW THIS HAS BEEN HARD. ON ALL OF US. BUT I NEEDED YOU TO SUFFER. LIKE I DID. THAT'S THE ONLY WAY YOU CAN SEE THE TRUTH.
THE ONLY WAY YOU'LL REMEMBER WHAT YOU DID.

PETE, I KNEW IF I JUST CAME AFTER YOU, OR THE PEOPLE YOU LOVED, YOU'D MAKE IT ANOTHER CHANCE TO PLAY HERO.

I NEEDED TO SHOW YOU THAT *YOU* ARE THE CAUSE OF THEIR SUFFERING. WITH YOUR SANCTIMONY AND YOUR HUBRIS, ALWAYS MAKING EVERYTHING WORSE.

AND *YOU*, DAD-- WELL, I KNEW THE GOBLIN WOULD NEVER *LET* YOU FEEL PAIN. SO I HAD TO TAKE HIM AWAY.

NOW PAIN IS ALL YOU ARE.

I THOUGHT IF I DID *ALL THAT*, IT WOULD GET THROUGH TO YOU BOTH, BUT YOU CAN'T EVEN *REMEMBER*. THAT'S HOW *POWERFUL* THE LIES ARE.

SO, THIS IS WHERE WE START. YOU'RE GOING TO LEAVE HERE AND TRY TO UNRAVEL ALL OF THIS.

AND AS YOU DIG DEEPER AND DEEPER, YOU'LL FIND IT...

THE TRUTH YOU'VE BEEN *RUNNING* FROM.

I--I LOVED YOU BOTH SO MUCH...

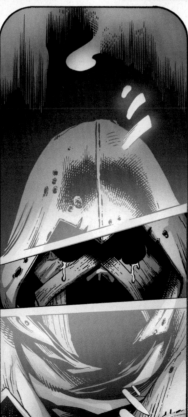

WHY DID YOU *DO* THIS TO ME?

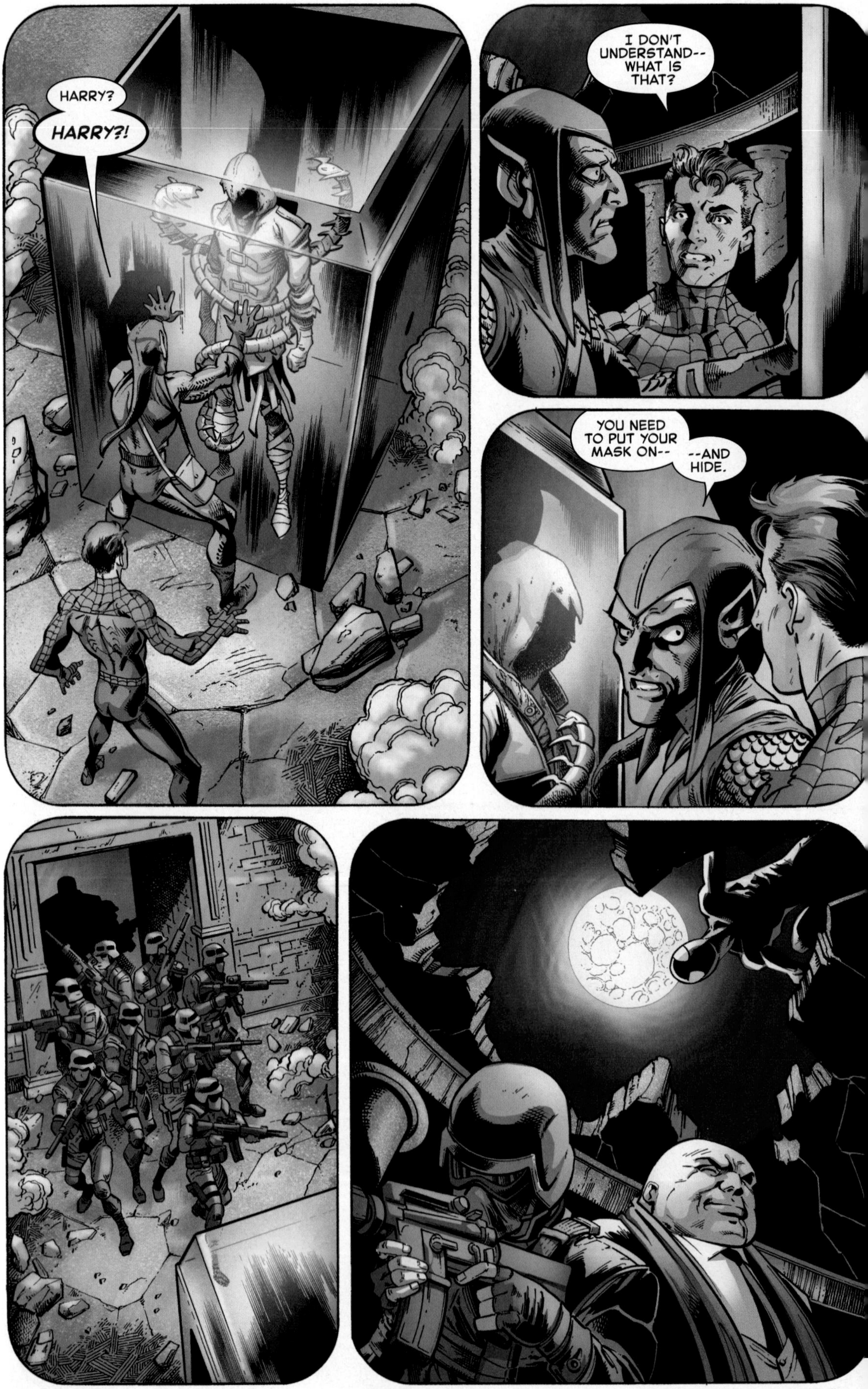
HARRY?
HARRY?!
I DON'T UNDERSTAND-- WHAT IS THAT?
YOU NEED TO PUT YOUR MASK ON--
--AND HIDE.

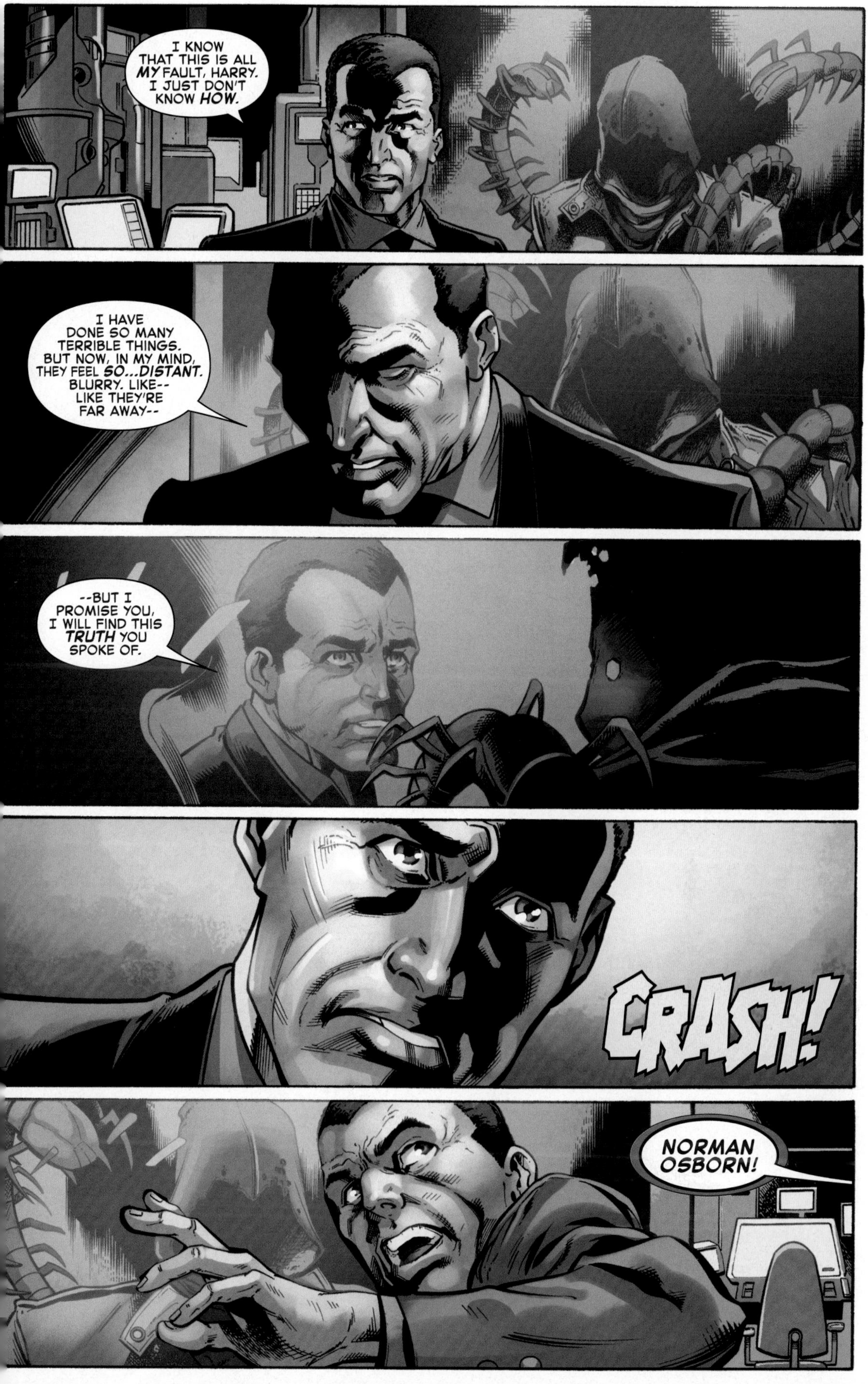
I KNOW THAT THIS IS ALL *MY* FAULT, HARRY. I JUST DON'T KNOW *HOW*.
I HAVE DONE SO MANY TERRIBLE THINGS. BUT NOW, IN MY MIND, THEY FEEL *SO...DISTANT*. BLURRY. LIKE-- LIKE THEY'RE FAR AWAY--
--BUT I PROMISE YOU, I WILL FIND THIS *TRUTH* YOU SPOKE OF.
CRASH!
NORMAN OSBORN!

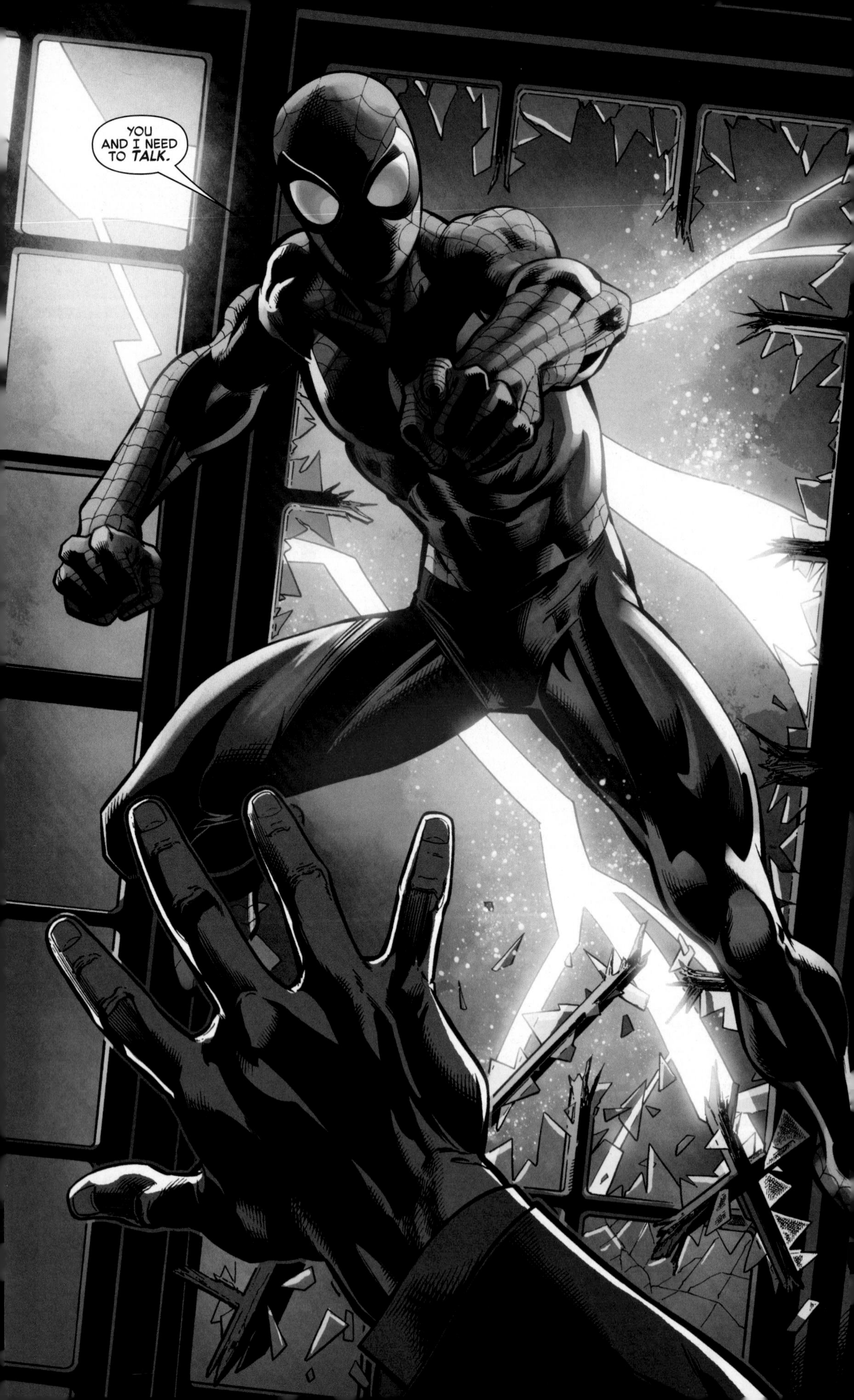
YOU AND I NEED TO TALK.

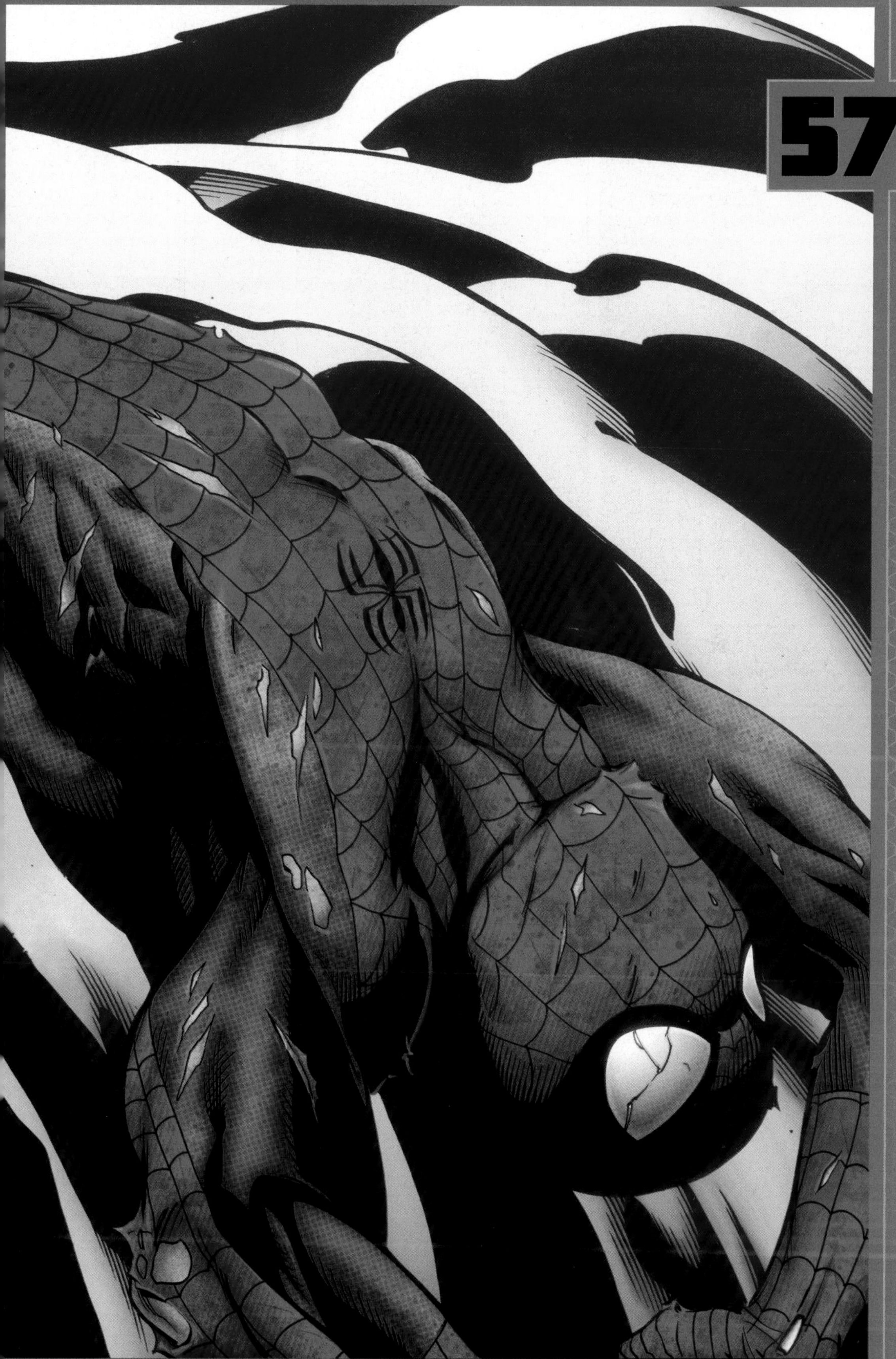
57

LAST REMAINS: POST-MORTEM PART 2

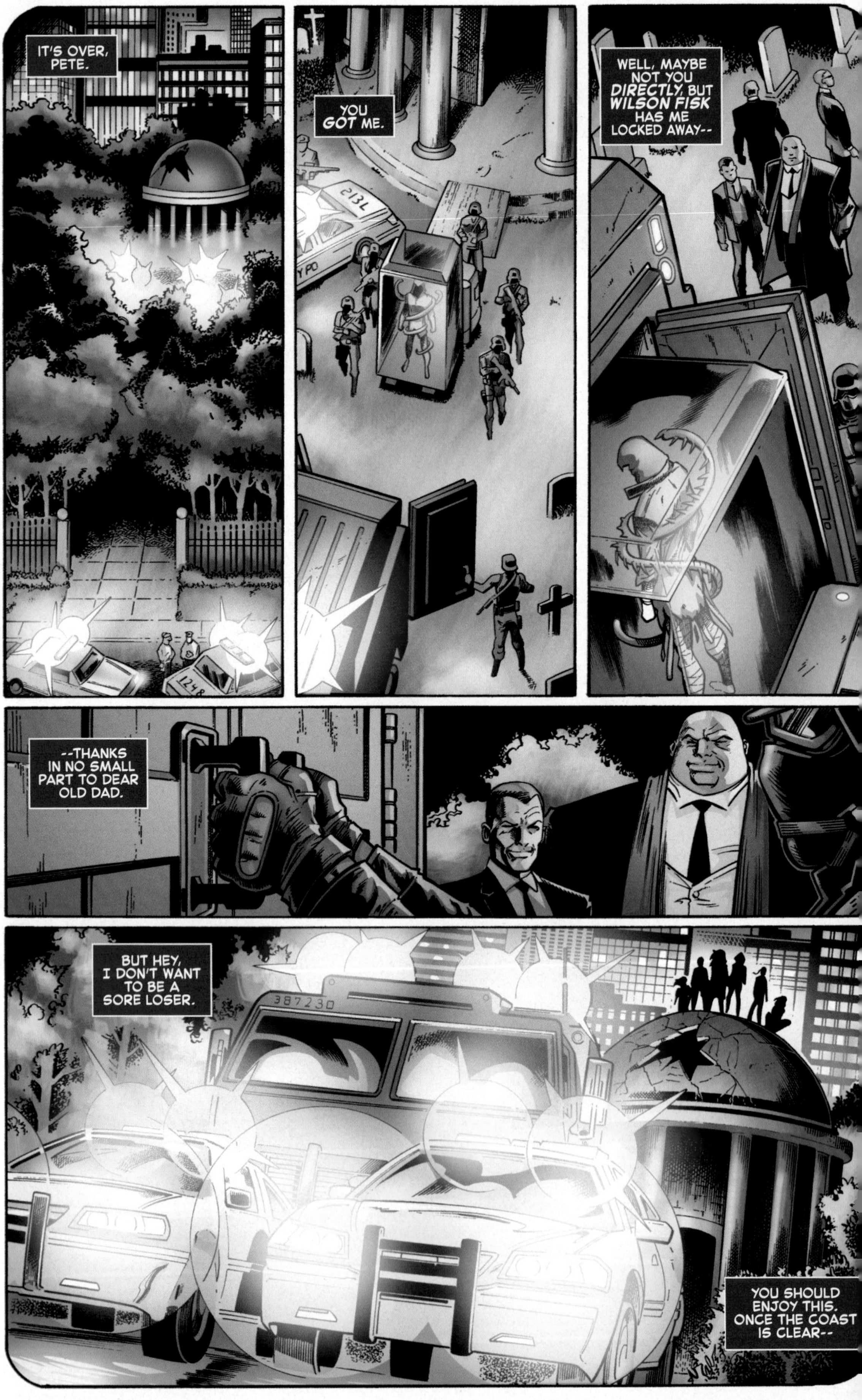
IT'S OVER, PETE.
YOU GOT ME.
WELL, MAYBE NOT YOU DIRECTLY, BUT WILSON FISK HAS ME LOCKED AWAY--
--THANKS IN NO SMALL PART TO DEAR OLD DAD.
BUT HEY, I DON'T WANT TO BE A SORE LOSER.
YOU SHOULD ENJOY THIS. ONCE THE COAST IS CLEAR--

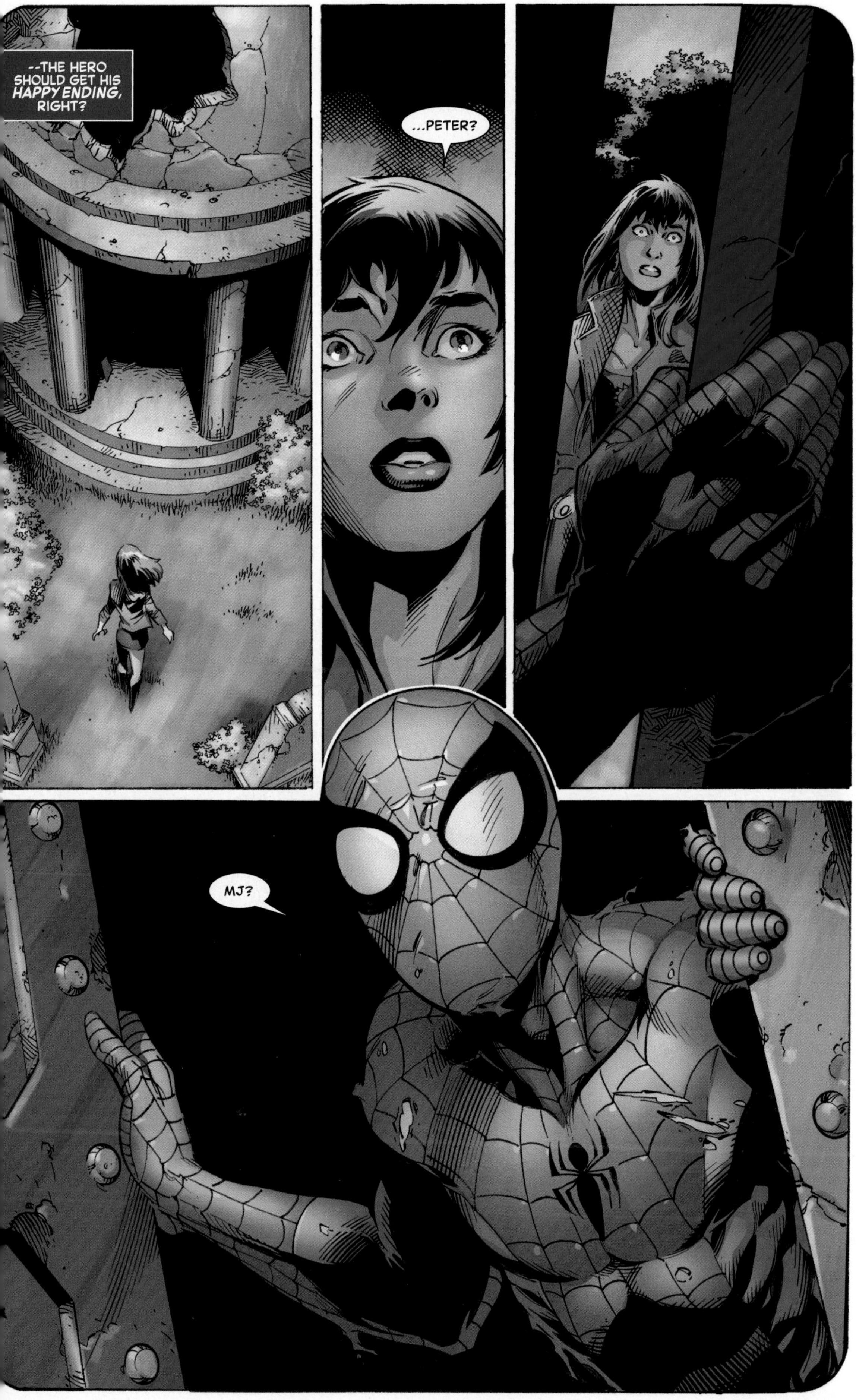
--THE HERO SHOULD GET HIS *HAPPY ENDING,* RIGHT?
...PETER?
MJ?

IT ALL HAPPENED SO FAST. I--I STILL CAN'T BELIEVE YOU'RE HERE...

IT'S REALLY *YOU*, ISN'T IT?

YEAH, TIGER, IT'S ME.

FOR A MINUTE IN THERE, I THOUGHT I'D--

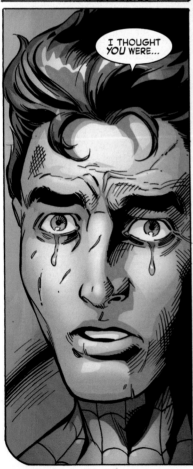

I THOUGHT *YOU* WERE...

OH GOD... PETER...

WHAT DID HE *DO* TO YOU?

YEAH--

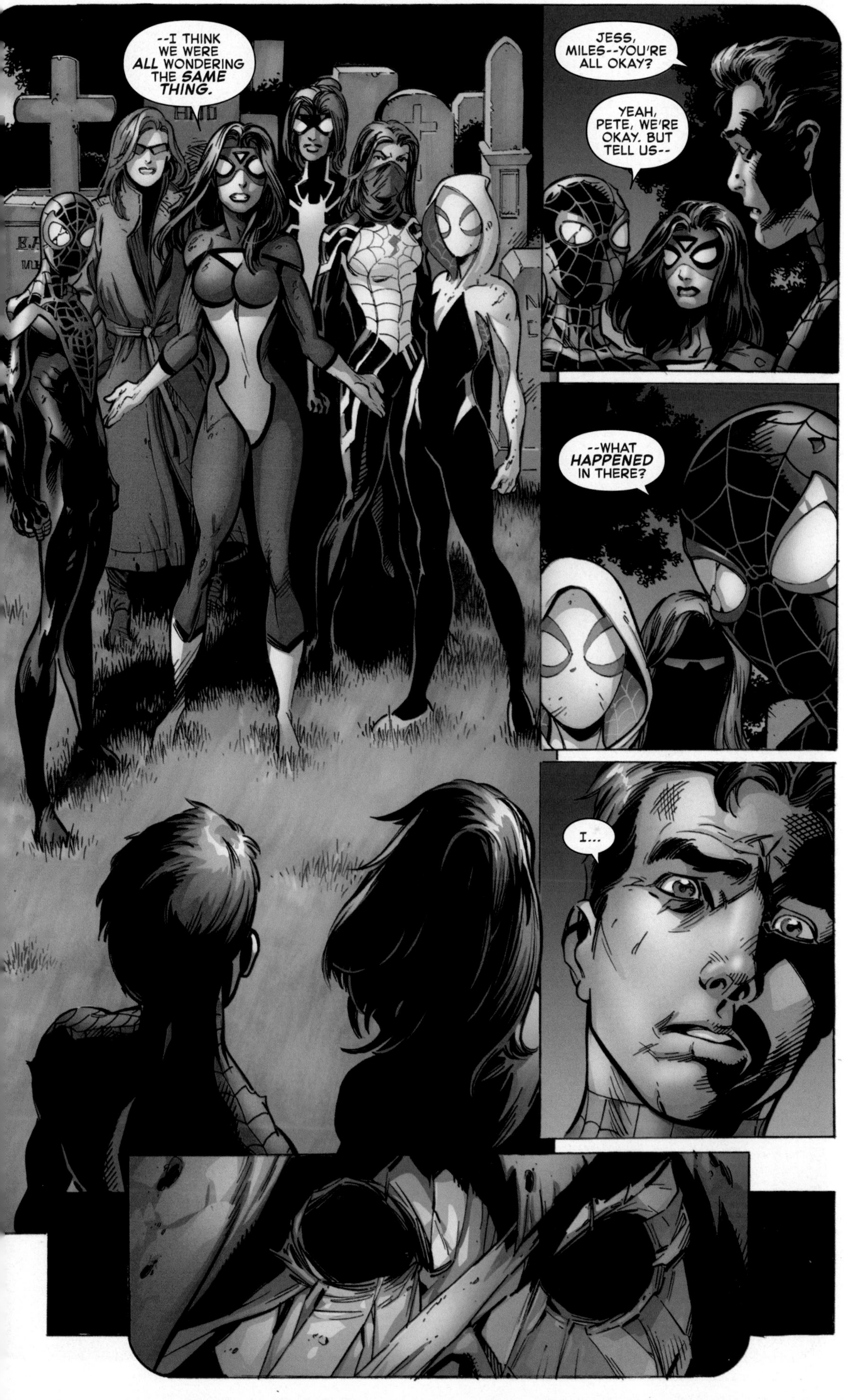
--I THINK WE WERE ALL WONDERING THE SAME THING.
JESS, MILES--YOU'RE ALL OKAY?
YEAH, PETE, WE'RE OKAY. BUT TELL US--
--WHAT HAPPENED IN THERE?
I...

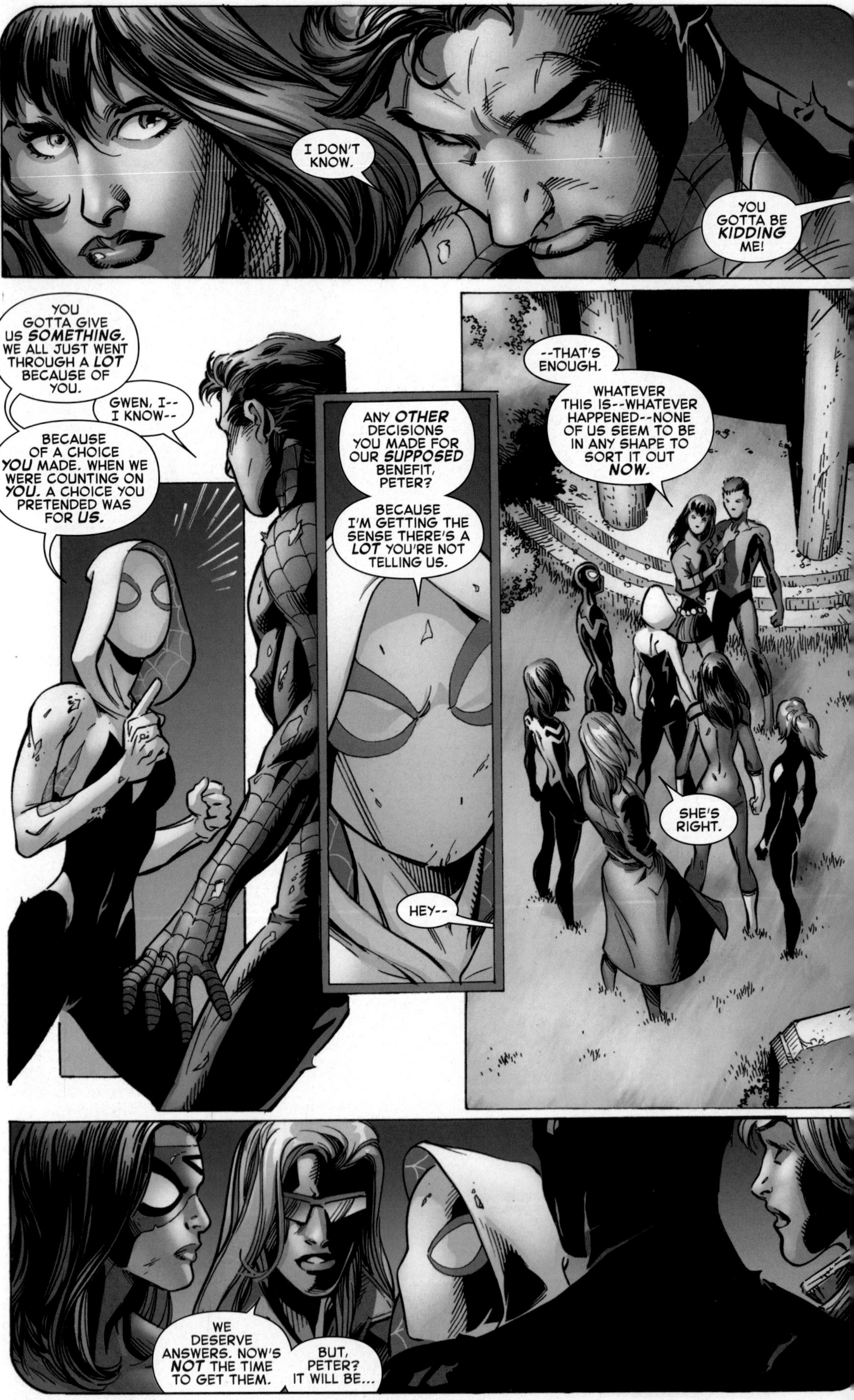
I DON'T KNOW.
YOU GOTTA BE KIDDING ME!
YOU GOTTA GIVE US SOMETHING. WE ALL JUST WENT THROUGH A LOT BECAUSE OF YOU.
GWEN, I-- I KNOW--
BECAUSE OF A CHOICE YOU MADE. WHEN WE WERE COUNTING ON YOU. A CHOICE YOU PRETENDED WAS FOR US.
ANY OTHER DECISIONS YOU MADE FOR OUR SUPPOSED BENEFIT, PETER?
BECAUSE I'M GETTING THE SENSE THERE'S A LOT YOU'RE NOT TELLING US.
HEY--
--THAT'S ENOUGH.
WHATEVER THIS IS--WHATEVER HAPPENED--NONE OF US SEEM TO BE IN ANY SHAPE TO SORT IT OUT NOW.
SHE'S RIGHT.
WE DESERVE ANSWERS. NOW'S NOT THE TIME TO GET THEM.
BUT, PETER? IT WILL BE...

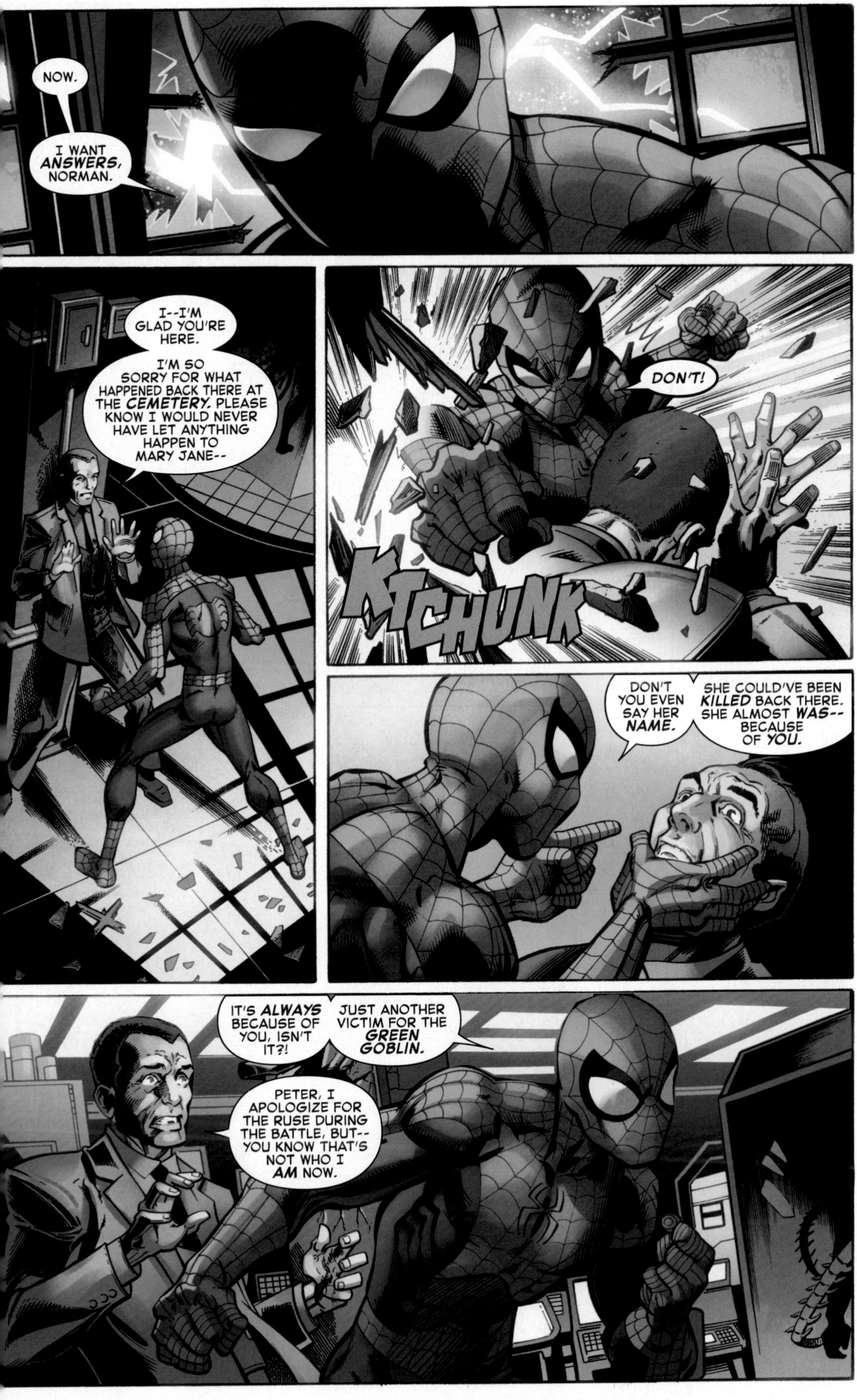

NOW.
I WANT ANSWERS, NORMAN.
I--I'M GLAD YOU'RE HERE.
I'M SO SORRY FOR WHAT HAPPENED BACK THERE AT THE CEMETERY. PLEASE KNOW I WOULD NEVER HAVE LET ANYTHING HAPPEN TO MARY JANE--
DON'T!
KTCHUNK
DON'T YOU EVEN SAY HER NAME.
SHE COULD'VE BEEN KILLED BACK THERE. SHE ALMOST WAS--BECAUSE OF YOU.
IT'S ALWAYS BECAUSE OF YOU, ISN'T IT?!
JUST ANOTHER VICTIM FOR THE GREEN GOBLIN.
PETER, I APOLOGIZE FOR THE RUSE DURING THE BATTLE, BUT--YOU KNOW THAT'S NOT WHO I AM NOW.

RIGHT. NORMAN OSBORN-- *SAVED.*

YOU KNOW, WHEN I THREW YOU OUT OF THAT *ESCAPE POD* AND LEFT YOU FOR THE *SIN-EATER,* I GUESS I LET MYSELF BELIEVE IT WOULD FINALLY CHANGE THINGS. *END* ALL THIS.

BUT HERE YOU ARE--

--THE SAME OLD LYING *MONSTER.*

I DON'T KNOW WHY I EXPECTED ANY LESS. HOW MANY TIMES HAVE WE BEEN *THROUGH* SOMETHING LIKE THIS?

YOU HAVE *AMNESIA* AND CAN'T REMEMBER BEING THE GOBLIN.

THEN YOU'RE ON A *PHARMACEUTICAL TREATMENT* THAT CURES YOUR *PSYCHOSIS.* THEN YO SUDDENLY THINK YOU'RE *CLETUS KASADY*...OR WAS IT *MASON BANKS?*

I'VE SEEN SO MANY DIFFERENT VERSIONS OF YOU I CAN HARDLY KEEP THEM *STRAIGHT.* THEY ALL LEAD TO THE SAME END THOUGH.

SOMEONE *DIES.* SOMEONE *ALWAYS* DIES.

YOU--YOU'RE *RIGHT,* OF COURSE, PETER. I WON'T INSULT YOU BY ATTEMPTING TO APOLOGIZE. THIS REGRET--THIS *GRIEF*--IT *CONSUMES* ME. BUT I KNOW IT PALES IN COMPARISON TO WHAT I'VE PUT *YOU* THROUGH.

AND I WON'T OFFEND YOU BY TELLING YOU THAT I WOULD GIVE ANYTHING TO GO BACK AND CHANGE IT ALL. TO BE THE MENTOR AND FATHER FIGURE THAT YOUNG MAN I MET ALL THOSE YEARS AGO DESERVED, INSTEAD OF HIS *TORMENTOR.*

I KNOW THERE'S NO REASON ON EARTH YOU WOULD EVER TRUST ME NOW. AND...I WAS A *FOOL.* I SHOULD *NEVER* HAVE DONE WHAT I DID, PUTTING YOUR LOVED ONES AT RISK. BUT--

--I DIDN'T KNOW *WHAT* TO DO. AND I HAD TO DO *SOMETHING,* PETER--

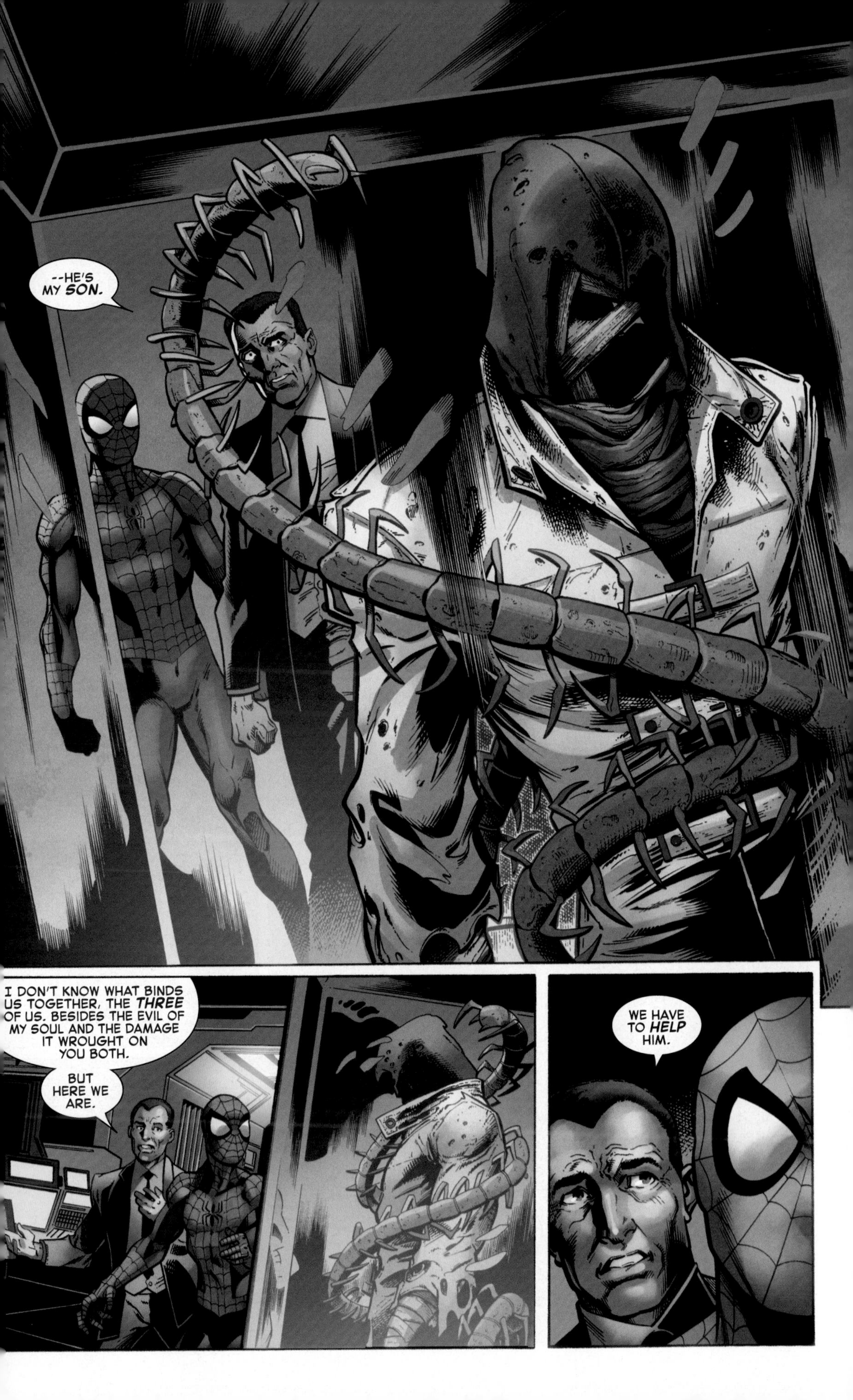
--HE'S MY SON.
I DON'T KNOW WHAT BINDS US TOGETHER, THE THREE OF US. BESIDES THE EVIL OF MY SOUL AND THE DAMAGE IT WROUGHT ON YOU BOTH.
BUT HERE WE ARE.
WE HAVE TO HELP HIM.

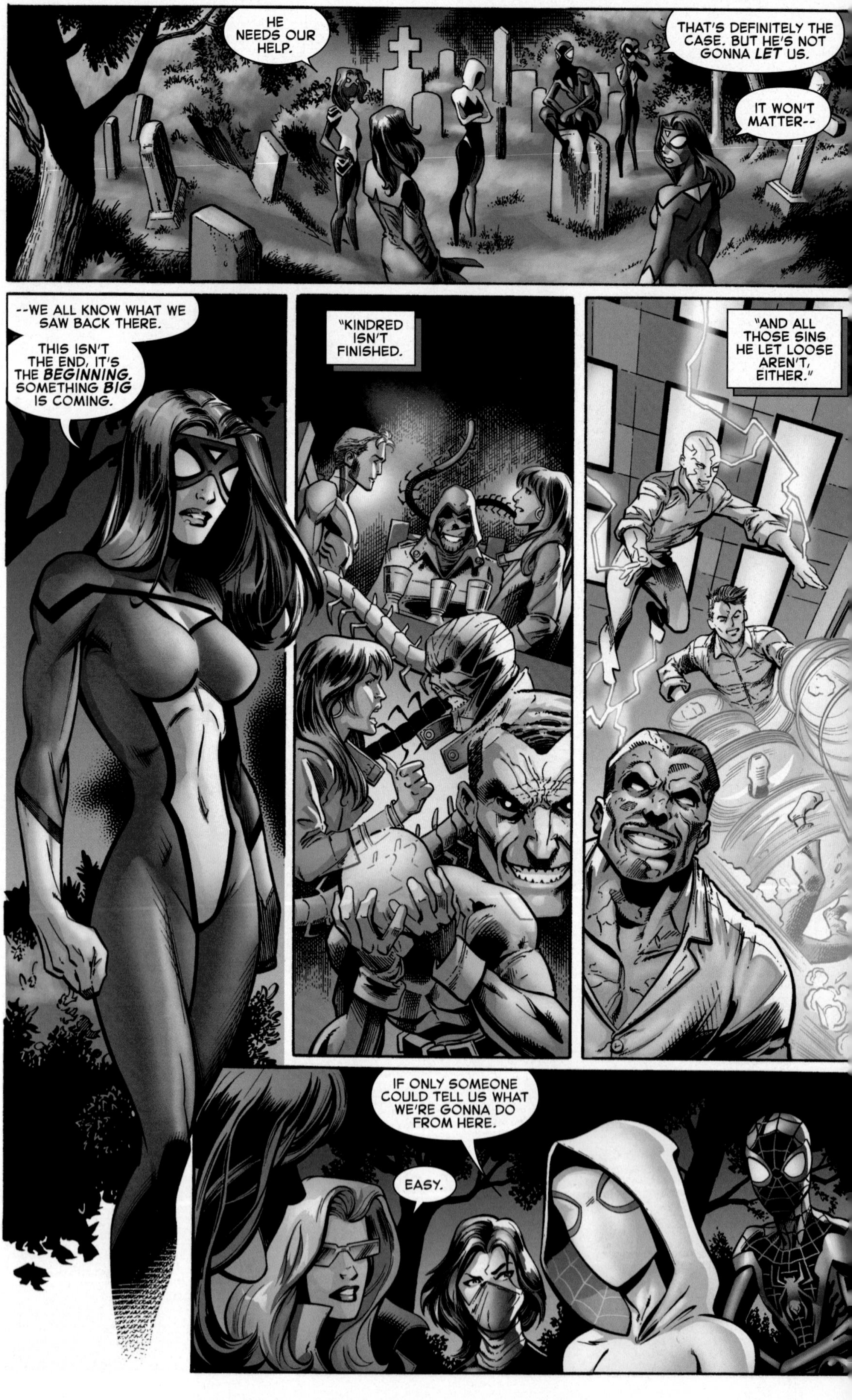
HE NEEDS OUR HELP.
THAT'S DEFINITELY THE CASE. BUT HE'S NOT GONNA LET US.
IT WON'T MATTER--
--WE ALL KNOW WHAT WE SAW BACK THERE.
THIS ISN'T THE END, IT'S THE BEGINNING. SOMETHING BIG IS COMING.
"KINDRED ISN'T FINISHED.
"AND ALL THOSE SINS HE LET LOOSE AREN'T, EITHER."
IF ONLY SOMEONE COULD TELL US WHAT WE'RE GONNA DO FROM HERE.
EASY.

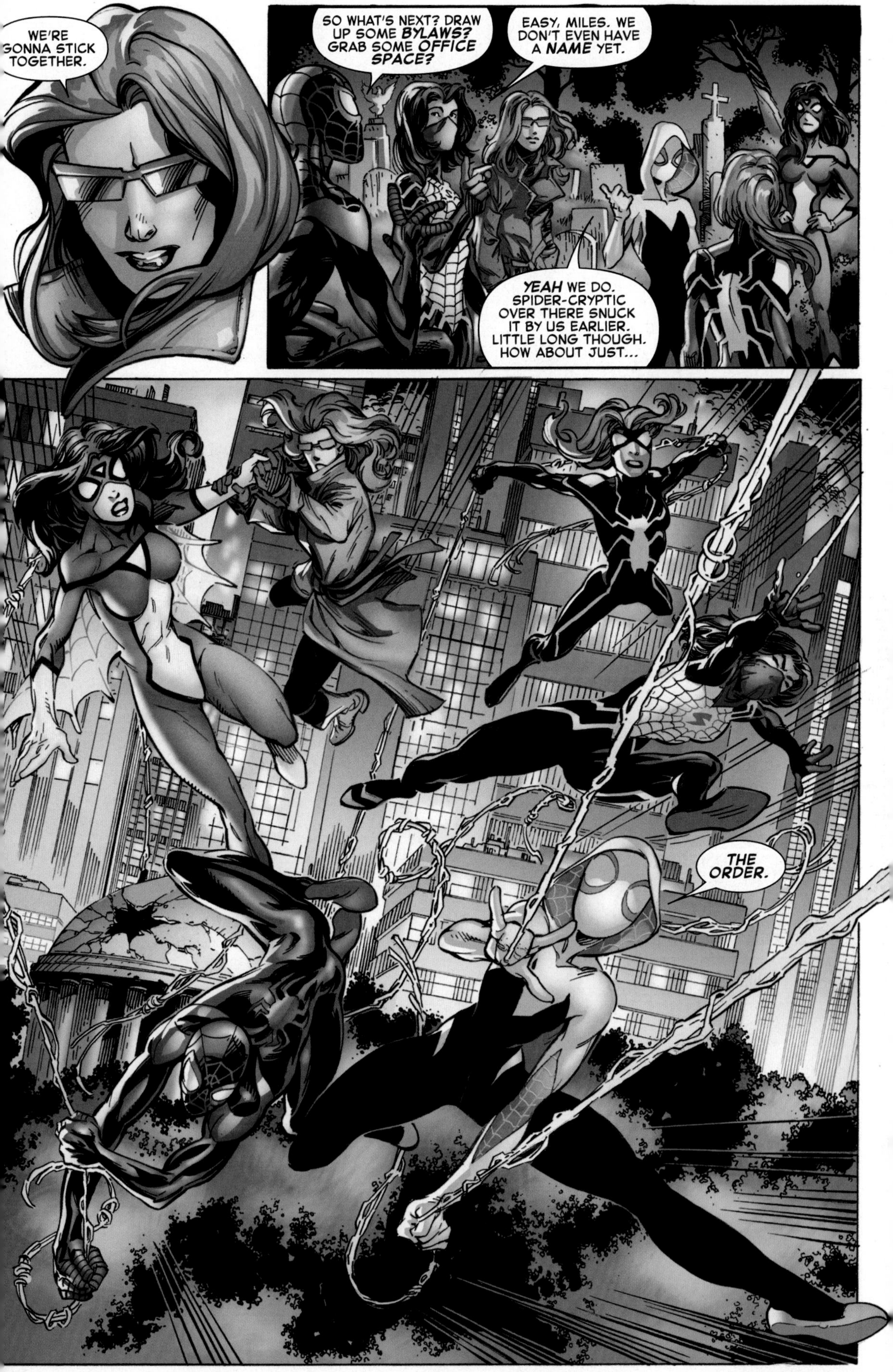
WE'RE GONNA STICK TOGETHER.
SO WHAT'S NEXT? DRAW UP SOME BYLAWS? GRAB SOME OFFICE SPACE?
EASY, MILES. WE DON'T EVEN HAVE A NAME YET.
YEAH WE DO. SPIDER-CRYPTIC OVER THERE SNUCK IT BY US EARLIER. LITTLE LONG THOUGH. HOW ABOUT JUST...
THE ORDER.

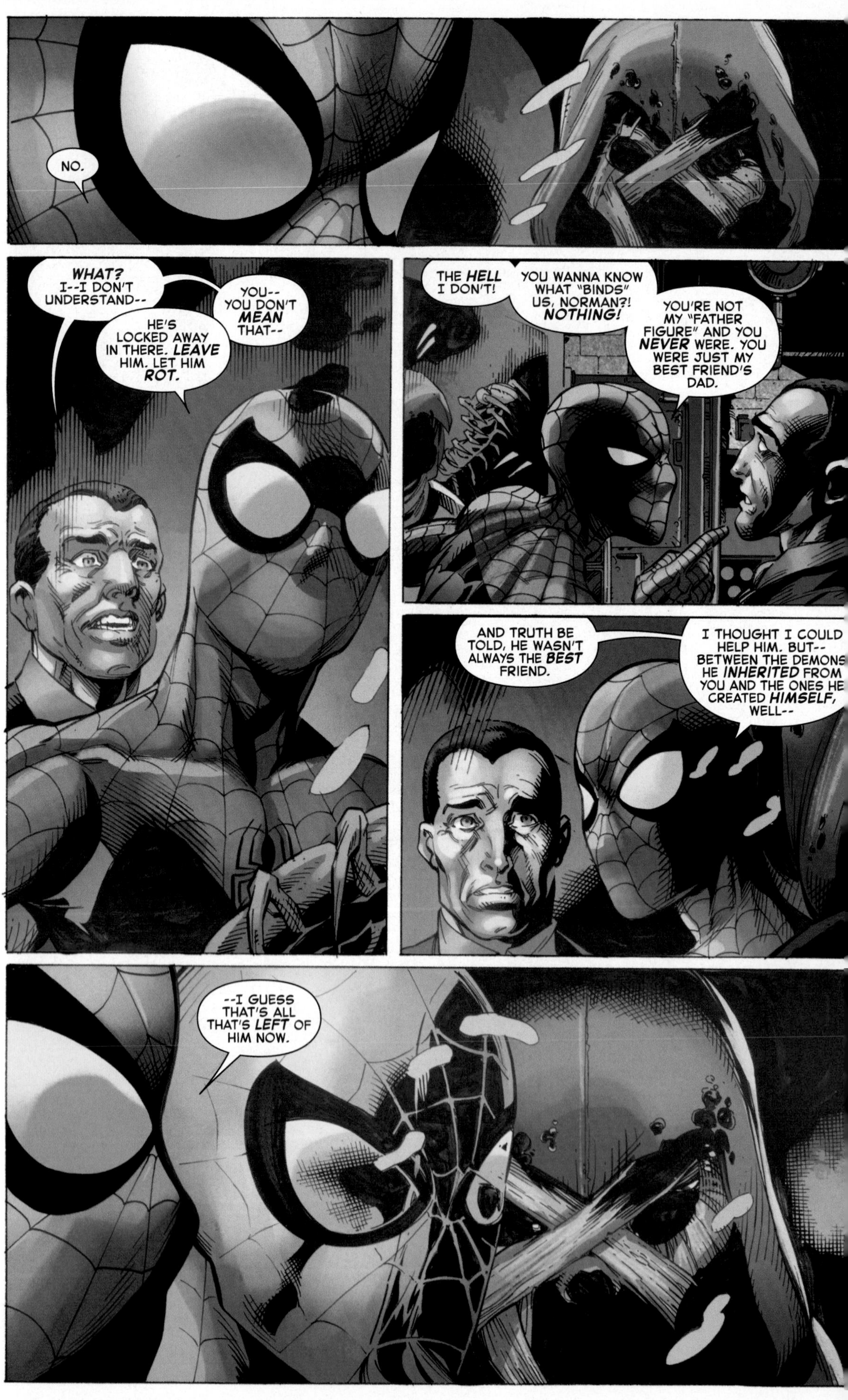
NO.
WHAT? I--I DON'T UNDERSTAND--
YOU-- YOU DON'T MEAN THAT--
HE'S LOCKED AWAY IN THERE. LEAVE HIM. LET HIM ROT.
THE HELL I DON'T!
YOU WANNA KNOW WHAT "BINDS" US, NORMAN?! NOTHING!
YOU'RE NOT MY "FATHER FIGURE" AND YOU NEVER WERE. YOU WERE JUST MY BEST FRIEND'S DAD.
AND TRUTH BE TOLD, HE WASN'T ALWAYS THE BEST FRIEND.
I THOUGHT I COULD HELP HIM. BUT-- BETWEEN THE DEMONS HE INHERITED FROM YOU AND THE ONES HE CREATED HIMSELF, WELL--
--I GUESS THAT'S ALL THAT'S LEFT OF HIM NOW.

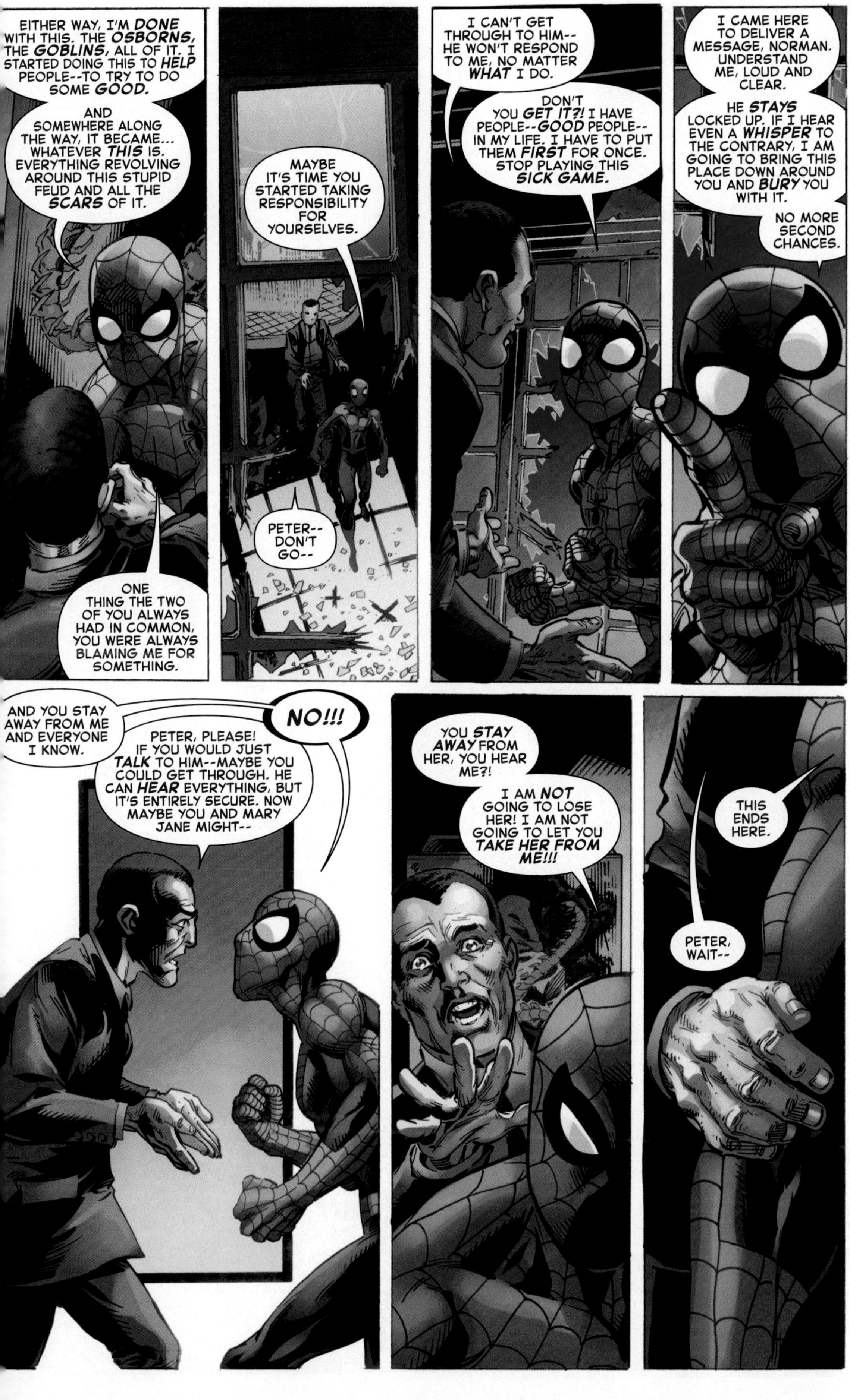
EITHER WAY, I'M DONE WITH THIS. THE OSBORNS, THE GOBLINS, ALL OF IT. I STARTED DOING THIS TO HELP PEOPLE--TO TRY TO DO SOME GOOD.
AND SOMEWHERE ALONG THE WAY, IT BECAME... WHATEVER THIS IS. EVERYTHING REVOLVING AROUND THIS STUPID FEUD AND ALL THE SCARS OF IT.
ONE THING THE TWO OF YOU ALWAYS HAD IN COMMON, YOU WERE ALWAYS BLAMING ME FOR SOMETHING.
MAYBE IT'S TIME YOU STARTED TAKING RESPONSIBILITY FOR YOURSELVES.
PETER-- DON'T GO--
I CAN'T GET THROUGH TO HIM-- HE WON'T RESPOND TO ME, NO MATTER WHAT I DO.
DON'T YOU GET IT?! I HAVE PEOPLE--GOOD PEOPLE-- IN MY LIFE. I HAVE TO PUT THEM FIRST FOR ONCE. STOP PLAYING THIS SICK GAME.
I CAME HERE TO DELIVER A MESSAGE, NORMAN. UNDERSTAND ME, LOUD AND CLEAR.
HE STAYS LOCKED UP. IF I HEAR EVEN A WHISPER TO THE CONTRARY, I AM GOING TO BRING THIS PLACE DOWN AROUND YOU AND BURY YOU WITH IT.
NO MORE SECOND CHANCES.
AND YOU STAY AWAY FROM ME AND EVERYONE I KNOW.
PETER, PLEASE! IF YOU WOULD JUST TALK TO HIM--MAYBE YOU COULD GET THROUGH. HE CAN HEAR EVERYTHING, BUT IT'S ENTIRELY SECURE. NOW MAYBE YOU AND MARY JANE MIGHT--
NO!!!
YOU STAY AWAY FROM HER, YOU HEAR ME?!
I AM NOT GOING TO LOSE HER! I AM NOT GOING TO LET YOU TAKE HER FROM ME!!!
THIS ENDS HERE.
PETER, WAIT--

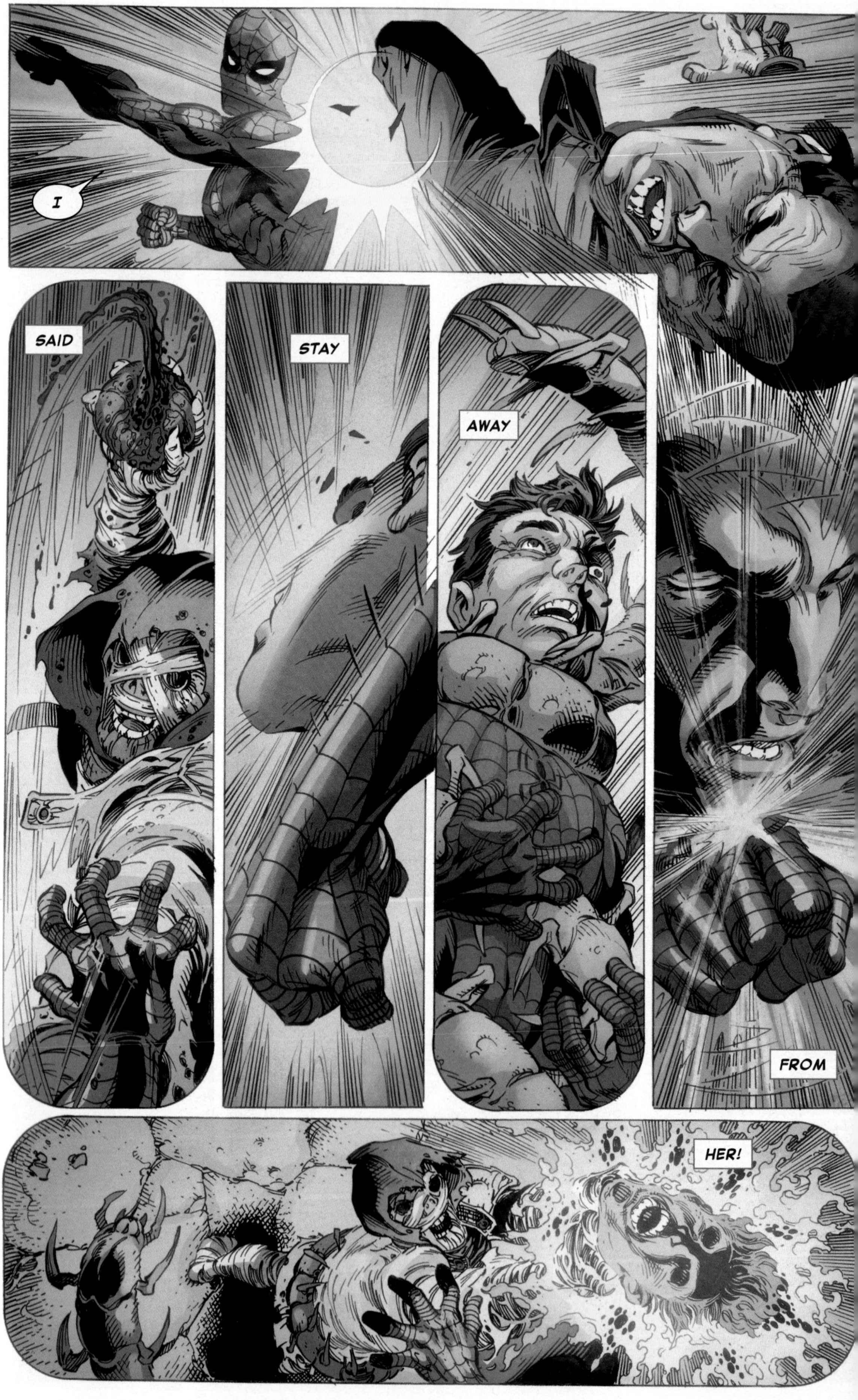
I
SAID
STAY
AWAY
FROM
HER!

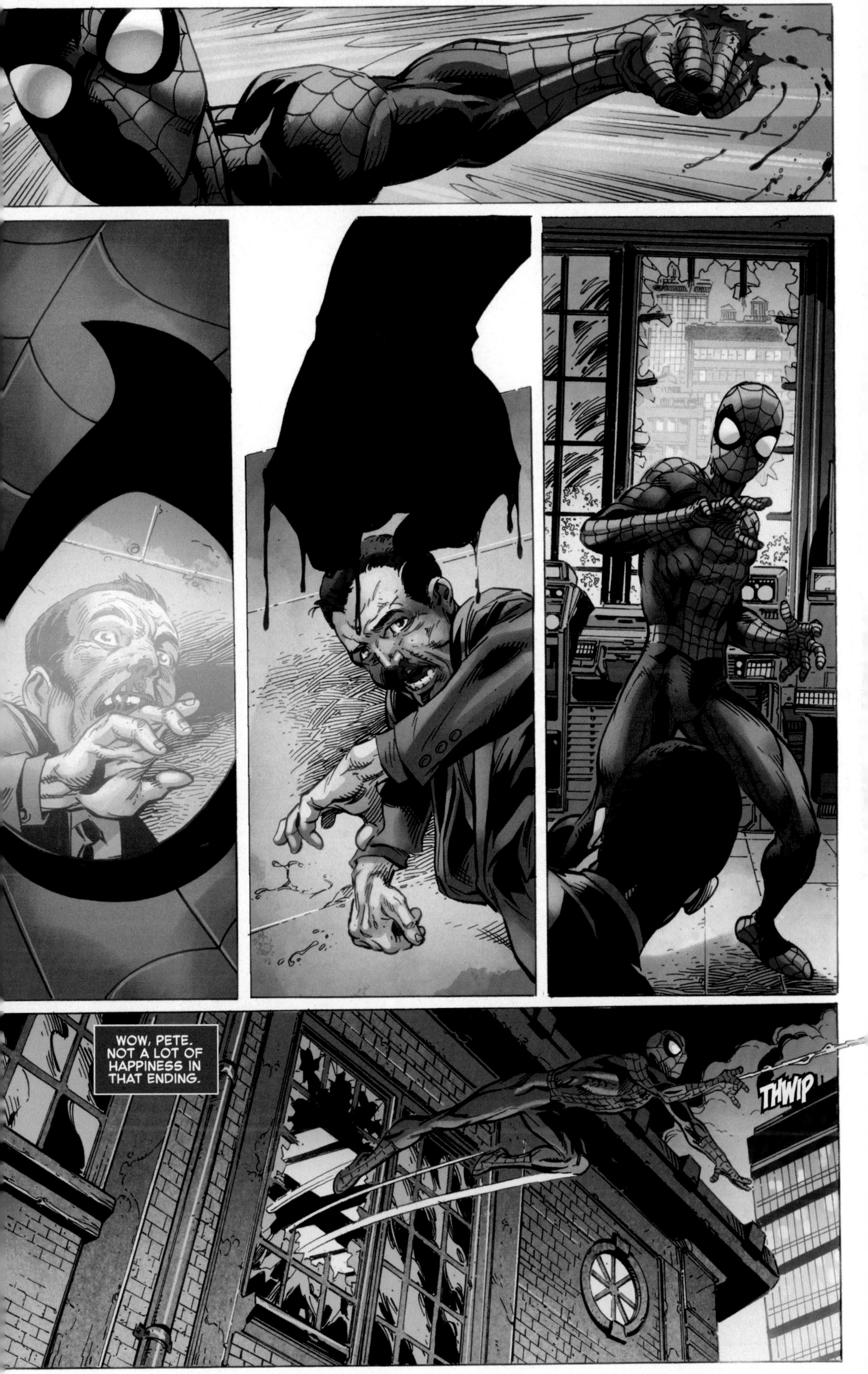
WOW, PETE. NOT A LOT OF HAPPINESS IN THAT ENDING.
THWIP

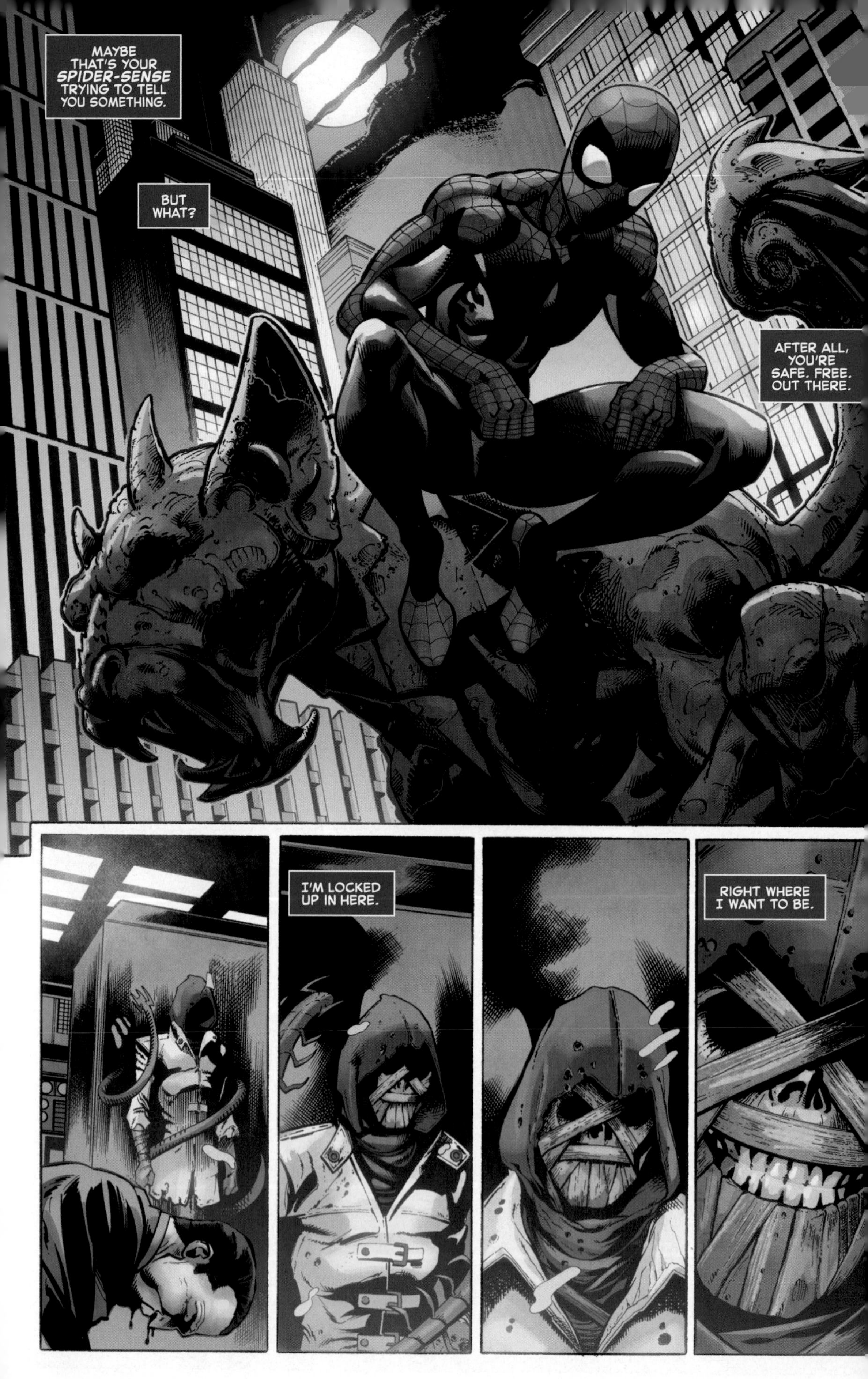
MAYBE THAT'S YOUR SPIDER-SENSE TRYING TO TELL YOU SOMETHING.
BUT WHAT?
AFTER ALL, YOU'RE SAFE. FREE. OUT THERE.
I'M LOCKED UP IN HERE.
RIGHT WHERE I WANT TO BE.

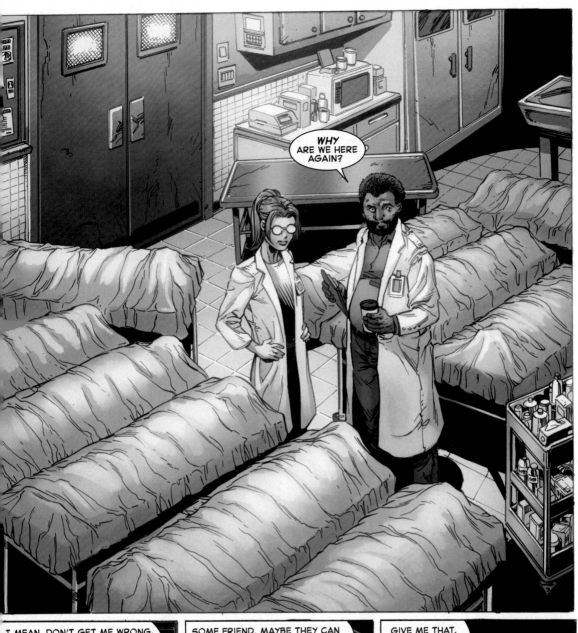

WHY ARE WE HERE AGAIN?

I MEAN, DON'T GET ME WRONG, IT'S *AWFUL* THEY ALL GOT DUG UP LIKE THIS. BUT EXAMINING LONG-DEAD CORPSES THAT HAVE ALREADY BEEN I.D.'d AND BURIED ISN'T USUALLY THE KINDA STUFF WE DO HERE.

FAVOR FOR A FRIEND.

SOME FRIEND. MAYBE THEY CAN TELL YOU WHAT THE *CONNECTION* HERE IS? BECAUSE THESE PEOPLE WERE BURIED IN DIFFERENT CEMETERIES, MOST OF THEM WEREN'T RELATED, AND--

GIVE ME THAT. WHY DON'T YOU GO AHEAD AND HEAD OUT FOR THE NIGHT? I CAN HANDLE THIS.

SUIT YOURSELF.

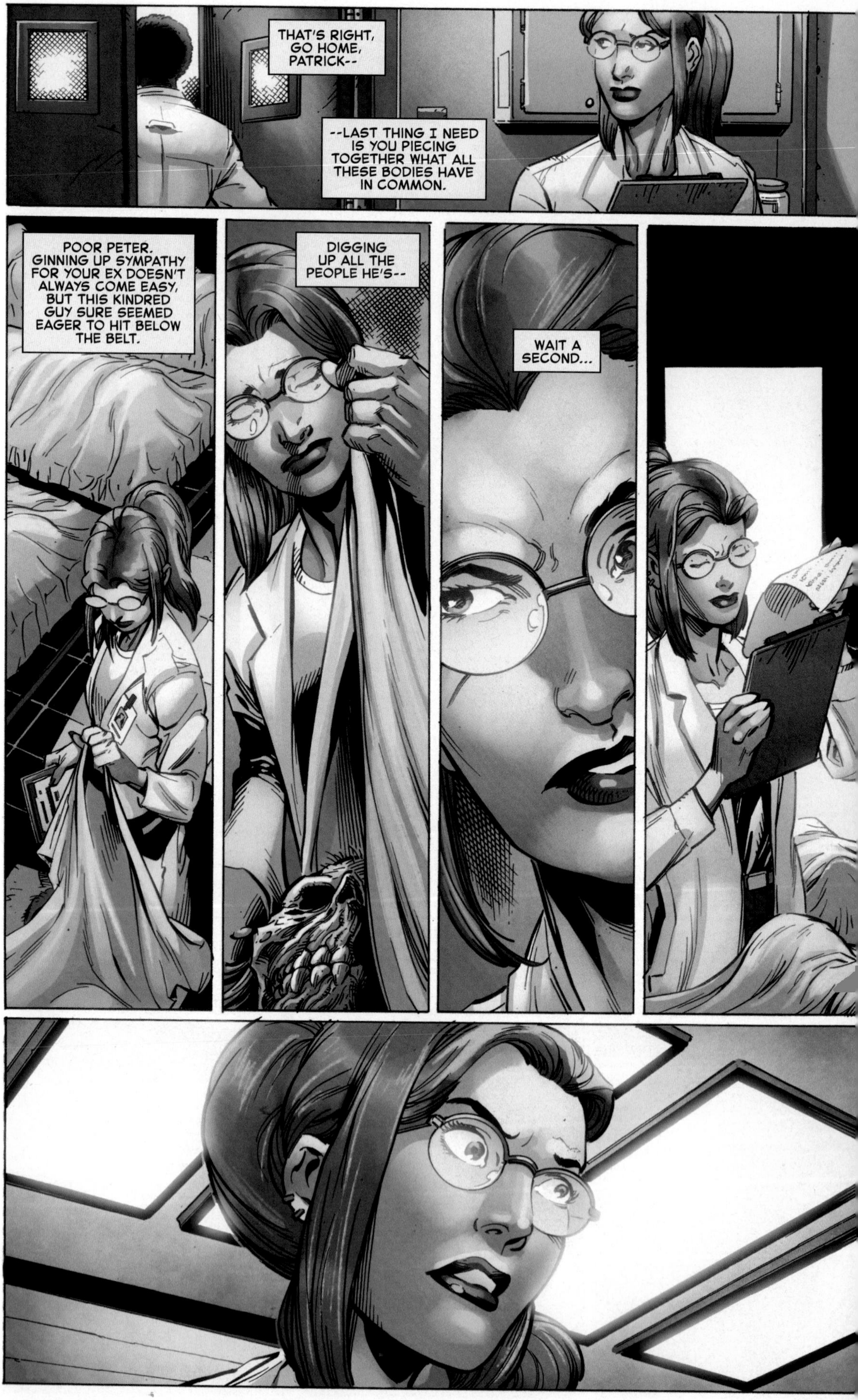
THAT'S RIGHT, GO HOME, PATRICK--
--LAST THING I NEED IS YOU PIECING TOGETHER WHAT ALL THESE BODIES HAVE IN COMMON.
POOR PETER. GINNING UP SYMPATHY FOR YOUR EX DOESN'T ALWAYS COME EASY, BUT THIS KINDRED GUY SURE SEEMED EAGER TO HIT BELOW THE BELT.
DIGGING UP ALL THE PEOPLE HE'S--
WAIT A SECOND...

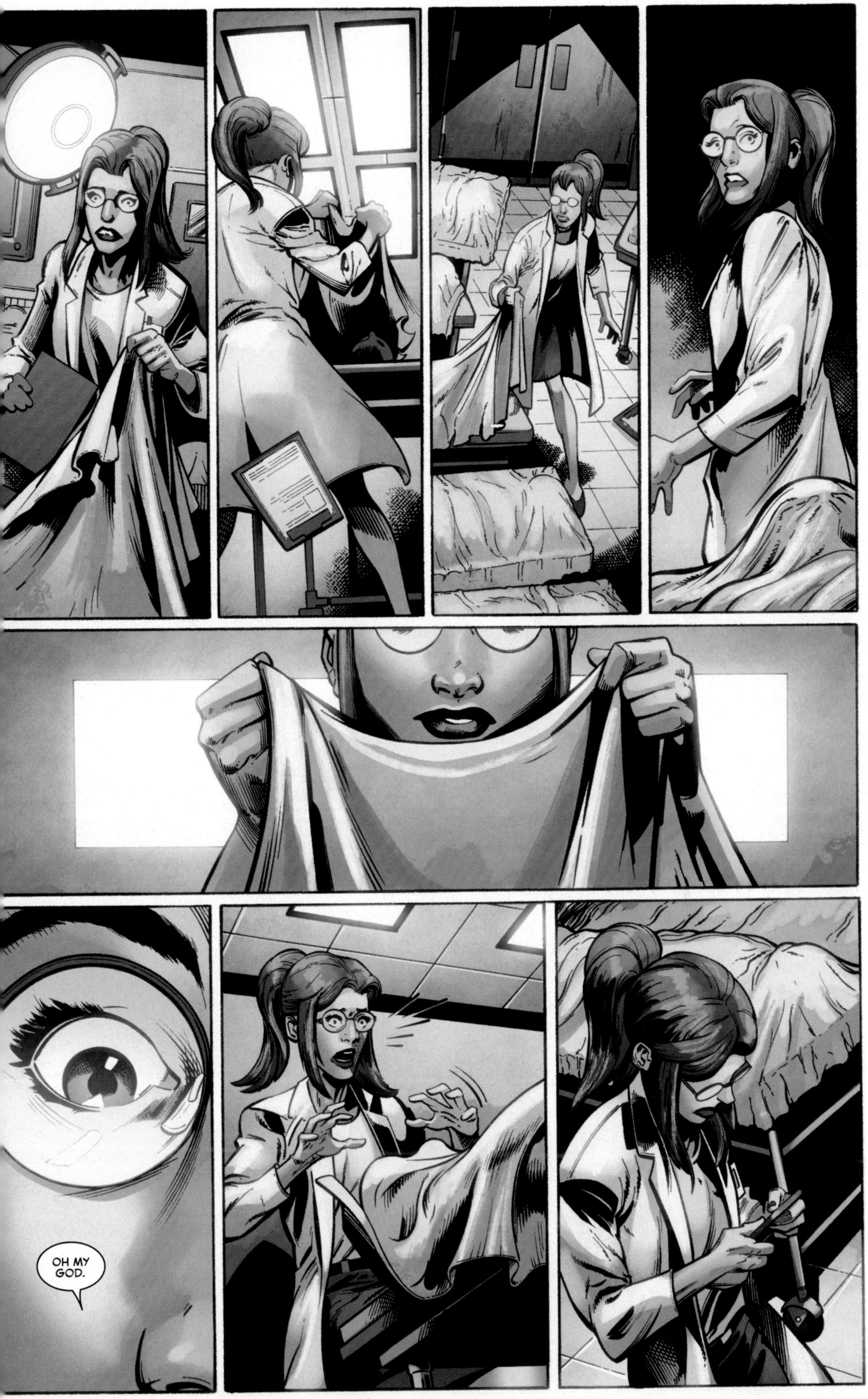
OH MY GOD.

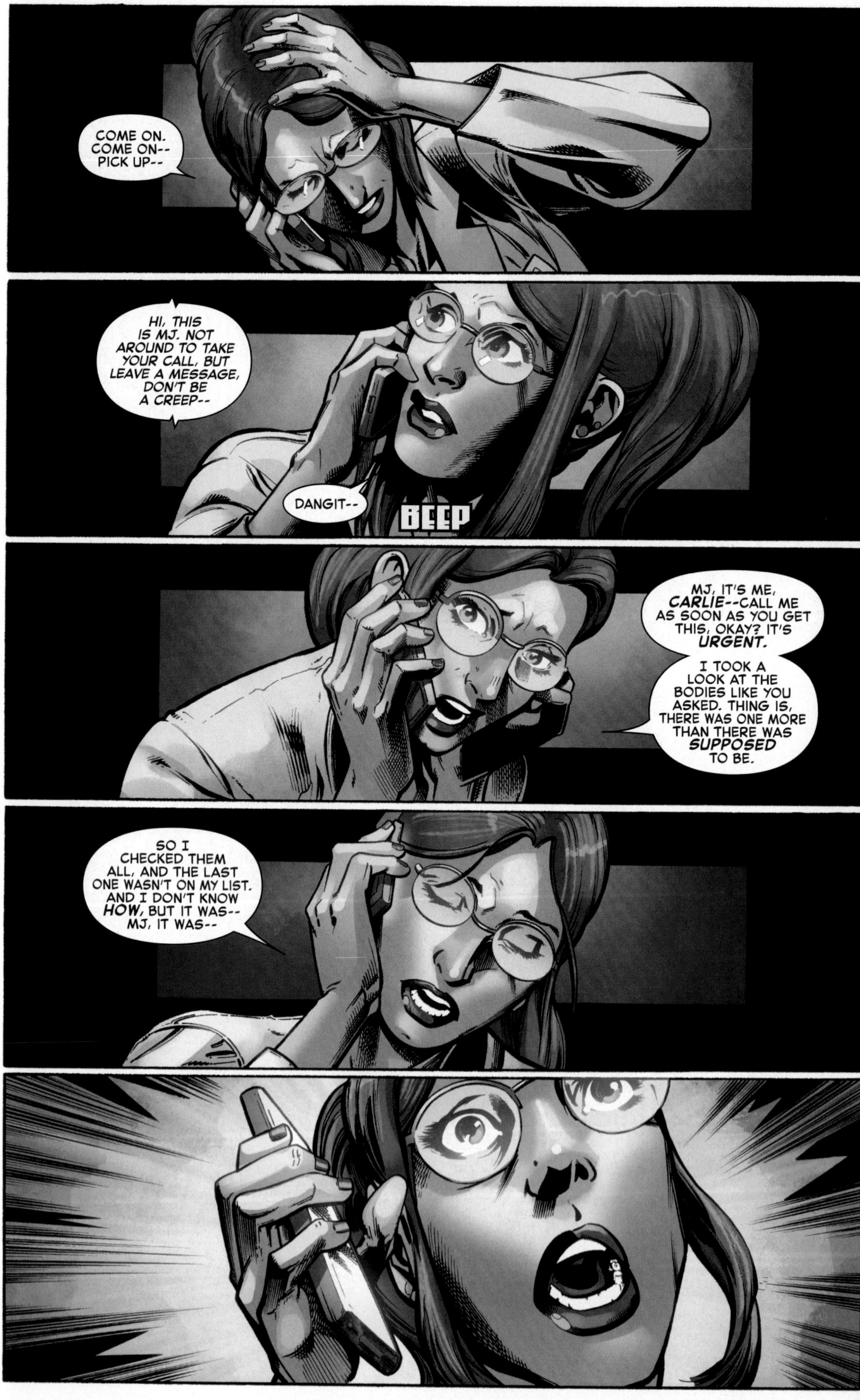
COME ON. COME ON-- PICK UP--
HI, THIS IS MJ. NOT AROUND TO TAKE YOUR CALL, BUT LEAVE A MESSAGE, DON'T BE A CREEP--
DANGIT--
BEEP
MJ, IT'S ME, CARLIE--CALL ME AS SOON AS YOU GET THIS, OKAY? IT'S URGENT.
I TOOK A LOOK AT THE BODIES LIKE YOU ASKED. THING IS, THERE WAS ONE MORE THAN THERE WAS SUPPOSED TO BE.
SO I CHECKED THEM ALL, AND THE LAST ONE WASN'T ON MY LIST. AND I DON'T KNOW HOW, BUT IT WAS-- MJ, IT WAS--

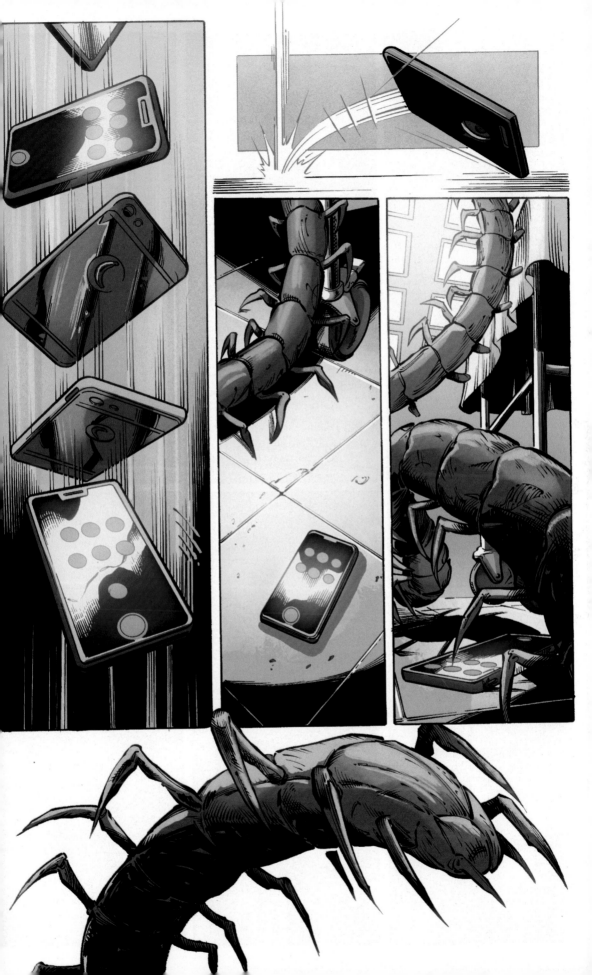

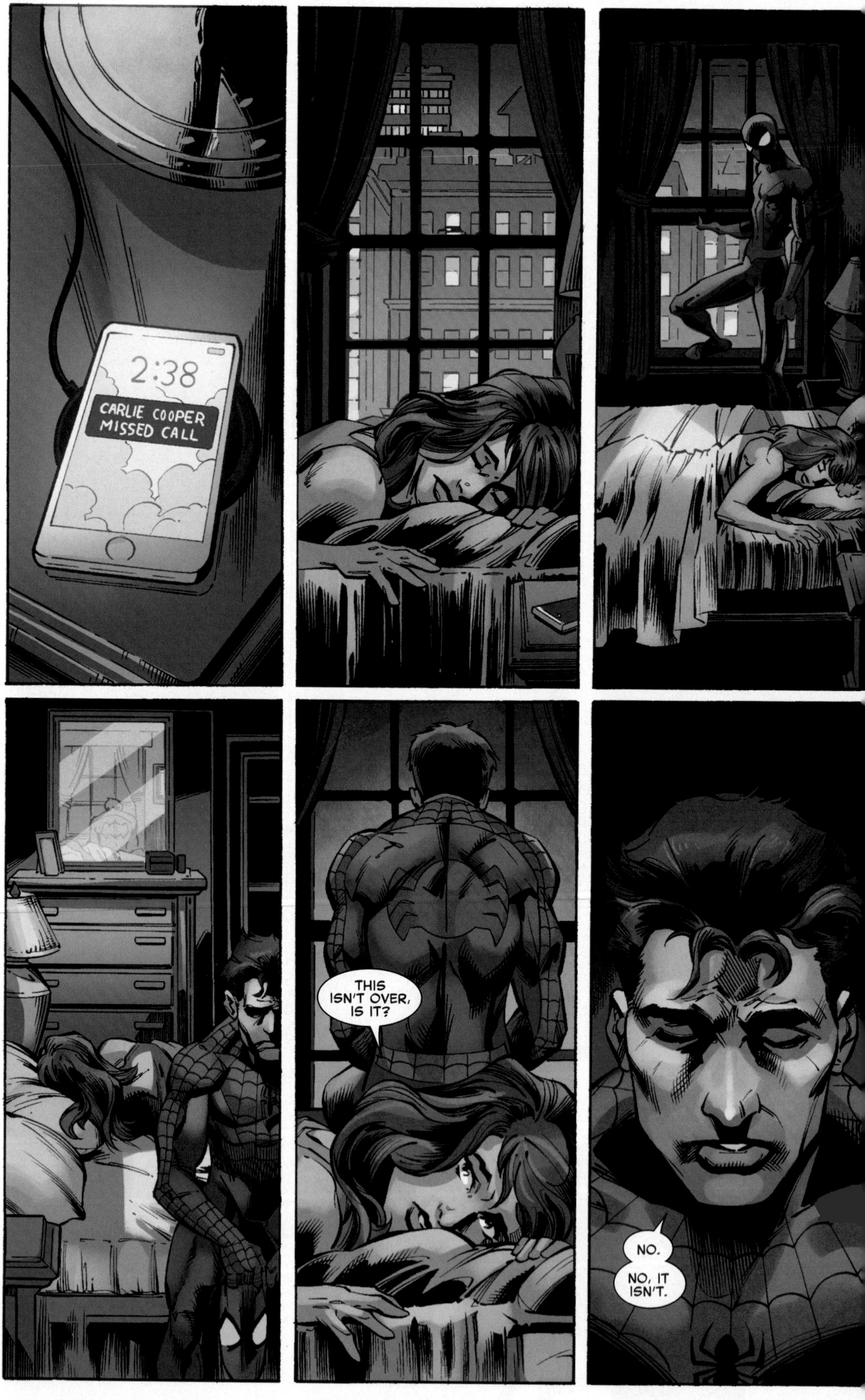
2:38
CARLIE COOPER
MISSED CALL
THIS ISN'T OVER, IS IT?
NO.
NO, IT ISN'T.

# 58

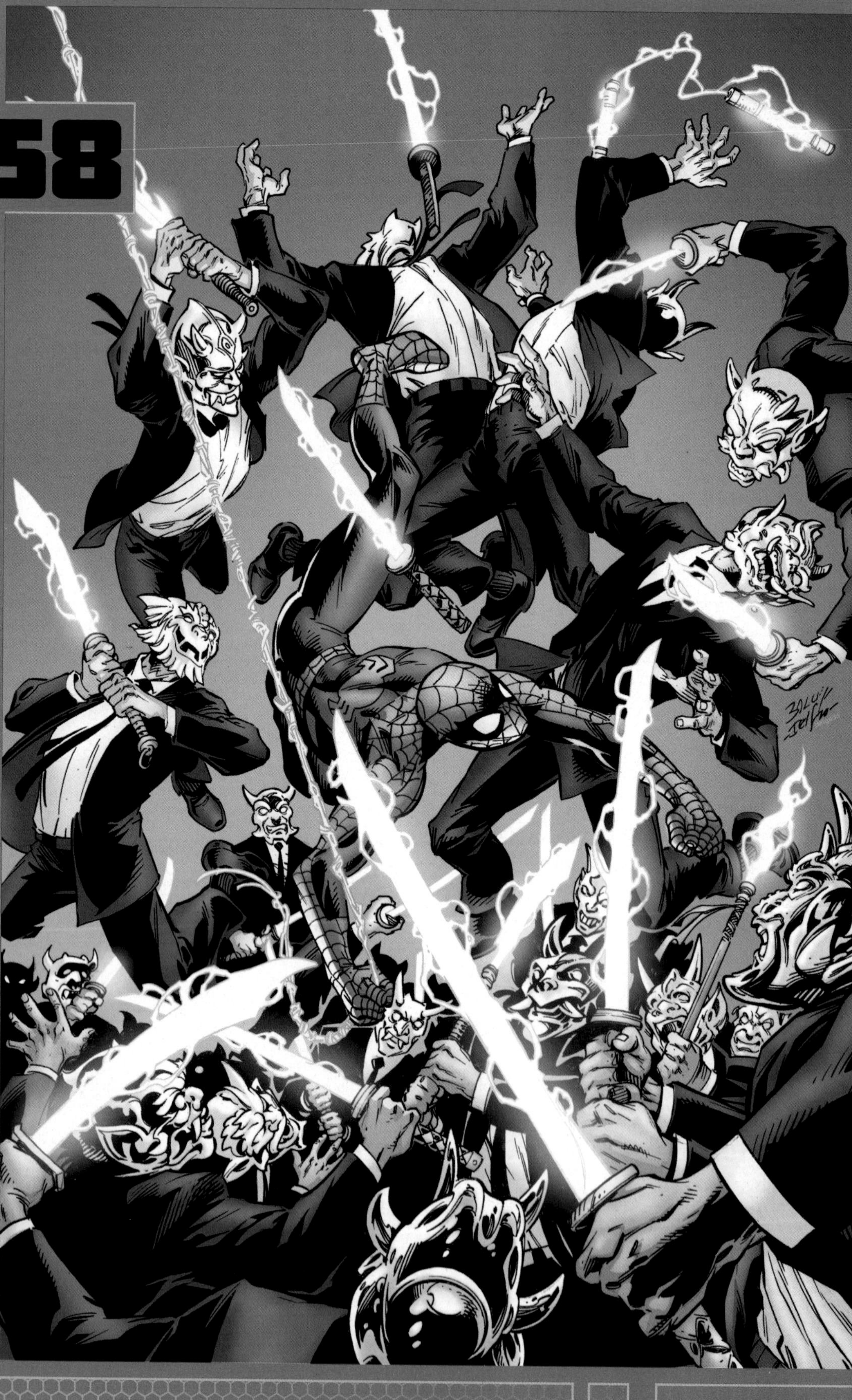

## NEGATIVE SPACE PART 1

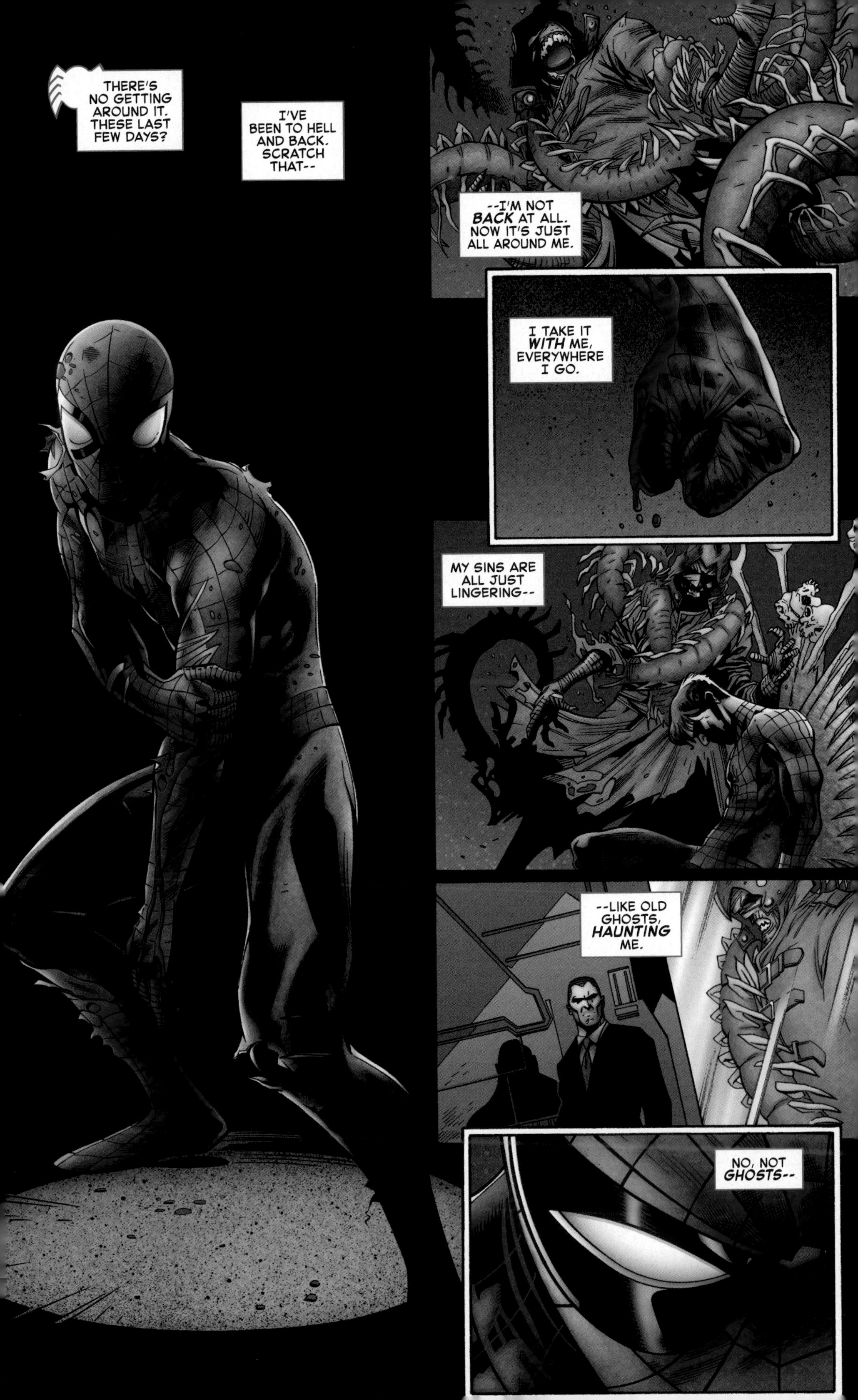
THERE'S NO GETTING AROUND IT. THESE LAST FEW DAYS?
I'VE BEEN TO HELL AND BACK. SCRATCH THAT--
--I'M NOT BACK AT ALL. NOW IT'S JUST ALL AROUND ME.
I TAKE IT WITH ME, EVERYWHERE I GO.
MY SINS ARE ALL JUST LINGERING--
--LIKE OLD GHOSTS, HAUNTING ME.
NO, NOT GHOSTS--

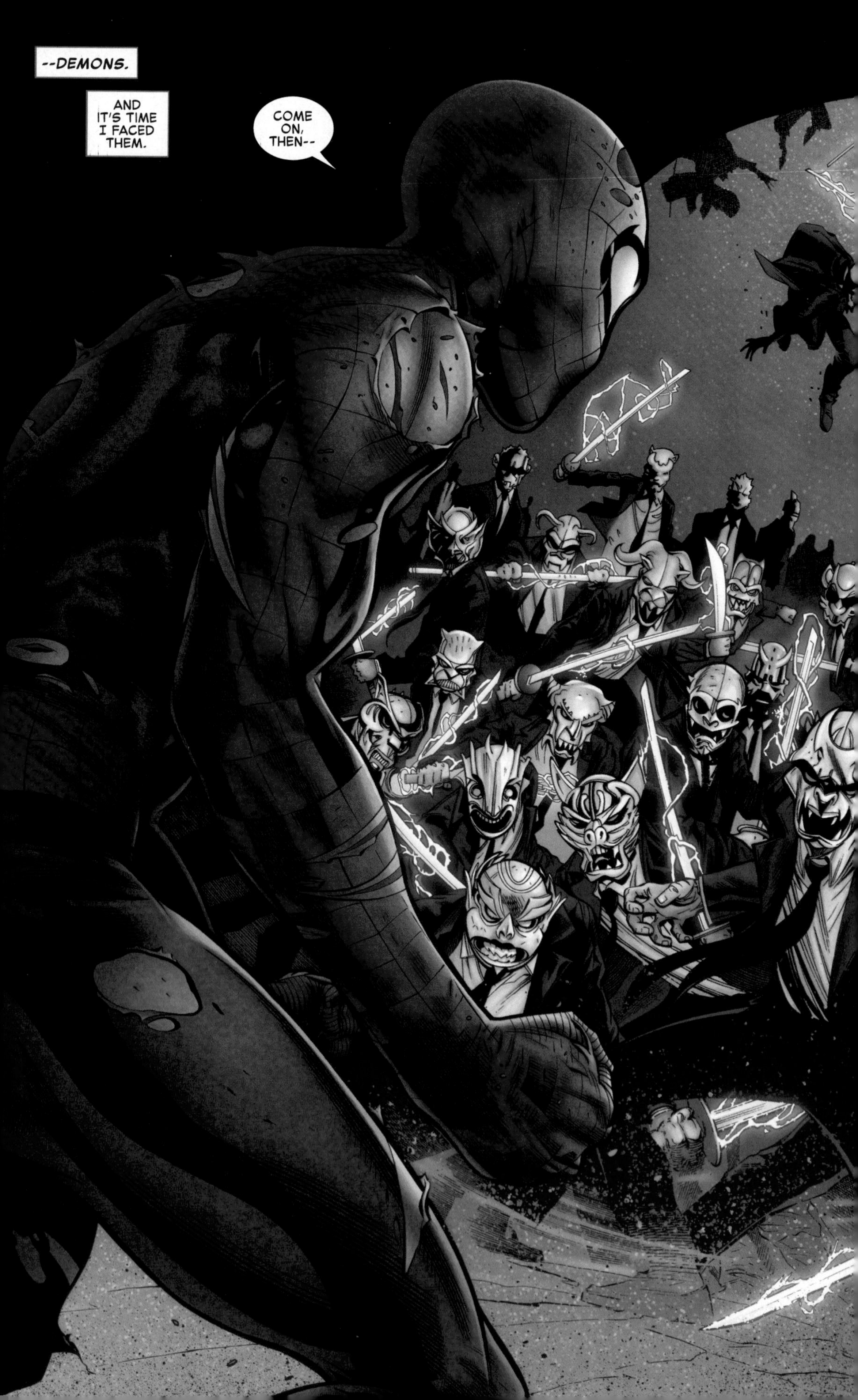
--DEMONS.
AND IT'S TIME I FACED THEM.
COME ON, THEN--

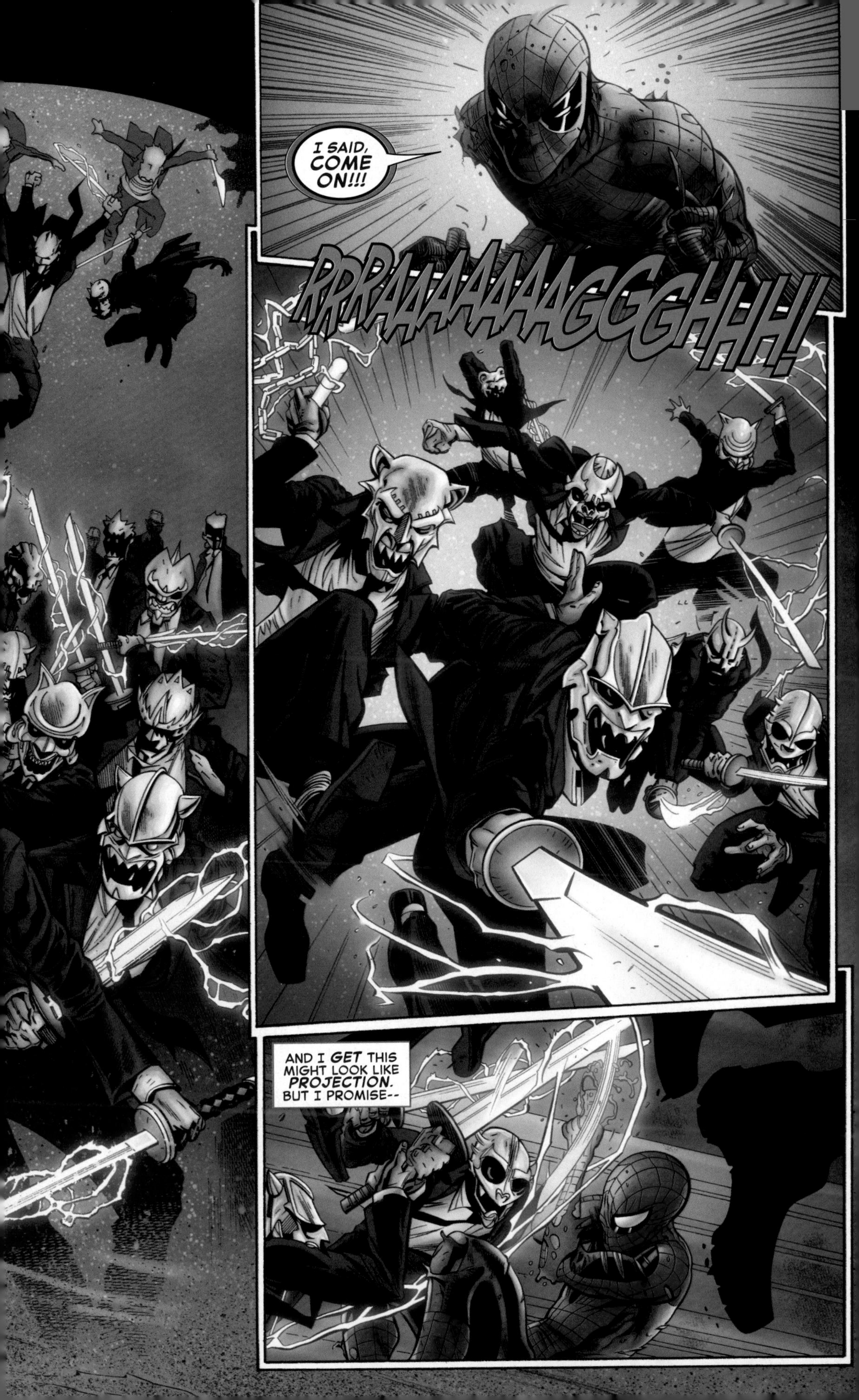
I SAID, COME ON!!!
RRRAAAAAAAAGGGHHH!
AND I GET THIS MIGHT LOOK LIKE PROJECTION. BUT I PROMISE--

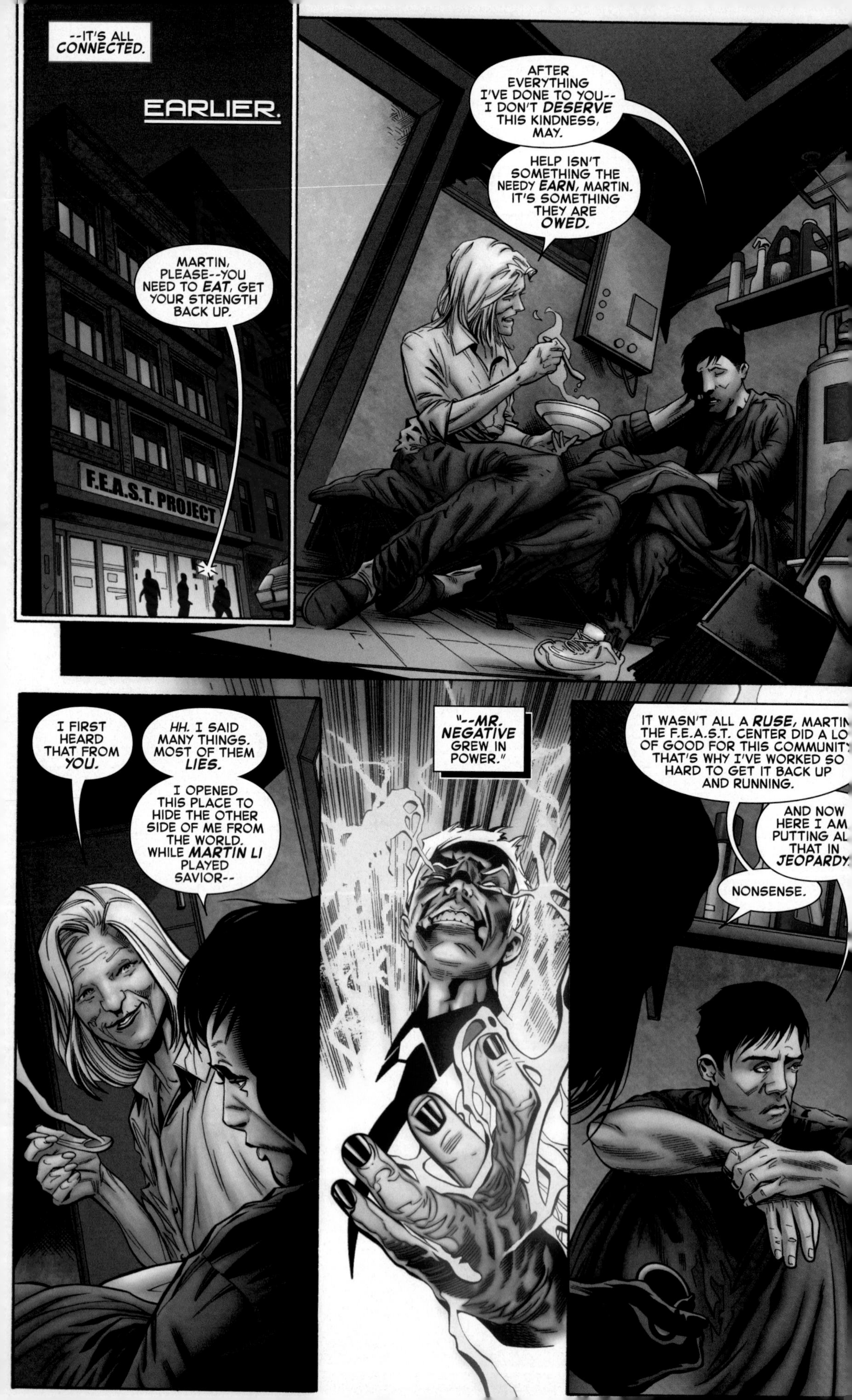
--IT'S ALL CONNECTED.
EARLIER.
MARTIN, PLEASE--YOU NEED TO EAT, GET YOUR STRENGTH BACK UP.
F.E.A.S.T. PROJECT
AFTER EVERYTHING I'VE DONE TO YOU-- I DON'T DESERVE THIS KINDNESS, MAY.
HELP ISN'T SOMETHING THE NEEDY EARN, MARTIN. IT'S SOMETHING THEY ARE OWED.
I FIRST HEARD THAT FROM YOU.
HH. I SAID MANY THINGS. MOST OF THEM LIES.
I OPENED THIS PLACE TO HIDE THE OTHER SIDE OF ME FROM THE WORLD. WHILE MARTIN LI PLAYED SAVIOR--
"--MR. NEGATIVE GREW IN POWER."
IT WASN'T ALL A RUSE, MARTIN THE F.E.A.S.T. CENTER DID A LO OF GOOD FOR THIS COMMUNITY THAT'S WHY I'VE WORKED SO HARD TO GET IT BACK UP AND RUNNING.
AND NOW HERE I AM PUTTING AL THAT IN JEOPARDY.
NONSENSE.

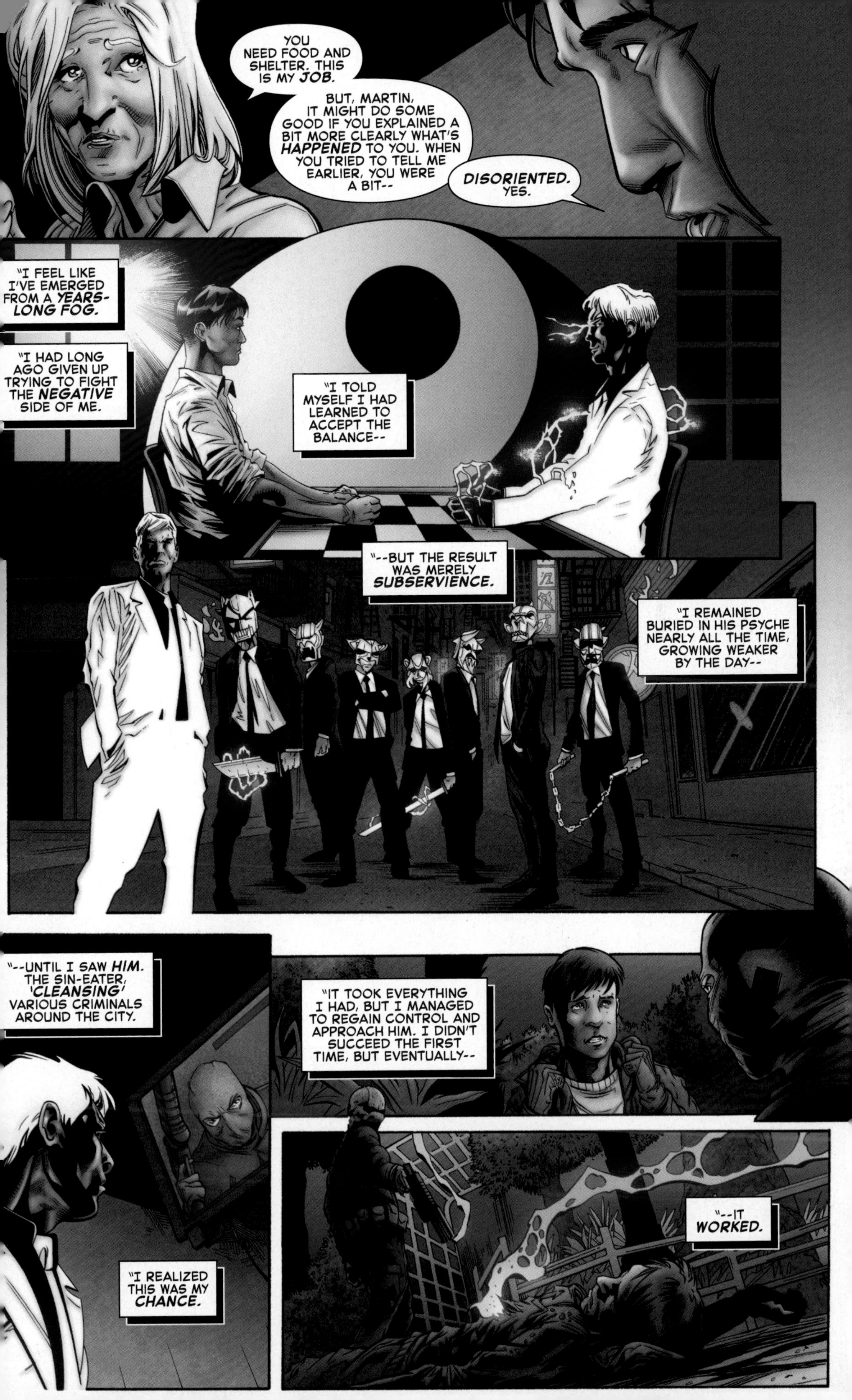
YOU NEED FOOD AND SHELTER. THIS IS MY JOB.
BUT, MARTIN, IT MIGHT DO SOME GOOD IF YOU EXPLAINED A BIT MORE CLEARLY WHAT'S HAPPENED TO YOU. WHEN YOU TRIED TO TELL ME EARLIER, YOU WERE A BIT--
DISORIENTED. YES.
"I FEEL LIKE I'VE EMERGED FROM A YEARS-LONG FOG.
"I HAD LONG AGO GIVEN UP TRYING TO FIGHT THE NEGATIVE SIDE OF ME.
"I TOLD MYSELF I HAD LEARNED TO ACCEPT THE BALANCE--
"--BUT THE RESULT WAS MERELY SUBSERVIENCE.
"I REMAINED BURIED IN HIS PSYCHE NEARLY ALL THE TIME, GROWING WEAKER BY THE DAY--
"--UNTIL I SAW HIM. THE SIN-EATER, 'CLEANSING' VARIOUS CRIMINALS AROUND THE CITY.
"I REALIZED THIS WAS MY CHANCE.
"IT TOOK EVERYTHING I HAD, BUT I MANAGED TO REGAIN CONTROL AND APPROACH HIM. I DIDN'T SUCCEED THE FIRST TIME, BUT EVENTUALLY--
"--IT WORKED.

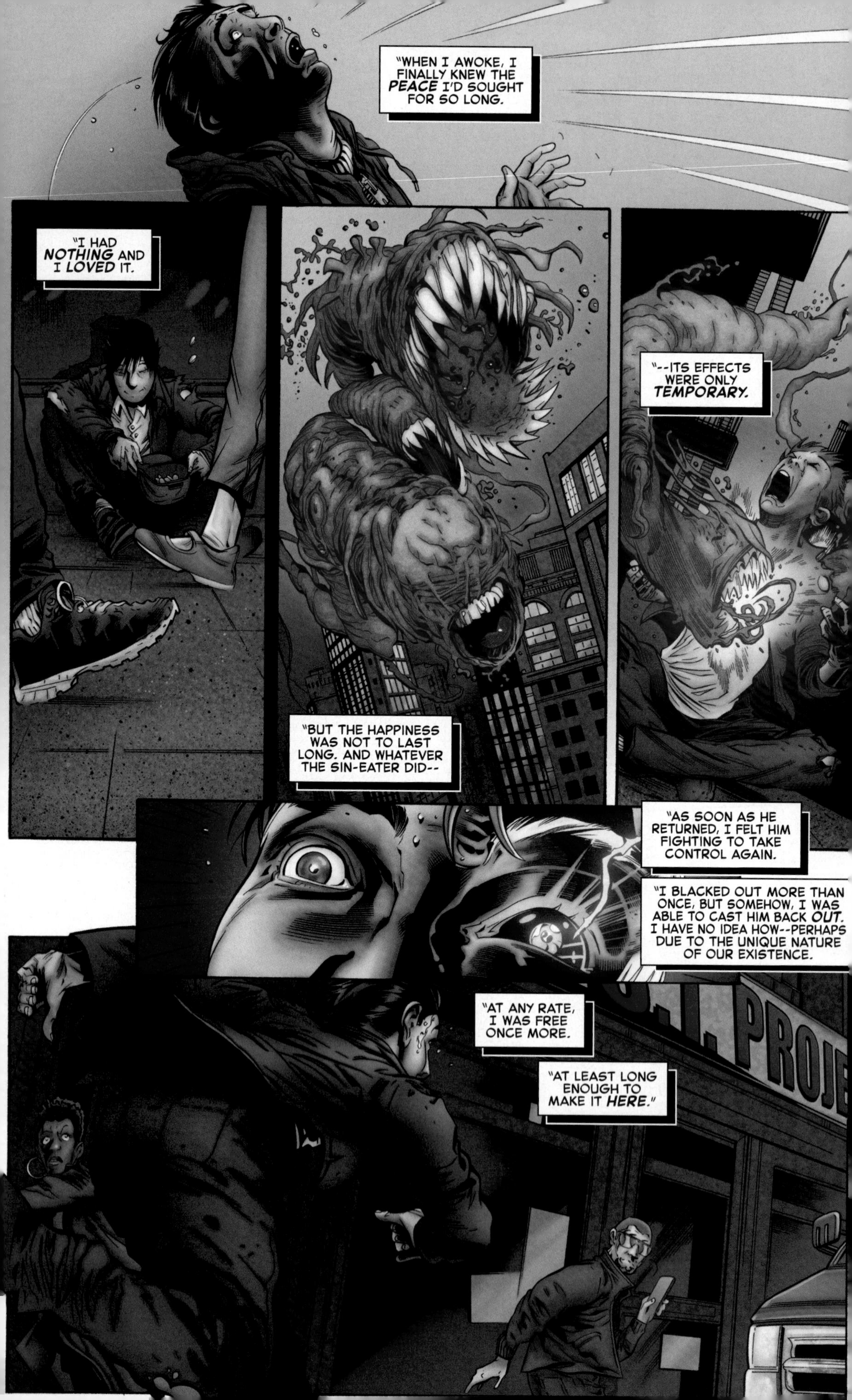
"WHEN I AWOKE, I FINALLY KNEW THE PEACE I'D SOUGHT FOR SO LONG.
"I HAD NOTHING AND I LOVED IT.
"BUT THE HAPPINESS WAS NOT TO LAST LONG. AND WHATEVER THE SIN-EATER DID--
"--ITS EFFECTS WERE ONLY TEMPORARY.
"AS SOON AS HE RETURNED, I FELT HIM FIGHTING TO TAKE CONTROL AGAIN.
"I BLACKED OUT MORE THAN ONCE, BUT SOMEHOW, I WAS ABLE TO CAST HIM BACK OUT. I HAVE NO IDEA HOW--PERHAPS DUE TO THE UNIQUE NATURE OF OUR EXISTENCE.
"AT ANY RATE, I WAS FREE ONCE MORE.
"AT LEAST LONG ENOUGH TO MAKE IT HERE."
PROJE

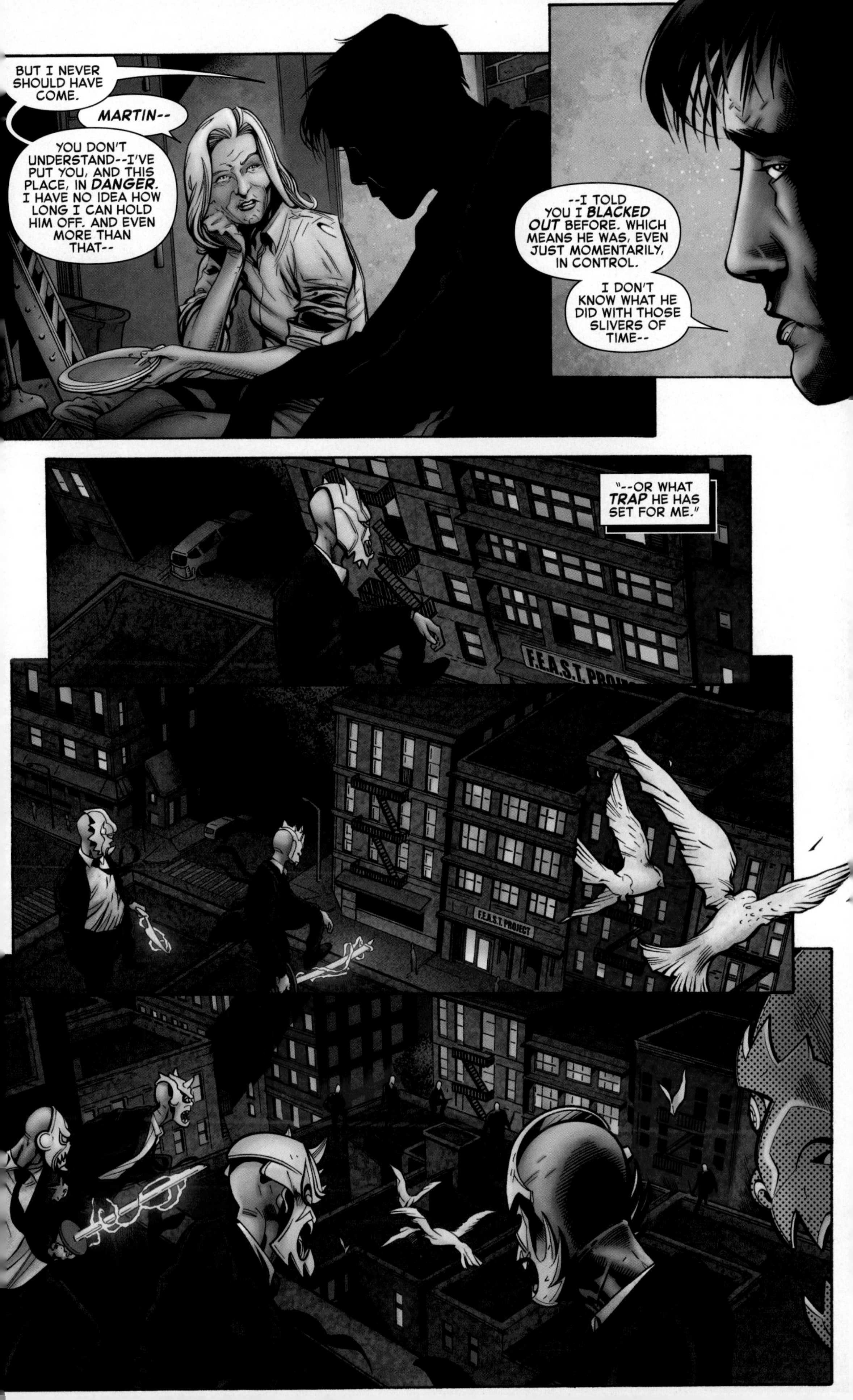
BUT I NEVER SHOULD HAVE COME.
MARTIN--
YOU DON'T UNDERSTAND--I'VE PUT YOU, AND THIS PLACE, IN DANGER. I HAVE NO IDEA HOW LONG I CAN HOLD HIM OFF. AND EVEN MORE THAN THAT--
--I TOLD YOU I BLACKED OUT BEFORE. WHICH MEANS HE WAS, EVEN JUST MOMENTARILY, IN CONTROL.
I DON'T KNOW WHAT HE DID WITH THOSE SLIVERS OF TIME--
"--OR WHAT TRAP HE HAS SET FOR ME."
F.E.A.S.T. PROJECT

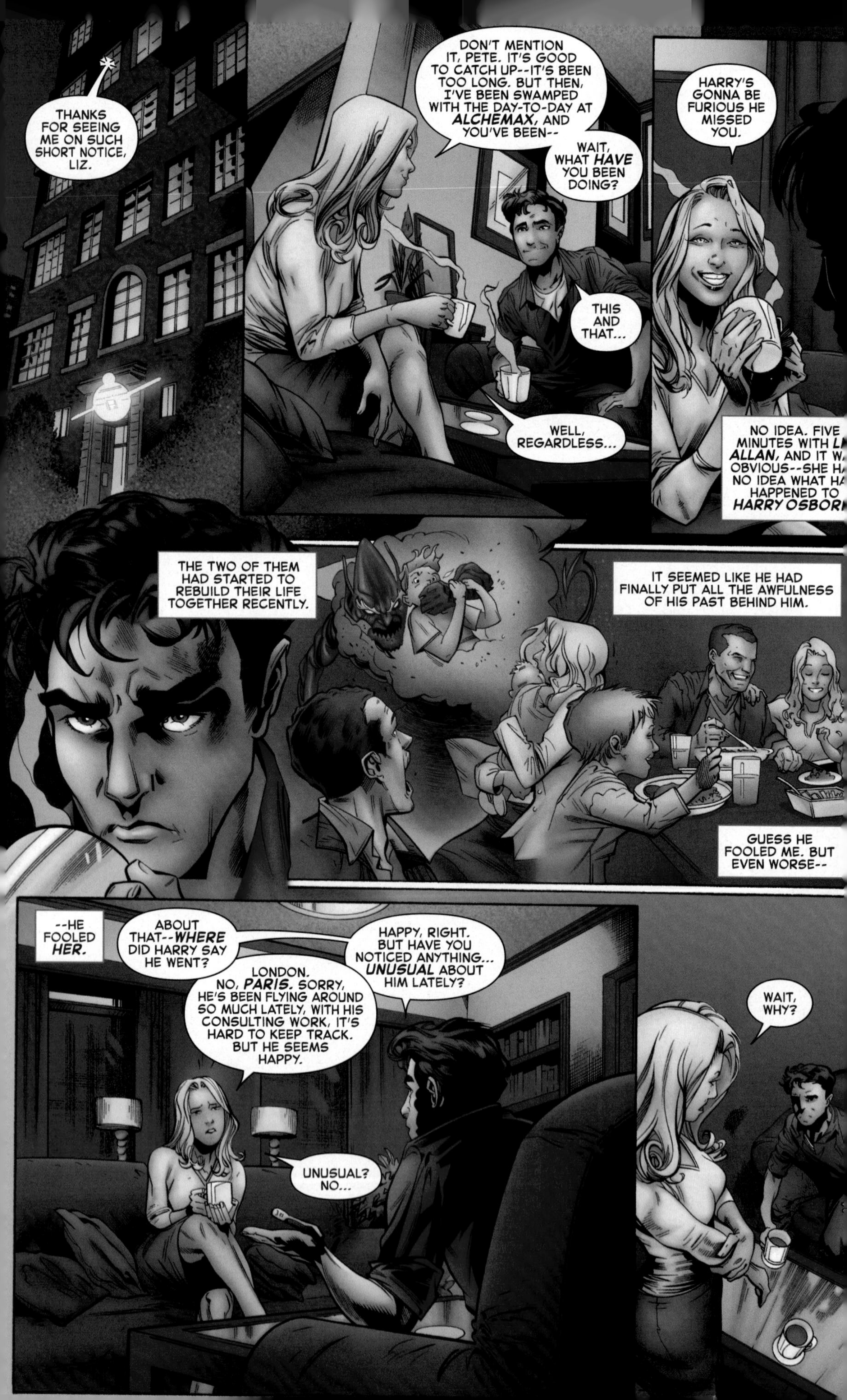
THANKS FOR SEEING ME ON SUCH SHORT NOTICE, LIZ.
DON'T MENTION IT, PETE. IT'S GOOD TO CATCH UP--IT'S BEEN TOO LONG. BUT THEN, I'VE BEEN SWAMPED WITH THE DAY-TO-DAY AT ALCHEMAX, AND YOU'VE BEEN--
WAIT, WHAT HAVE YOU BEEN DOING?
THIS AND THAT...
WELL, REGARDLESS...
HARRY'S GONNA BE FURIOUS HE MISSED YOU.
NO IDEA. FIVE MINUTES WITH
ALLAN, AND IT WA
OBVIOUS--SHE HA
NO IDEA WHAT HA
HAPPENED TO
HARRY OSBOR
THE TWO OF THEM HAD STARTED TO REBUILD THEIR LIFE TOGETHER RECENTLY.
IT SEEMED LIKE HE HAD FINALLY PUT ALL THE AWFULNESS OF HIS PAST BEHIND HIM.
GUESS HE FOOLED ME. BUT EVEN WORSE--
--HE FOOLED HER.
ABOUT THAT--WHERE DID HARRY SAY HE WENT?
LONDON. NO, PARIS. SORRY, HE'S BEEN FLYING AROUND SO MUCH LATELY, WITH HIS CONSULTING WORK, IT'S HARD TO KEEP TRACK. BUT HE SEEMS HAPPY.
HAPPY, RIGHT. BUT HAVE YOU NOTICED ANYTHING... UNUSUAL ABOUT HIM LATELY?
UNUSUAL? NO...
WAIT, WHY?

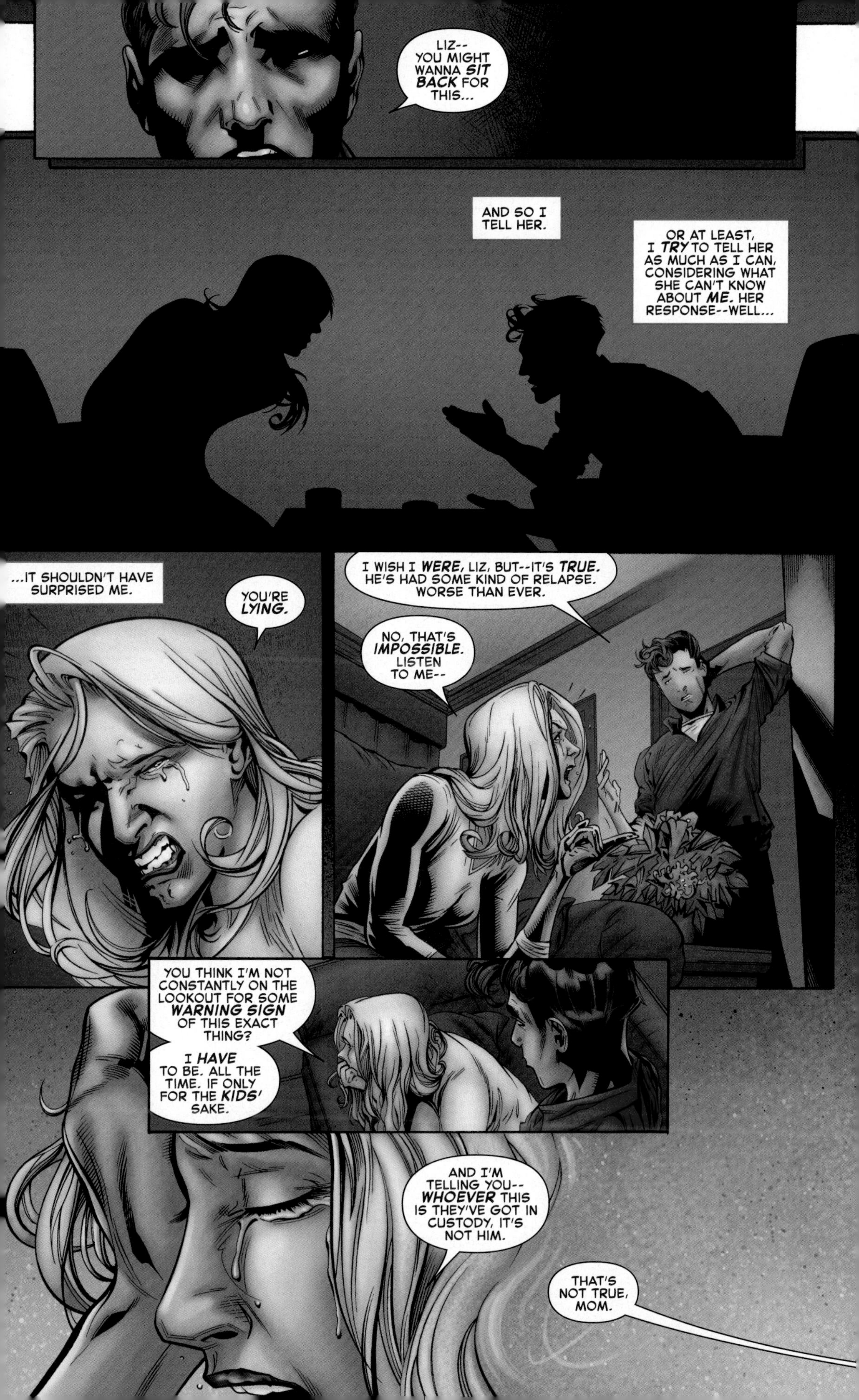
LIZ-- YOU MIGHT WANNA SIT BACK FOR THIS...
AND SO I TELL HER.
OR AT LEAST, I TRY TO TELL HER AS MUCH AS I CAN, CONSIDERING WHAT SHE CAN'T KNOW ABOUT ME. HER RESPONSE--WELL...
...IT SHOULDN'T HAVE SURPRISED ME.
YOU'RE LYING.
I WISH I WERE, LIZ, BUT--IT'S TRUE. HE'S HAD SOME KIND OF RELAPSE. WORSE THAN EVER.
NO, THAT'S IMPOSSIBLE. LISTEN TO ME--
YOU THINK I'M NOT CONSTANTLY ON THE LOOKOUT FOR SOME WARNING SIGN OF THIS EXACT THING?
I HAVE TO BE. ALL THE TIME. IF ONLY FOR THE KIDS' SAKE.
AND I'M TELLING YOU-- WHOEVER THIS IS THEY'VE GOT IN CUSTODY, IT'S NOT HIM.
THAT'S NOT TRUE, MOM.

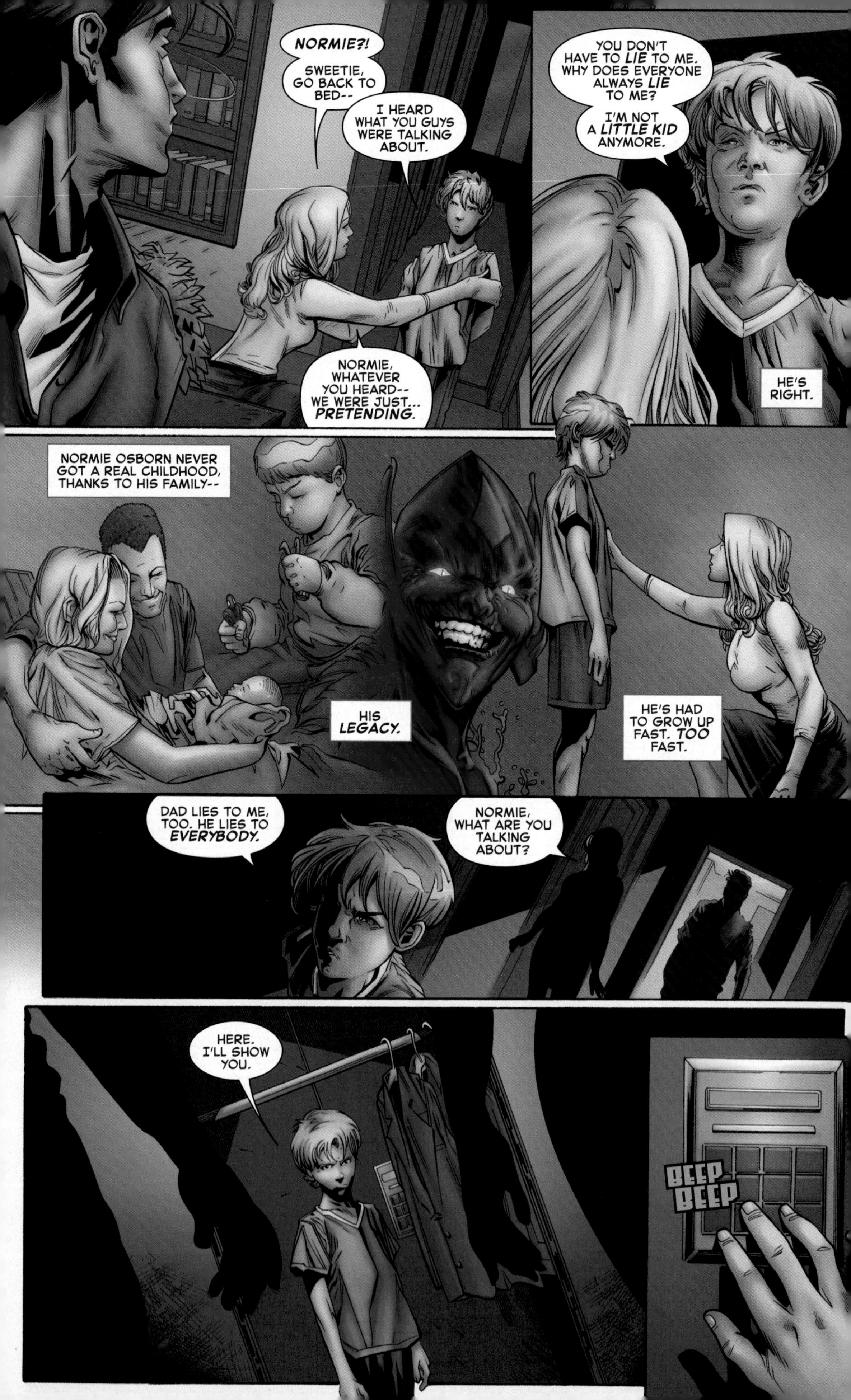
NORMIE?!
SWEETIE, GO BACK TO BED--
I HEARD WHAT YOU GUYS WERE TALKING ABOUT.
NORMIE, WHATEVER YOU HEARD-- WE WERE JUST... PRETENDING.
YOU DON'T HAVE TO LIE TO ME. WHY DOES EVERYONE ALWAYS LIE TO ME?
I'M NOT A LITTLE KID ANYMORE.
HE'S RIGHT.
NORMIE OSBORN NEVER GOT A REAL CHILDHOOD, THANKS TO HIS FAMILY--
HIS LEGACY.
HE'S HAD TO GROW UP FAST. TOO FAST.
DAD LIES TO ME, TOO. HE LIES TO EVERYBODY.
NORMIE, WHAT ARE YOU TALKING ABOUT?
HERE. I'LL SHOW YOU.
BEEP BEEP

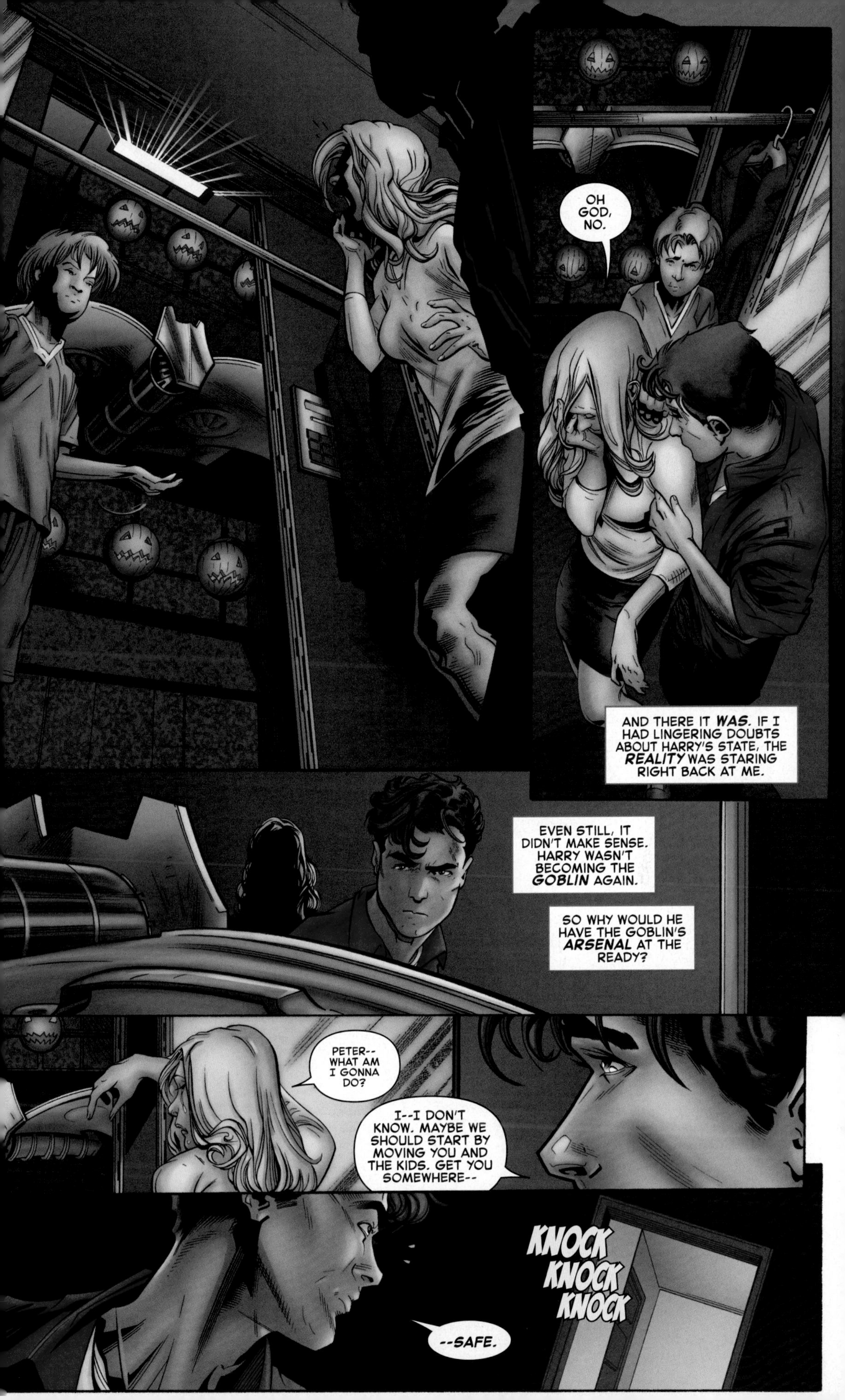
OH GOD, NO.
AND THERE IT WAS. IF I HAD LINGERING DOUBTS ABOUT HARRY'S STATE, THE REALITY WAS STARING RIGHT BACK AT ME.
EVEN STILL, IT DIDN'T MAKE SENSE. HARRY WASN'T BECOMING THE GOBLIN AGAIN.
SO WHY WOULD HE HAVE THE GOBLIN'S ARSENAL AT THE READY?
PETER-- WHAT AM I GONNA DO?
I--I DON'T KNOW. MAYBE WE SHOULD START BY MOVING YOU AND THE KIDS. GET YOU SOMEWHERE--
KNOCK KNOCK KNOCK
--SAFE.

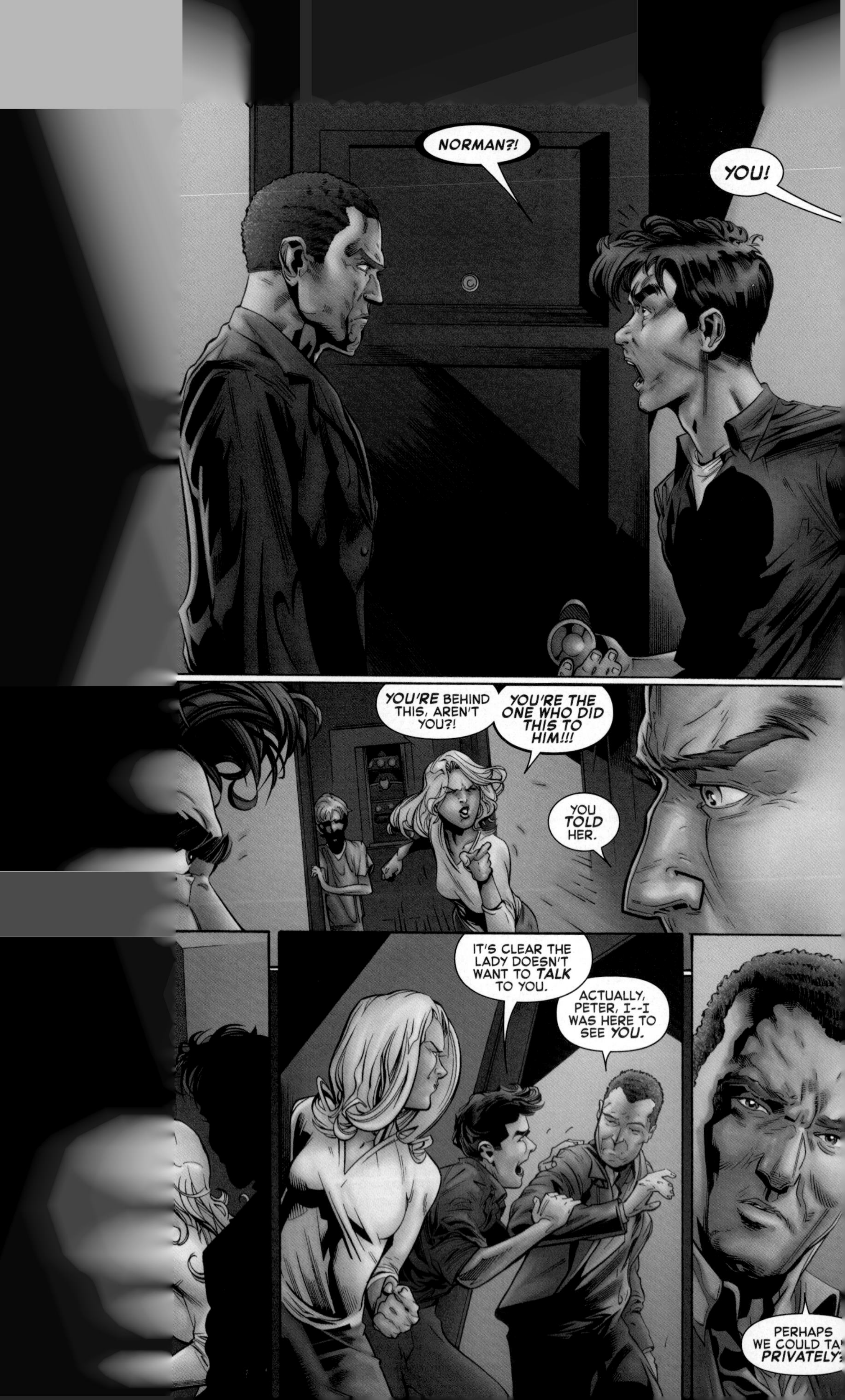
NORMAN?!
YOU!
YOU'RE BEHIND THIS, AREN'T YOU?!
YOU'RE THE ONE WHO DID THIS TO HIM!!!
YOU TOLD HER.
IT'S CLEAR THE LADY DOESN'T WANT TO TALK TO YOU.
ACTUALLY, PETER, I--I WAS HERE TO SEE YOU.
PERHAPS WE COULD TA
PRIVATELY

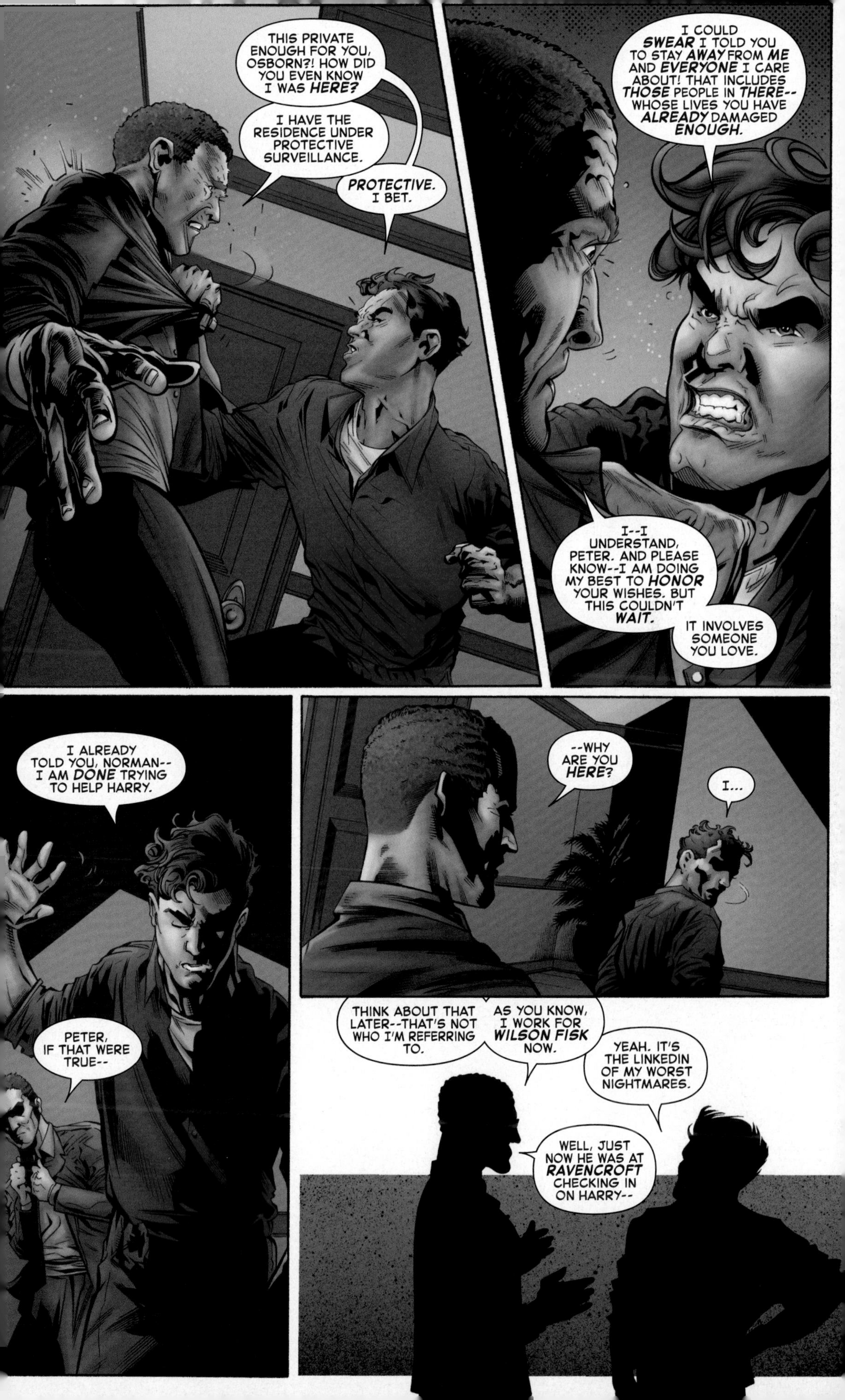
THIS PRIVATE ENOUGH FOR YOU, OSBORN?! HOW DID YOU EVEN KNOW I WAS *HERE?*
I HAVE THE RESIDENCE UNDER PROTECTIVE SURVEILLANCE.
*PROTECTIVE.* I BET.
I COULD *SWEAR* I TOLD YOU TO STAY *AWAY* FROM *ME* AND *EVERYONE* I CARE ABOUT! THAT INCLUDES *THOSE* PEOPLE IN *THERE--* WHOSE LIVES YOU HAVE *ALREADY* DAMAGED *ENOUGH.*
I--I UNDERSTAND, PETER. AND PLEASE KNOW--I AM DOING MY BEST TO *HONOR* YOUR WISHES. BUT THIS COULDN'T *WAIT.*
IT INVOLVES SOMEONE YOU LOVE.
I ALREADY TOLD YOU, NORMAN-- I AM *DONE* TRYING TO HELP HARRY.
PETER, IF THAT WERE TRUE--
--WHY ARE YOU *HERE?*
I...
THINK ABOUT THAT LATER--THAT'S NOT WHO I'M REFERRING TO.
AS YOU KNOW, I WORK FOR *WILSON FISK* NOW.
YEAH. IT'S THE LINKEDIN OF MY WORST NIGHTMARES.
WELL, JUST NOW HE WAS AT *RAVENCROFT* CHECKING IN ON HARRY--

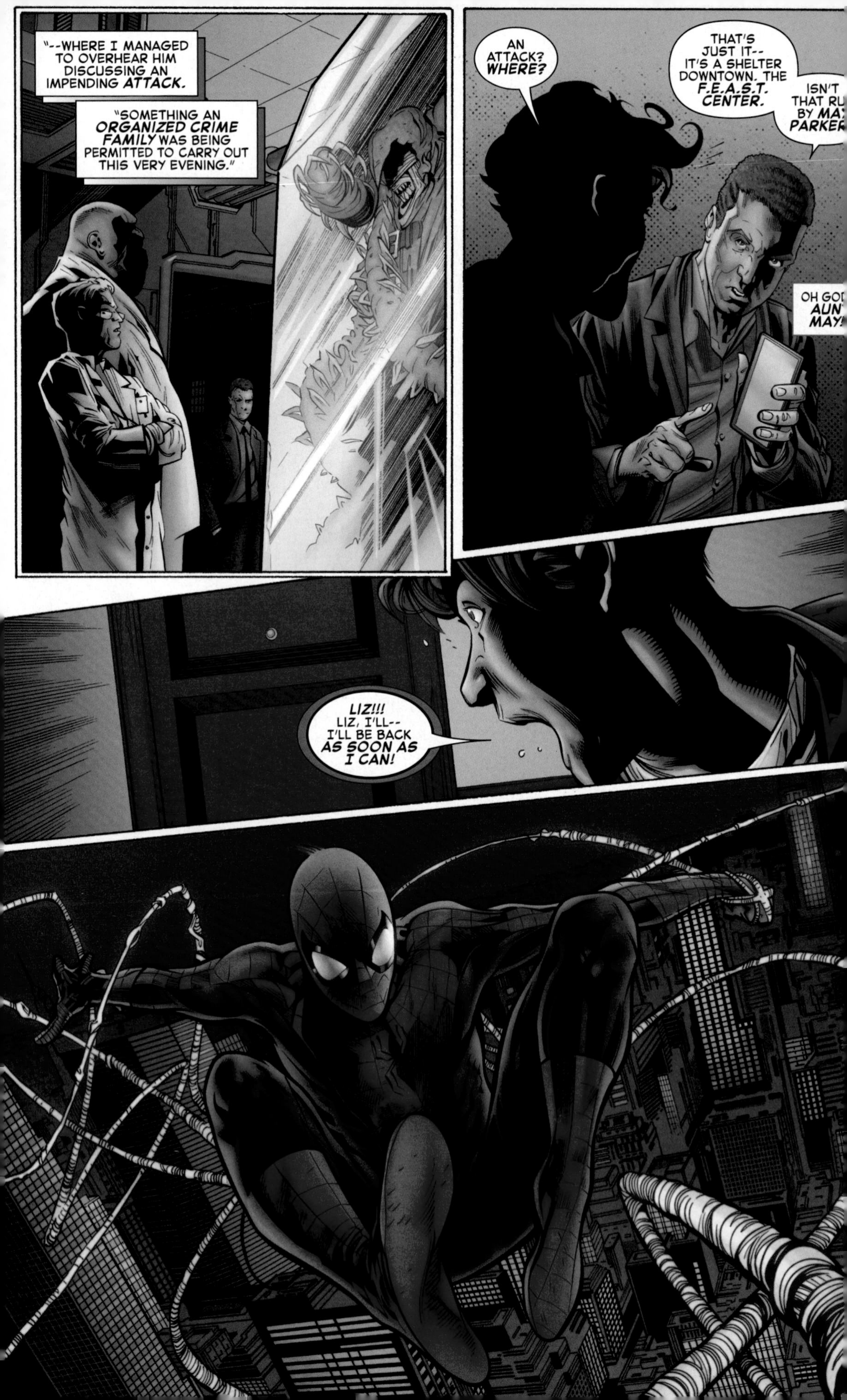
"--WHERE I MANAGED TO OVERHEAR HIM DISCUSSING AN IMPENDING ATTACK.
"SOMETHING AN ORGANIZED CRIME FAMILY WAS BEING PERMITTED TO CARRY OUT THIS VERY EVENING."
AN ATTACK? WHERE?
THAT'S JUST IT-- IT'S A SHELTER DOWNTOWN. THE F.E.A.S.T. CENTER.
LIZ!!! LIZ, I'LL-- I'LL BE BACK AS SOON AS I CAN!

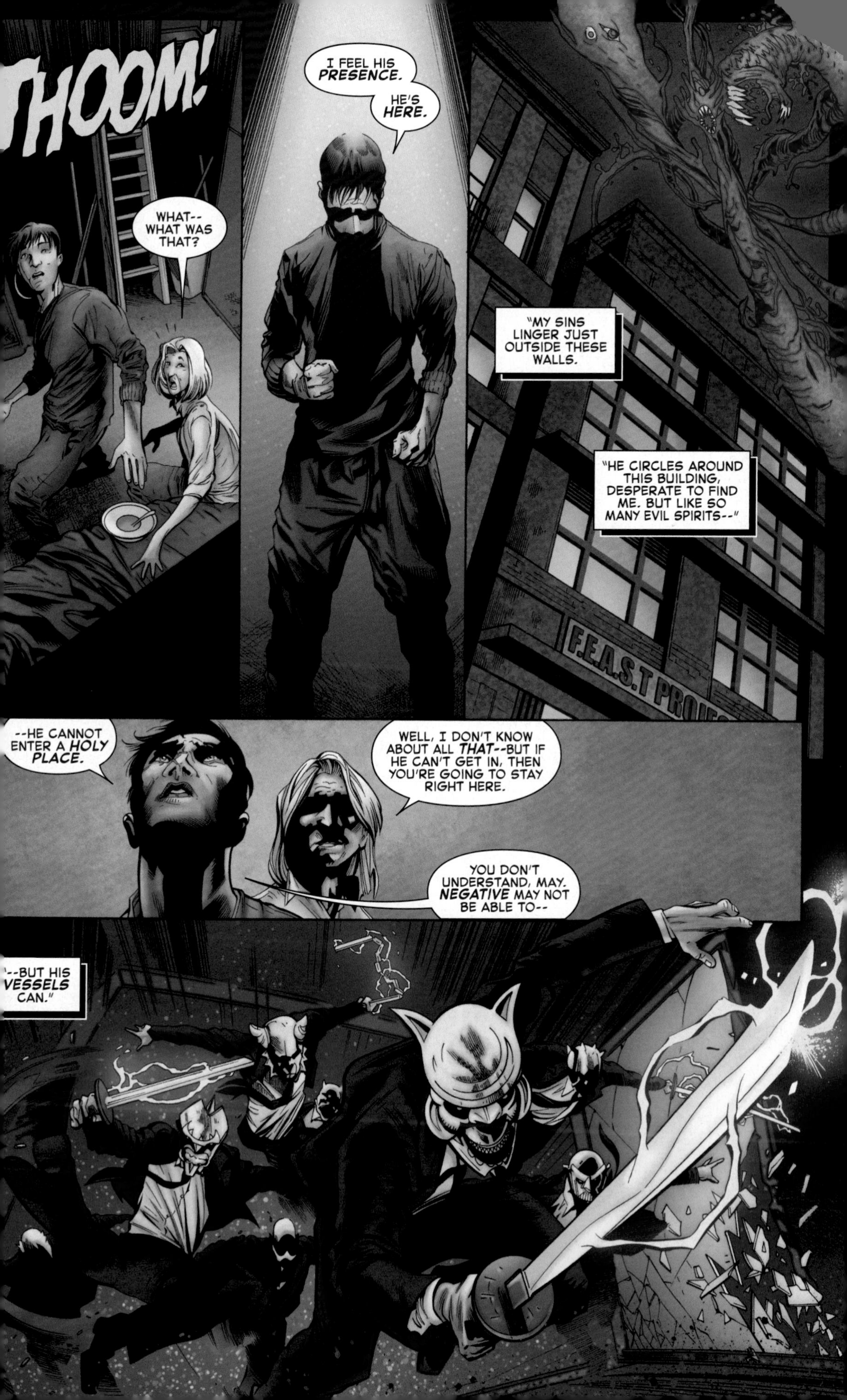
THOOM!
WHAT-- WHAT WAS THAT?
I FEEL HIS PRESENCE.
HE'S HERE.
"MY SINS LINGER JUST OUTSIDE THESE WALLS.
"HE CIRCLES AROUND THIS BUILDING, DESPERATE TO FIND ME. BUT LIKE SO MANY EVIL SPIRITS--"
F.E.A.S.T PROJE
--HE CANNOT ENTER A HOLY PLACE.
WELL, I DON'T KNOW ABOUT ALL THAT--BUT IF HE CAN'T GET IN, THEN YOU'RE GOING TO STAY RIGHT HERE.
YOU DON'T UNDERSTAND, MAY. NEGATIVE MAY NOT BE ABLE TO--
"--BUT HIS VESSELS CAN."

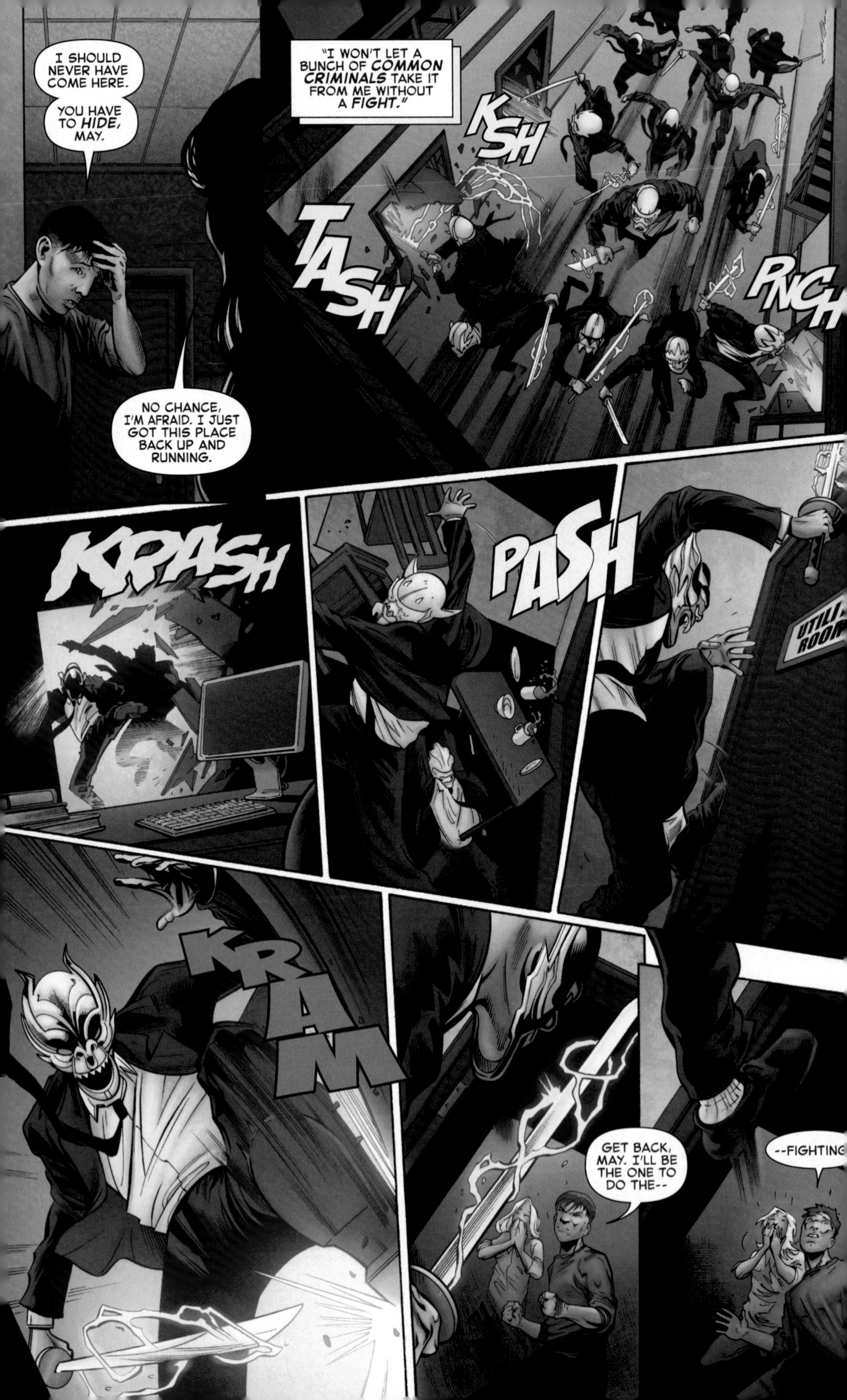
I SHOULD NEVER HAVE COME HERE.
YOU HAVE TO HIDE, MAY.
NO CHANCE, I'M AFRAID. I JUST GOT THIS PLACE BACK UP AND RUNNING.
"I WON'T LET A BUNCH OF COMMON CRIMINALS TAKE IT FROM ME WITHOUT A FIGHT."
KSH
TASH
PNCH
KRASH
PASH
UTILI ROOM
KRAM
GET BACK, MAY. I'LL BE THE ONE TO DO THE--
--FIGHTING

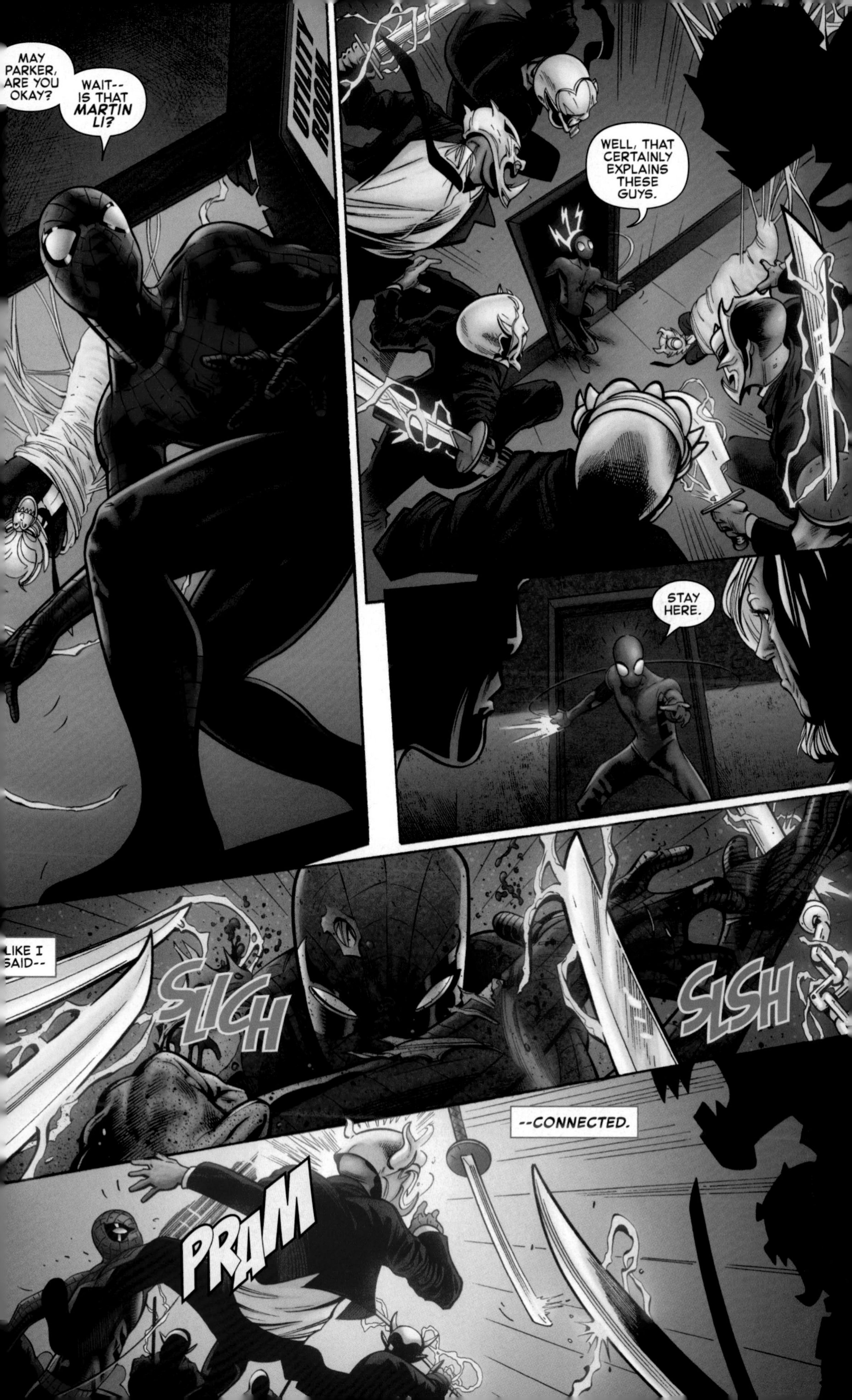

UTILITY ROOM
MAY PARKER, ARE YOU OKAY?
WAIT-- IS THAT MARTIN LI?
WELL, THAT CERTAINLY EXPLAINS THESE GUYS.
STAY HERE.
LIKE I SAID--
SLICH
SLSH
--CONNECTED.
PRAM

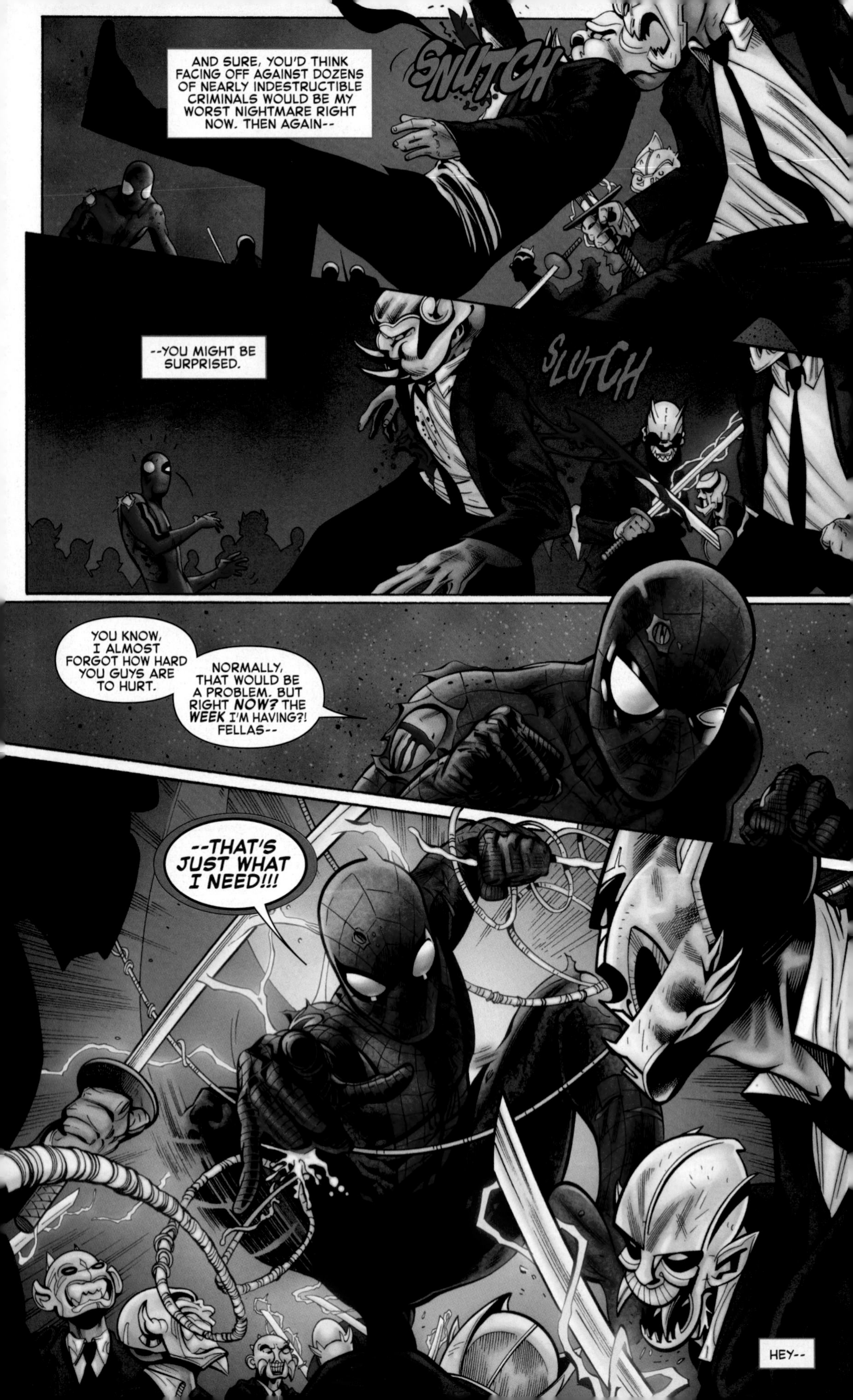
AND SURE, YOU'D THINK FACING OFF AGAINST DOZENS OF NEARLY INDESTRUCTIBLE CRIMINALS WOULD BE MY WORST NIGHTMARE RIGHT NOW. THEN AGAIN--
SNUTCH
--YOU MIGHT BE SURPRISED.
SLUTCH
YOU KNOW, I ALMOST FORGOT HOW HARD YOU GUYS ARE TO HURT.
NORMALLY, THAT WOULD BE A PROBLEM. BUT RIGHT NOW? THE WEEK I'M HAVING?! FELLAS--
--THAT'S JUST WHAT I NEED!!!
HEY--

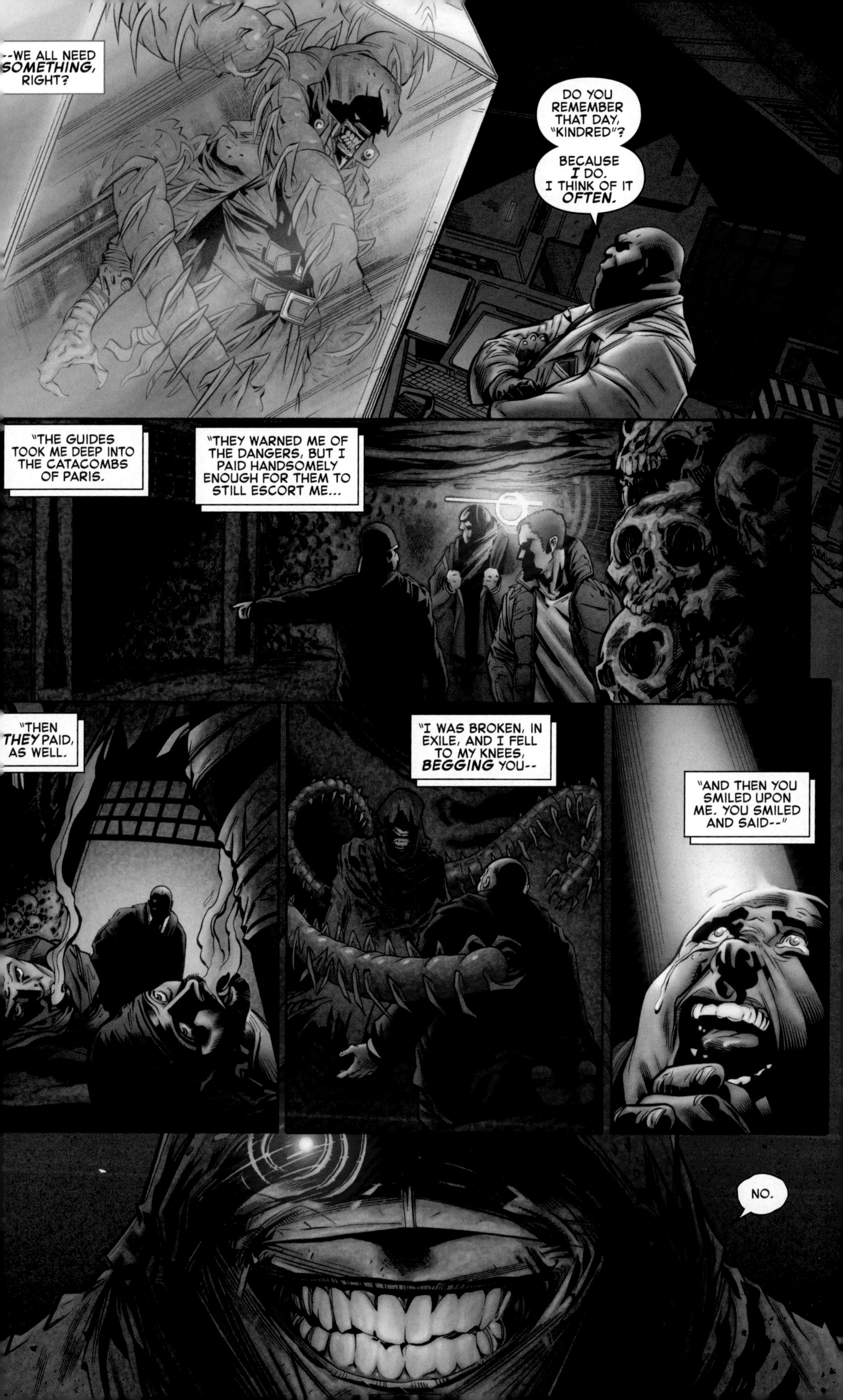
--WE ALL NEED SOMETHING, RIGHT?
DO YOU REMEMBER THAT DAY, "KINDRED"?
BECAUSE I DO. I THINK OF IT OFTEN.
"THE GUIDES TOOK ME DEEP INTO THE CATACOMBS OF PARIS.
"THEY WARNED ME OF THE DANGERS, BUT I PAID HANDSOMELY ENOUGH FOR THEM TO STILL ESCORT ME...
"THEN THEY PAID, AS WELL.
"I WAS BROKEN, IN EXILE, AND I FELL TO MY KNEES, BEGGING YOU--
"AND THEN YOU SMILED UPON ME. YOU SMILED AND SAID--"
NO.

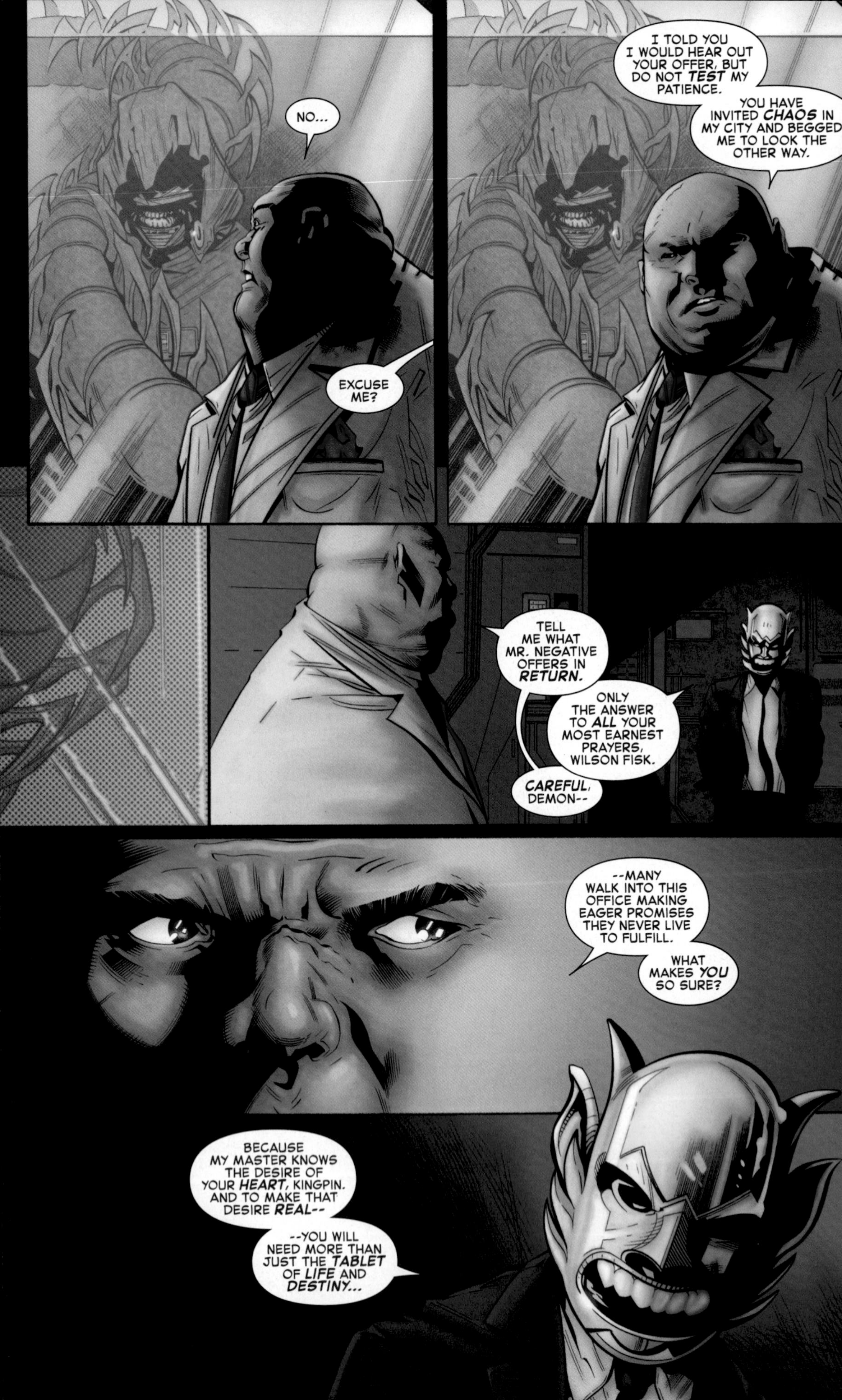

NO...
EXCUSE ME?
I TOLD YOU I WOULD HEAR OUT YOUR OFFER, BUT DO NOT TEST MY PATIENCE.
YOU HAVE INVITED CHAOS IN MY CITY AND BEGGED ME TO LOOK THE OTHER WAY.
TELL ME WHAT MR. NEGATIVE OFFERS IN RETURN.
ONLY THE ANSWER TO ALL YOUR MOST EARNEST PRAYERS, WILSON FISK.
CAREFUL, DEMON--
--MANY WALK INTO THIS OFFICE MAKING EAGER PROMISES THEY NEVER LIVE TO FULFILL.
WHAT MAKES YOU SO SURE?
BECAUSE MY MASTER KNOWS THE DESIRE OF YOUR HEART, KINGPIN. AND TO MAKE THAT DESIRE REAL--
--YOU WILL NEED MORE THAN JUST THE TABLET OF LIFE AND DESTINY...

# 59

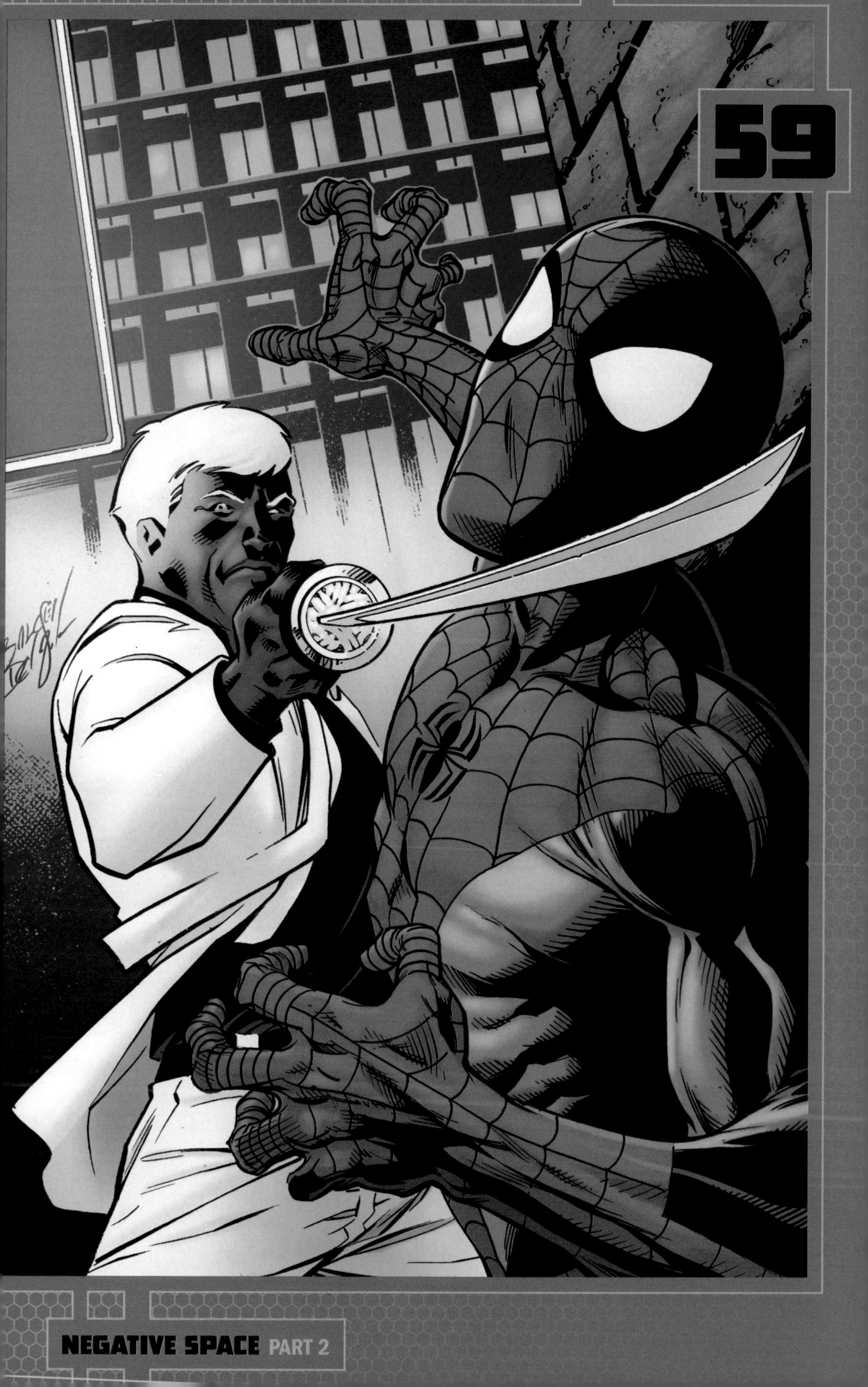

## NEGATIVE SPACE PART 2

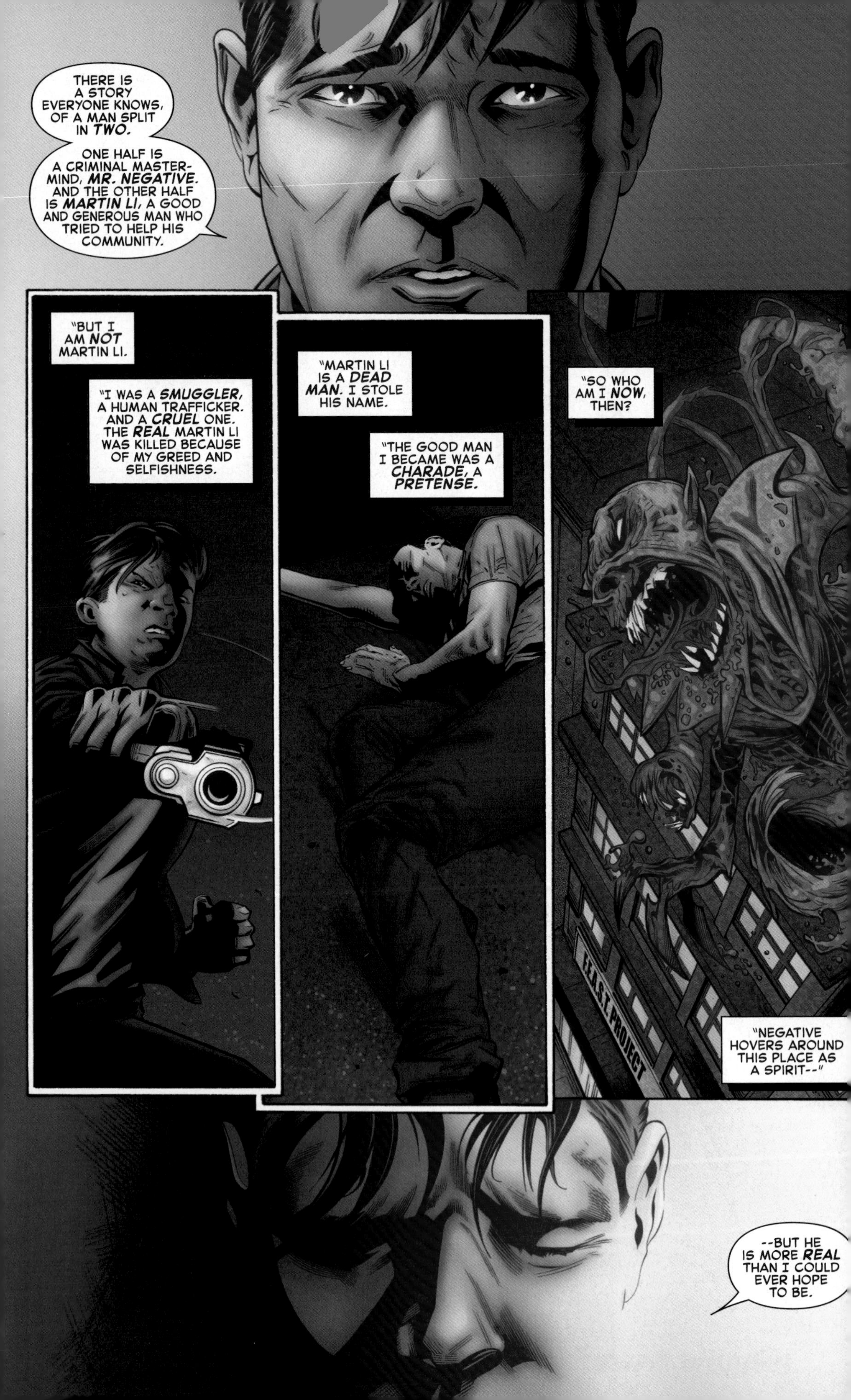
THERE IS A STORY EVERYONE KNOWS, OF A MAN SPLIT IN TWO.
ONE HALF IS A CRIMINAL MASTER-MIND, MR. NEGATIVE. AND THE OTHER HALF IS MARTIN LI, A GOOD AND GENEROUS MAN WHO TRIED TO HELP HIS COMMUNITY.
"BUT I AM NOT MARTIN LI.
"I WAS A SMUGGLER, A HUMAN TRAFFICKER. AND A CRUEL ONE. THE REAL MARTIN LI WAS KILLED BECAUSE OF MY GREED AND SELFISHNESS.
"MARTIN LI IS A DEAD MAN. I STOLE HIS NAME.
"THE GOOD MAN I BECAME WAS A CHARADE, A PRETENSE.
"SO WHO AM I NOW, THEN?
F.E.A.S.T. PROJECT
"NEGATIVE HOVERS AROUND THIS PLACE AS A SPIRIT--"
--BUT HE IS MORE REAL THAN I COULD EVER HOPE TO BE.

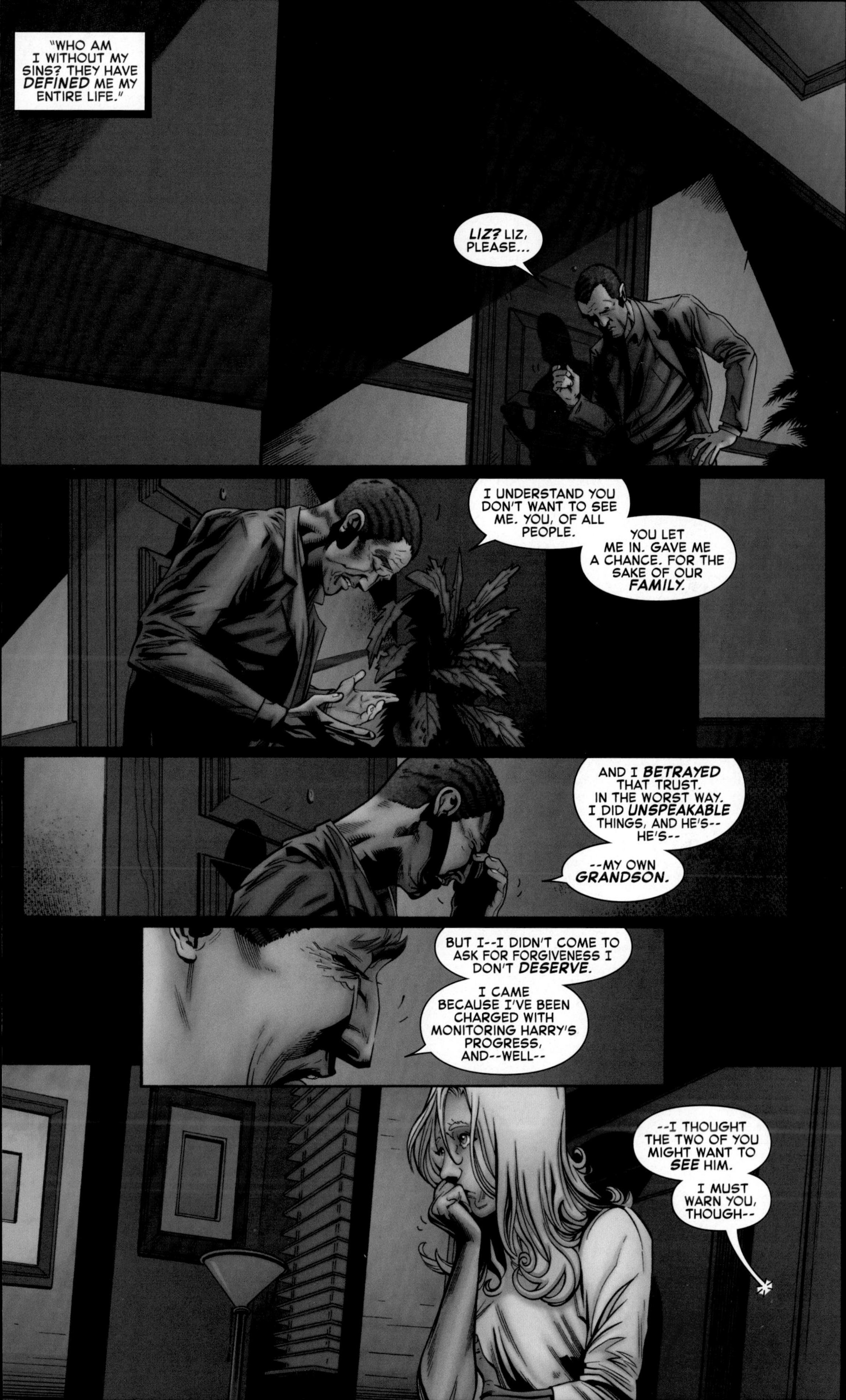
"WHO AM I WITHOUT MY SINS? THEY HAVE DEFINED ME MY ENTIRE LIFE."
LIZ? LIZ, PLEASE...
I UNDERSTAND YOU DON'T WANT TO SEE ME. YOU, OF ALL PEOPLE.
YOU LET ME IN. GAVE ME A CHANCE. FOR THE SAKE OF OUR FAMILY.
AND I BETRAYED THAT TRUST. IN THE WORST WAY. I DID UNSPEAKABLE THINGS, AND HE'S--HE'S--
--MY OWN GRANDSON.
BUT I--I DIDN'T COME TO ASK FOR FORGIVENESS I DON'T DESERVE.
I CAME BECAUSE I'VE BEEN CHARGED WITH MONITORING HARRY'S PROGRESS, AND--WELL--
--I THOUGHT THE TWO OF YOU MIGHT WANT TO SEE HIM.
I MUST WARN YOU, THOUGH--

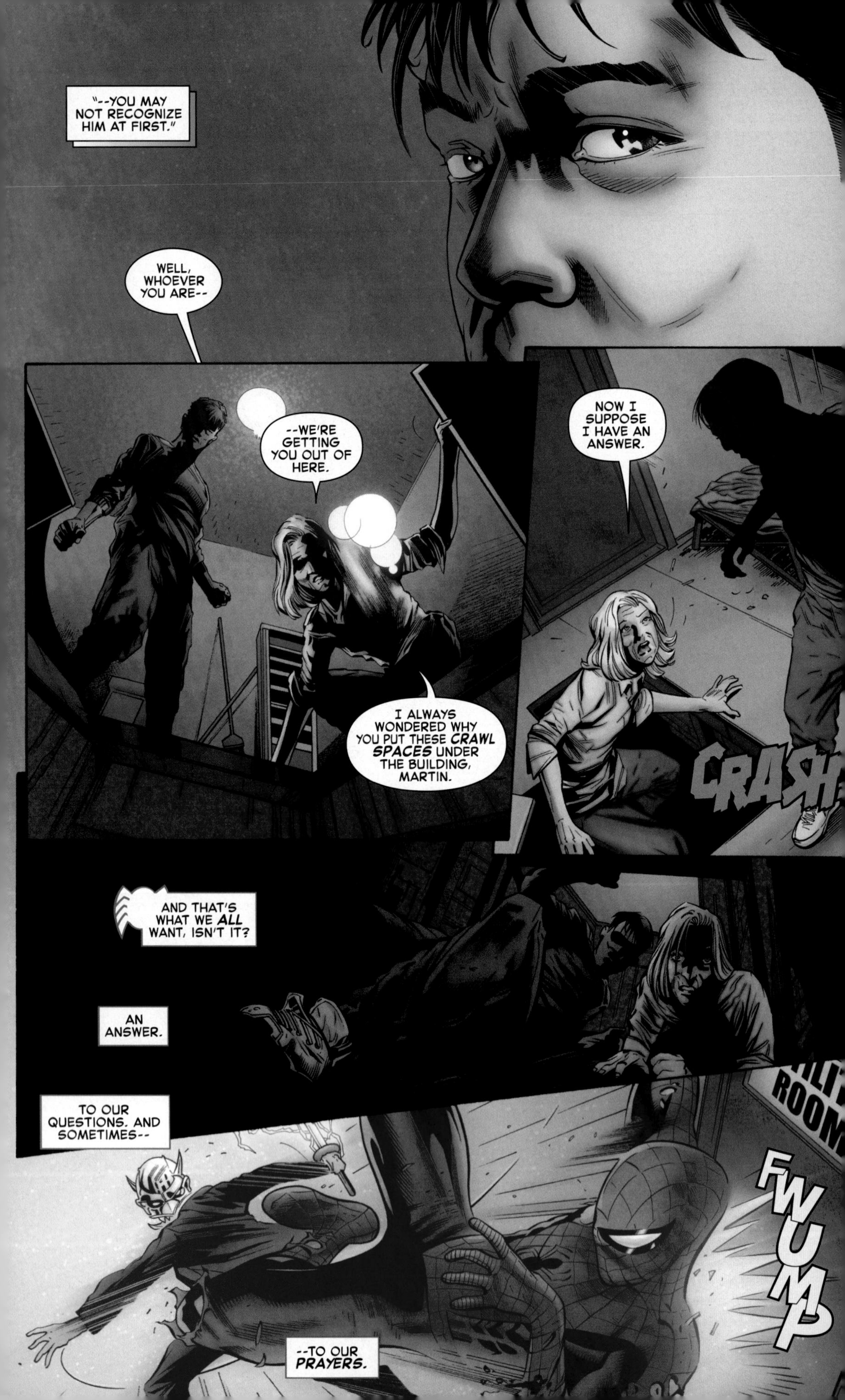
"--YOU MAY NOT RECOGNIZE HIM AT FIRST."
WELL, WHOEVER YOU ARE--
--WE'RE GETTING YOU OUT OF HERE.
I ALWAYS WONDERED WHY YOU PUT THESE *CRAWL SPACES* UNDER THE BUILDING, MARTIN.
NOW I SUPPOSE I HAVE AN ANSWER.
CRASH
AND THAT'S WHAT WE *ALL* WANT, ISN'T IT?
AN ANSWER.
TO OUR QUESTIONS. AND SOMETIMES--
ROOM
FWUMP
--TO OUR *PRAYERS*.

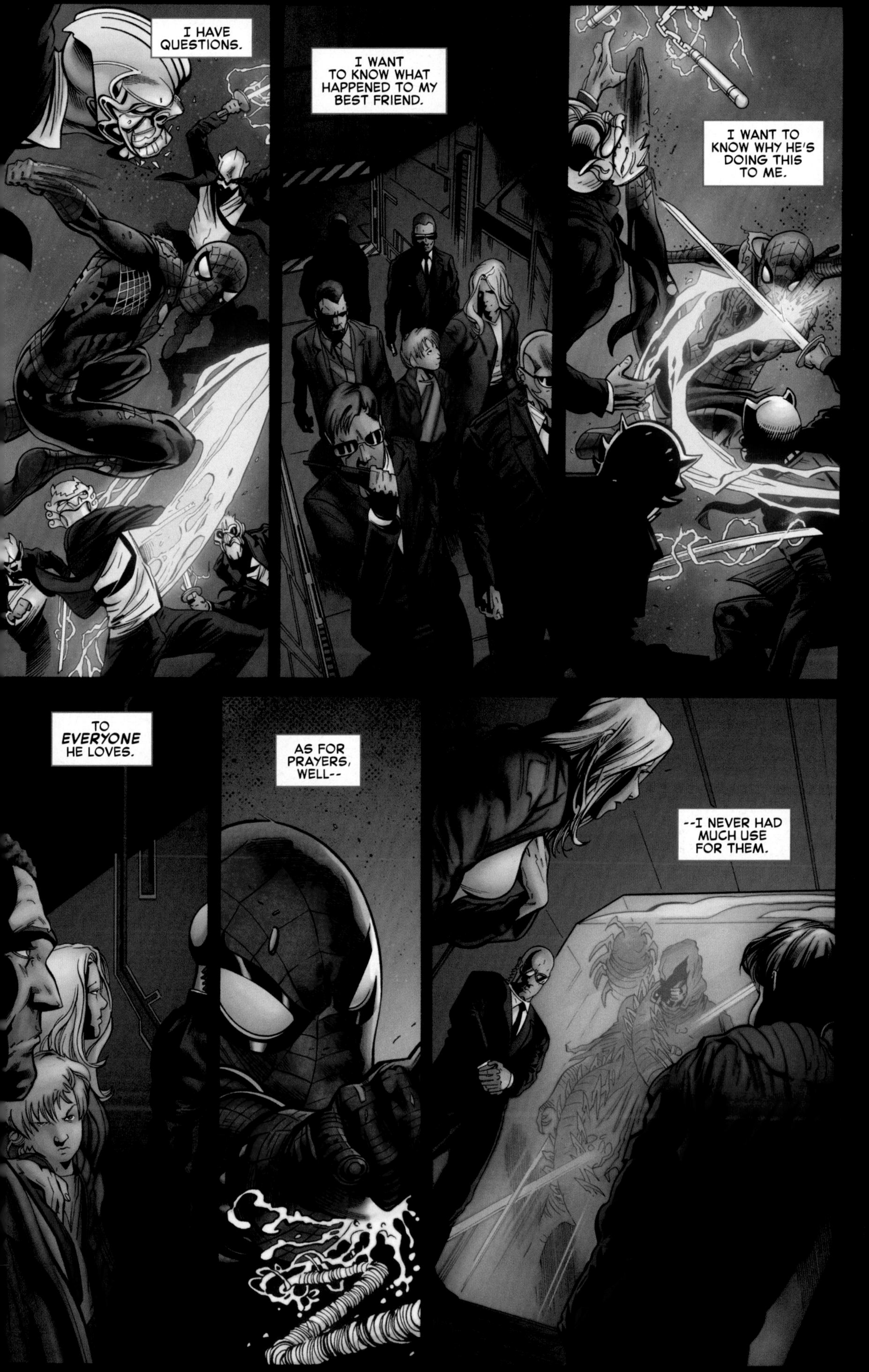
I HAVE QUESTIONS.
I WANT TO KNOW WHAT HAPPENED TO MY BEST FRIEND.
I WANT TO KNOW WHY HE'S DOING THIS TO ME.
TO *EVERYONE* HE LOVES.
AS FOR PRAYERS, WELL--
--I NEVER HAD MUCH USE FOR THEM.

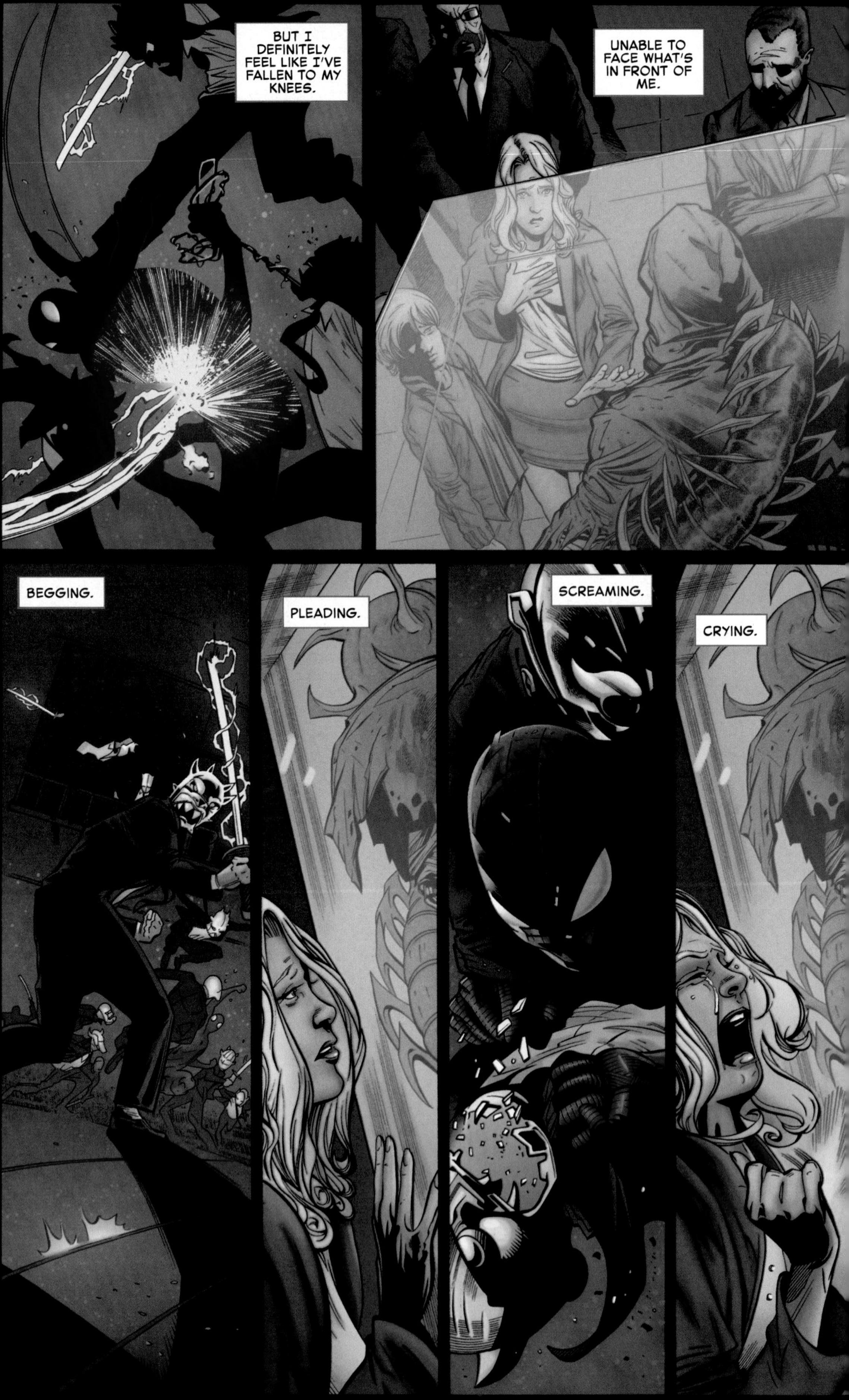
BUT I DEFINITELY FEEL LIKE I'VE FALLEN TO MY KNEES.
UNABLE TO FACE WHAT'S IN FRONT OF ME.
BEGGING.
PLEADING.
SCREAMING.
CRYING.

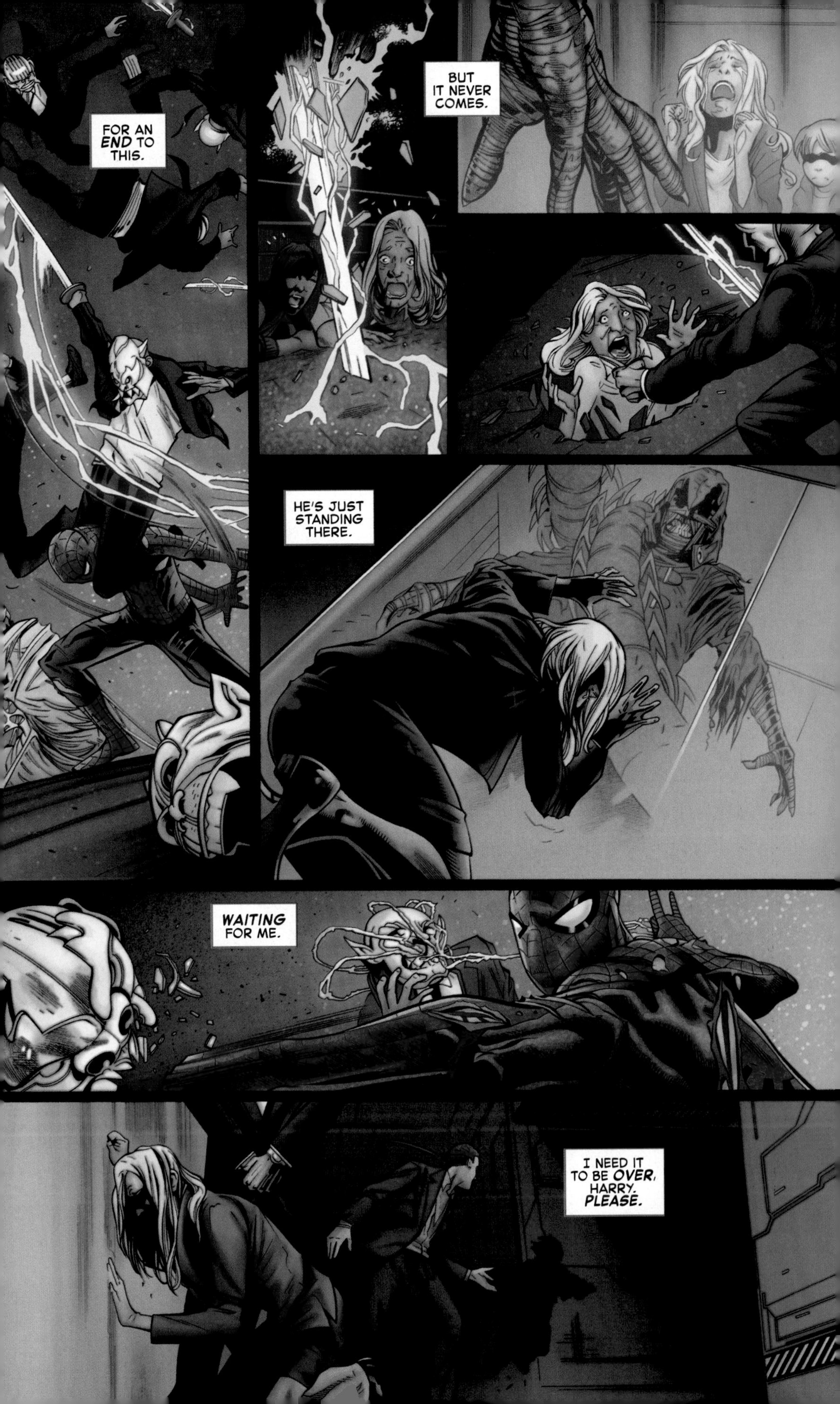
FOR AN END TO THIS.
BUT IT NEVER COMES.
HE'S JUST STANDING THERE.
WAITING FOR ME.
I NEED IT TO BE OVER, HARRY. PLEASE.

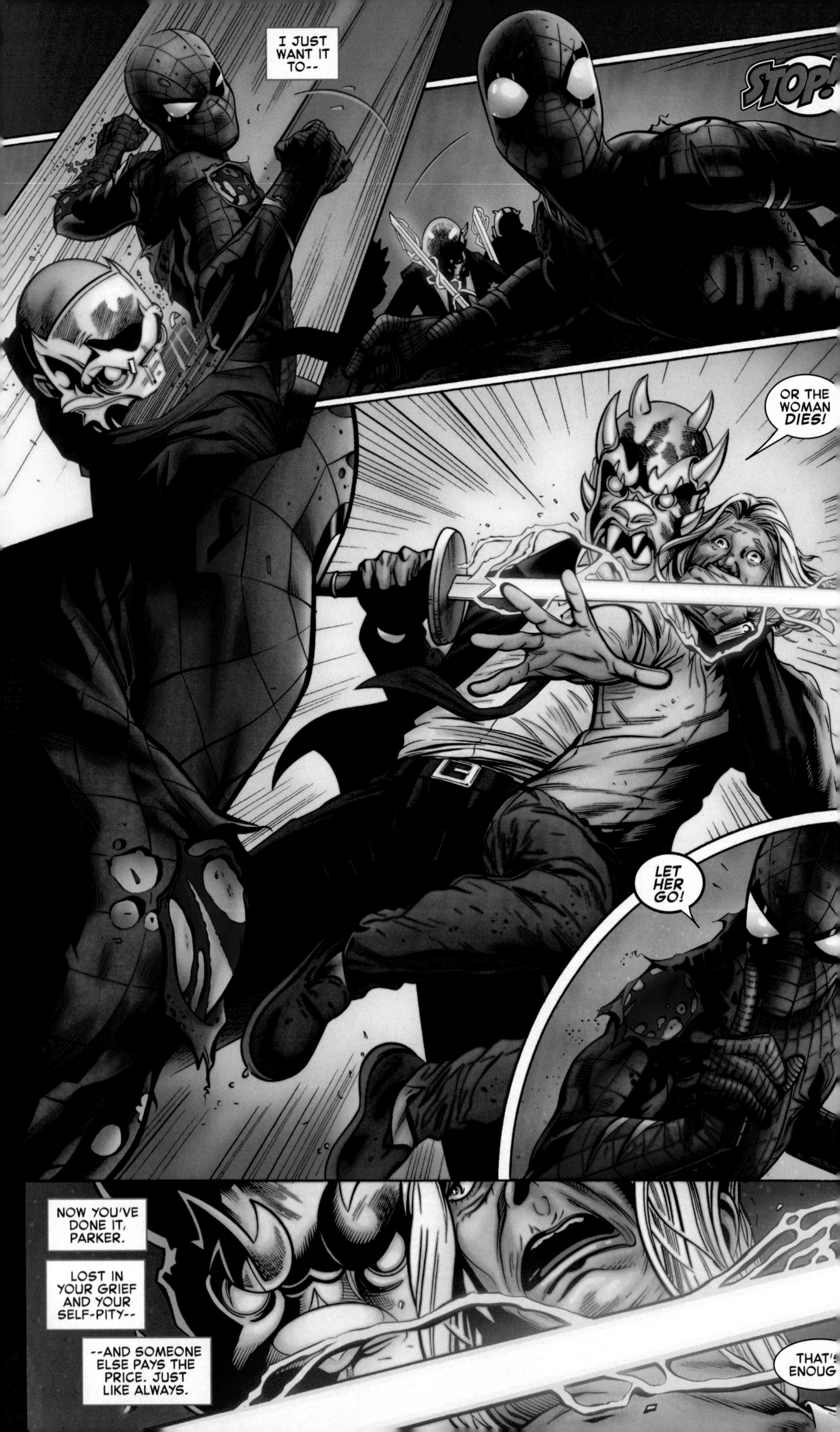
I JUST WANT IT TO--
STOP!
OR THE WOMAN DIES!
LET HER GO!
NOW YOU'VE DONE IT, PARKER.
LOST IN YOUR GRIEF AND YOUR SELF-PITY--
--AND SOMEONE ELSE PAYS THE PRICE. JUST LIKE ALWAYS.
THAT'S ENOUG

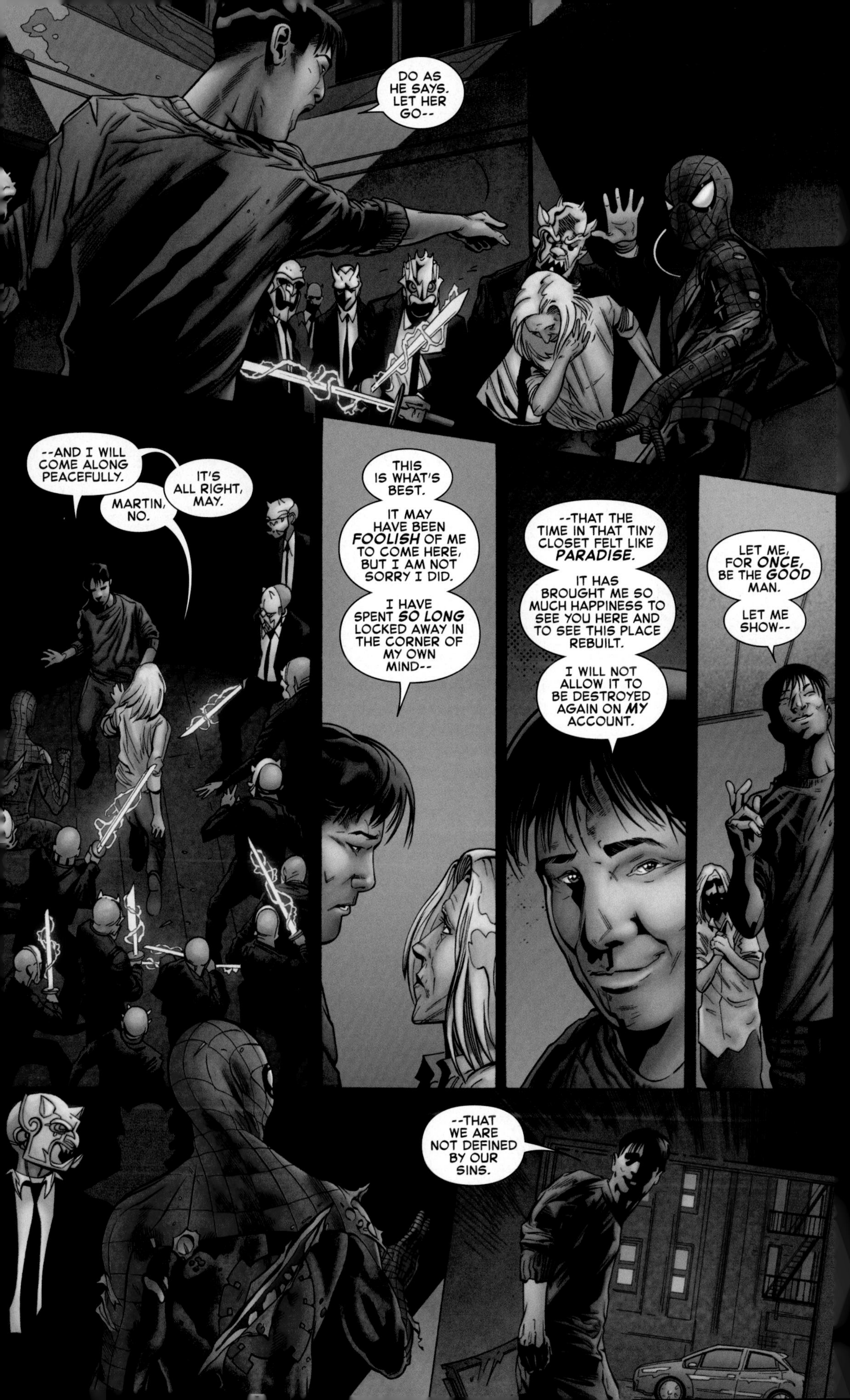

DO AS HE SAYS. LET HER GO--
--AND I WILL COME ALONG PEACEFULLY.
MARTIN, NO.
IT'S ALL RIGHT, MAY.
THIS IS WHAT'S BEST.
IT MAY HAVE BEEN FOOLISH OF ME TO COME HERE, BUT I AM NOT SORRY I DID.
I HAVE SPENT SO LONG LOCKED AWAY IN THE CORNER OF MY OWN MIND--
--THAT THE TIME IN THAT TINY CLOSET FELT LIKE PARADISE.
IT HAS BROUGHT ME SO MUCH HAPPINESS TO SEE YOU HERE AND TO SEE THIS PLACE REBUILT.
I WILL NOT ALLOW IT TO BE DESTROYED AGAIN ON MY ACCOUNT.
LET ME, FOR ONCE, BE THE GOOD MAN.
LET ME SHOW--
--THAT WE ARE NOT DEFINED BY OUR SINS.

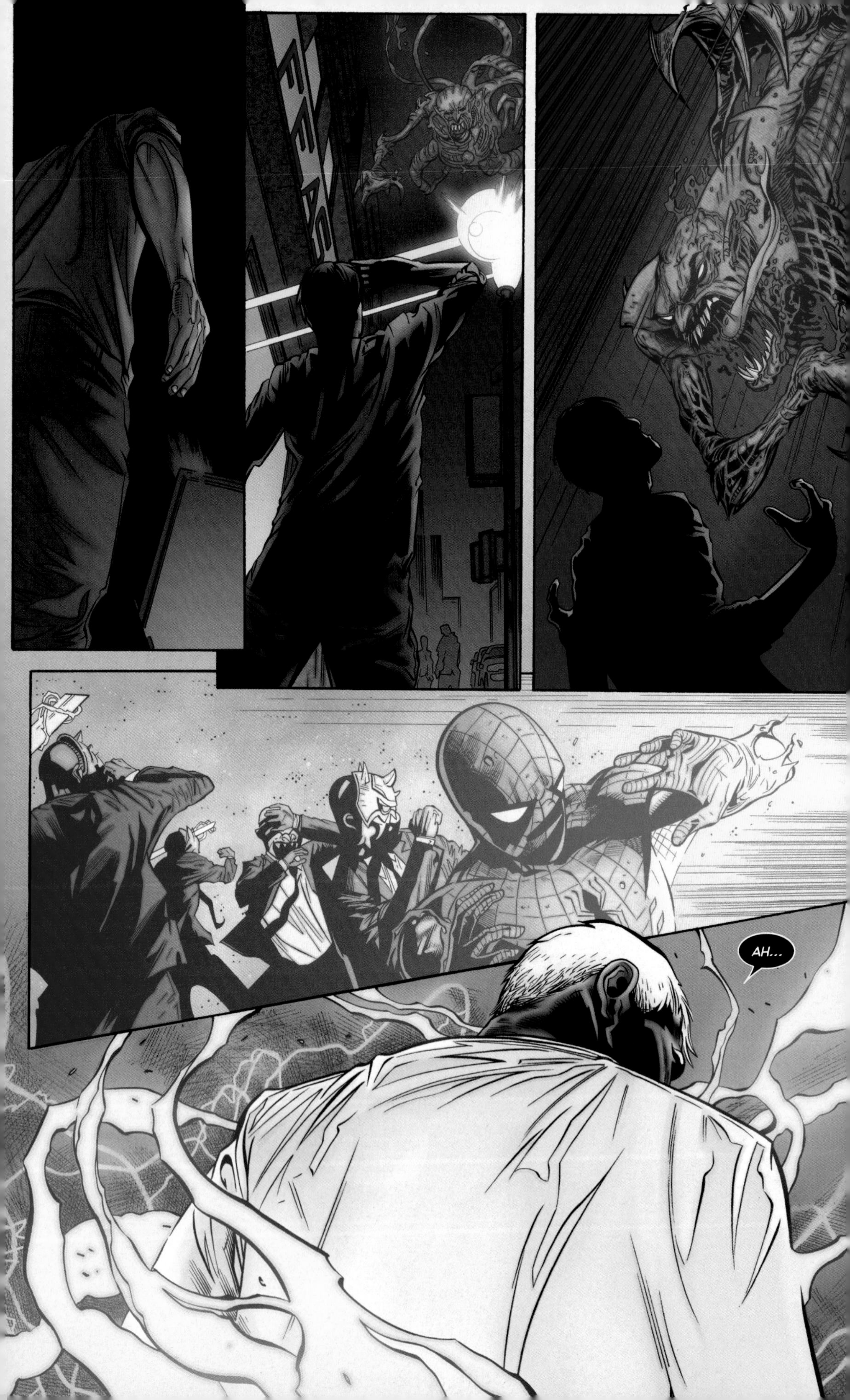
AH...

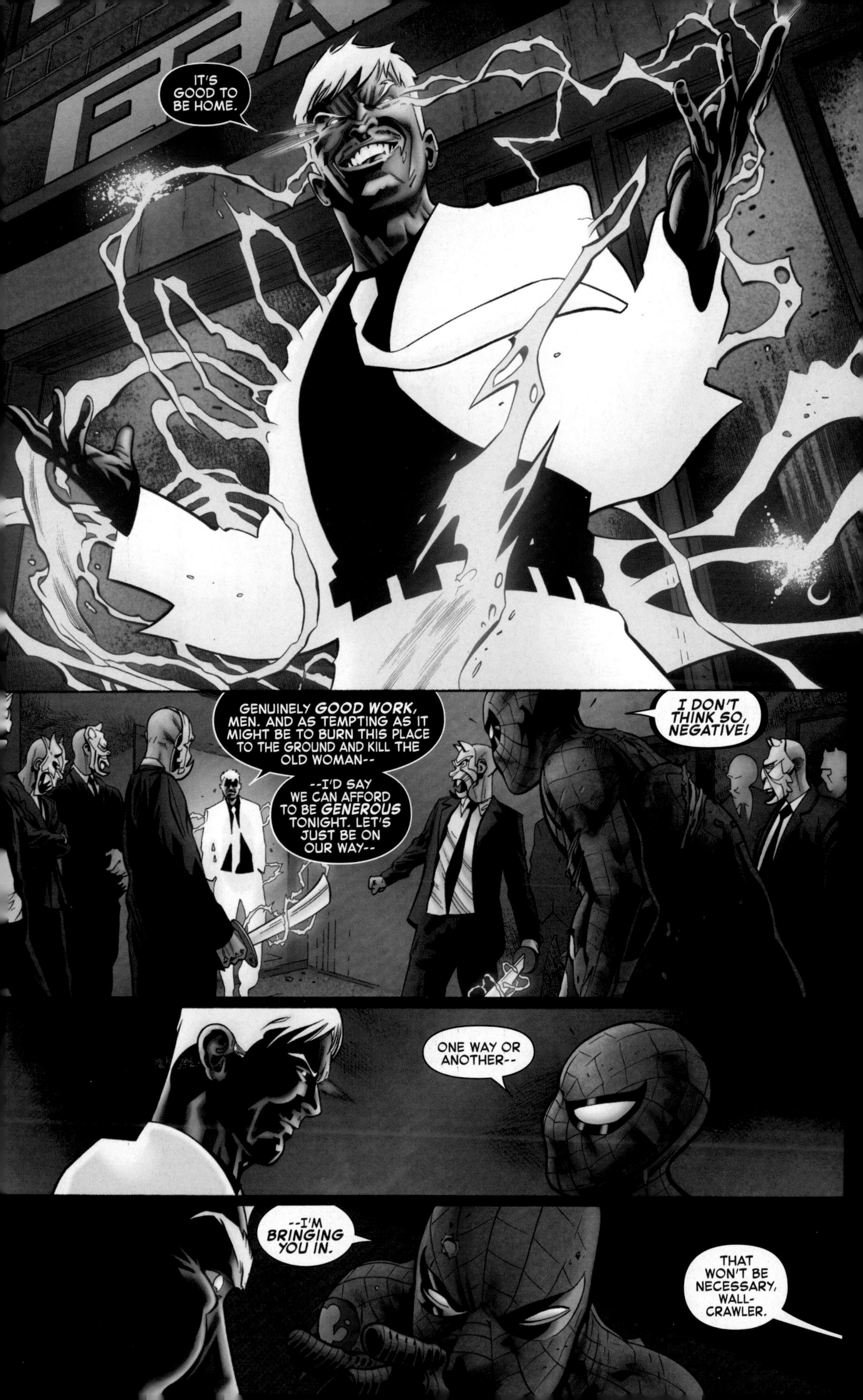
IT'S GOOD TO BE HOME.
GENUINELY GOOD WORK, MEN. AND AS TEMPTING AS IT MIGHT BE TO BURN THIS PLACE TO THE GROUND AND KILL THE OLD WOMAN--
--I'D SAY WE CAN AFFORD TO BE GENEROUS TONIGHT. LET'S JUST BE ON OUR WAY--
I DON'T THINK SO, NEGATIVE!
ONE WAY OR ANOTHER--
--I'M BRINGING YOU IN.
THAT WON'T BE NECESSARY, WALL-CRAWLER.

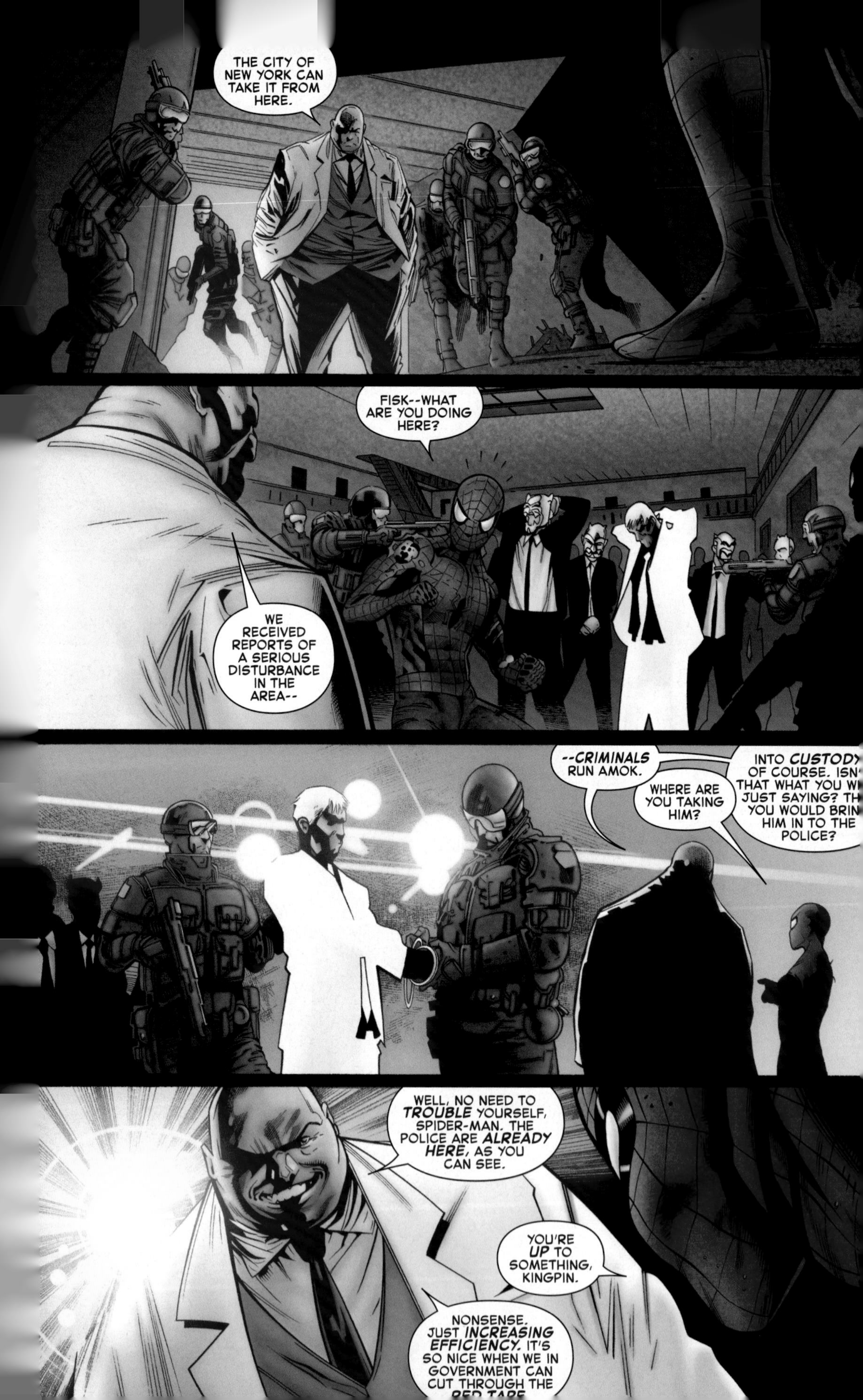
THE CITY OF NEW YORK CAN TAKE IT FROM HERE.
FISK--WHAT ARE YOU DOING HERE?
WE RECEIVED REPORTS OF A SERIOUS DISTURBANCE IN THE AREA--
--CRIMINALS RUN AMOK.
WHERE ARE YOU TAKING HIM?
INTO CUSTODY OF COURSE. ISN THAT WHAT YOU W JUST SAYING? TH YOU WOULD BRIN HIM IN TO THE POLICE?
WELL, NO NEED TO TROUBLE YOURSELF, SPIDER-MAN. THE POLICE ARE ALREADY HERE, AS YOU CAN SEE.
YOU'RE UP TO SOMETHING, KINGPIN.
NONSENSE. JUST INCREASING EFFICIENCY. IT'S SO NICE WHEN WE IN GOVERNMENT CAN CUT THROUGH THE

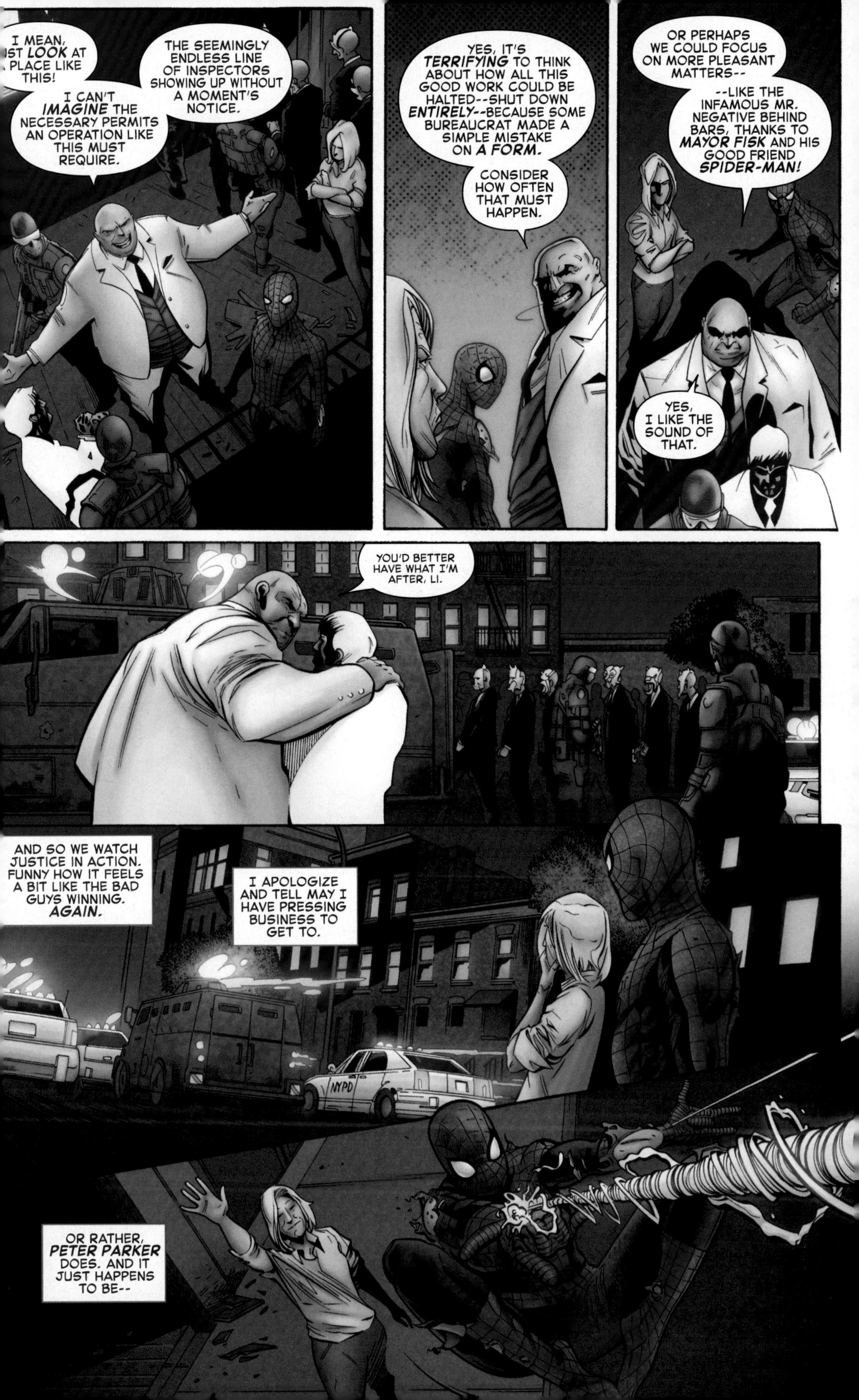

I MEAN, ...ST LOOK AT ...PLACE LIKE THIS!
I CAN'T IMAGINE THE NECESSARY PERMITS AN OPERATION LIKE THIS MUST REQUIRE.
THE SEEMINGLY ENDLESS LINE OF INSPECTORS SHOWING UP WITHOUT A MOMENT'S NOTICE.
YES, IT'S TERRIFYING TO THINK ABOUT HOW ALL THIS GOOD WORK COULD BE HALTED--SHUT DOWN ENTIRELY--BECAUSE SOME BUREAUCRAT MADE A SIMPLE MISTAKE ON A FORM.
CONSIDER HOW OFTEN THAT MUST HAPPEN.
OR PERHAPS WE COULD FOCUS ON MORE PLEASANT MATTERS--
--LIKE THE INFAMOUS MR. NEGATIVE BEHIND BARS, THANKS TO MAYOR FISK AND HIS GOOD FRIEND SPIDER-MAN!
YES, I LIKE THE SOUND OF THAT.
YOU'D BETTER HAVE WHAT I'M AFTER, LI.
AND SO WE WATCH JUSTICE IN ACTION. FUNNY HOW IT FEELS A BIT LIKE THE BAD GUYS WINNING. AGAIN.
I APOLOGIZE AND TELL MAY I HAVE PRESSING BUSINESS TO GET TO.
NYPD
OR RATHER, PETER PARKER DOES. AND IT JUST HAPPENS TO BE--

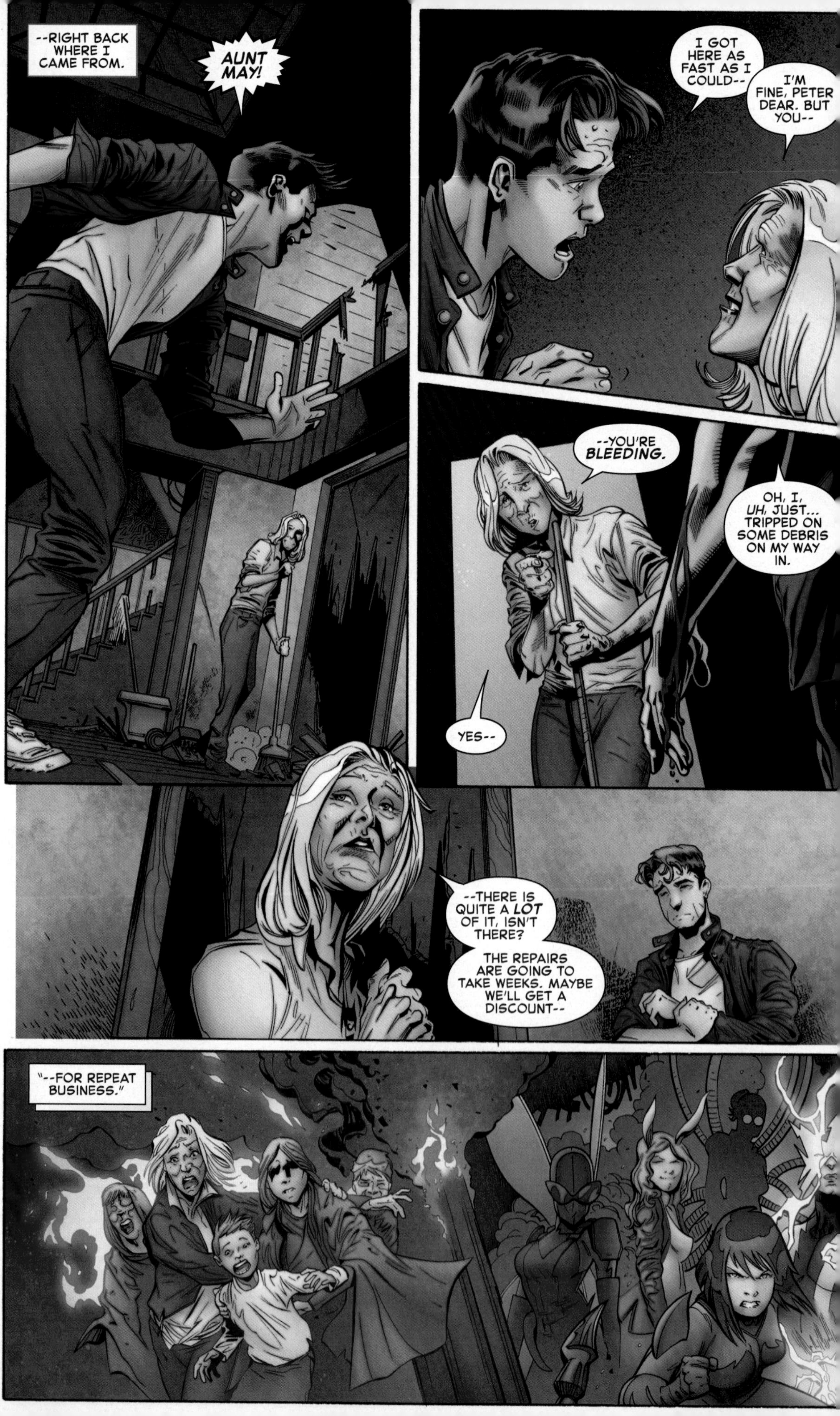
--RIGHT BACK WHERE I CAME FROM.
AUNT MAY!
I GOT HERE AS FAST AS I COULD--
I'M FINE, PETER DEAR. BUT YOU--
--YOU'RE BLEEDING.
OH, I, UH, JUST... TRIPPED ON SOME DEBRIS ON MY WAY IN.
YES--
--THERE IS QUITE A LOT OF IT, ISN'T THERE?
THE REPAIRS ARE GOING TO TAKE WEEKS. MAYBE WE'LL GET A DISCOUNT--
"--FOR REPEAT BUSINESS."

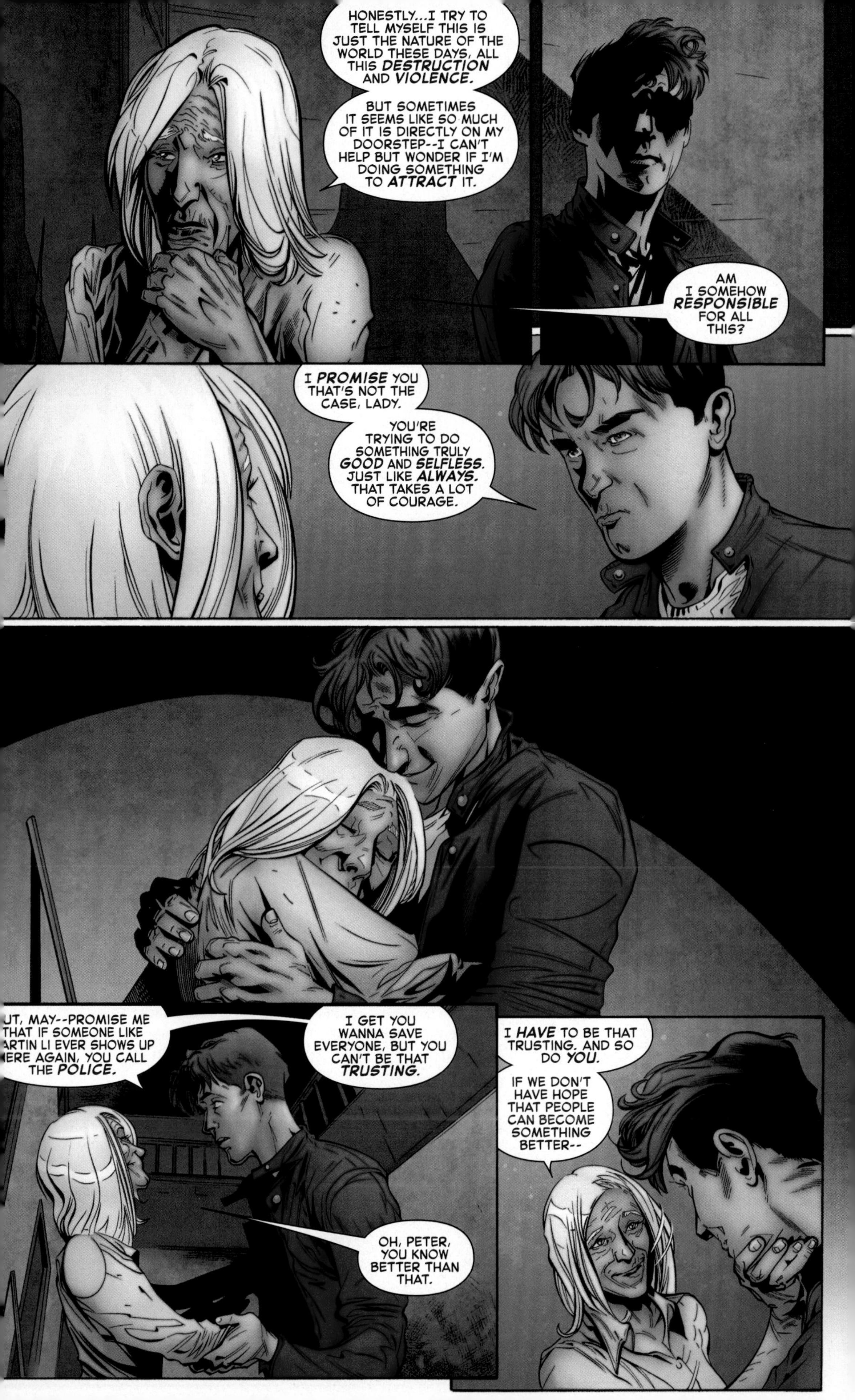

HONESTLY...I TRY TO TELL MYSELF THIS IS JUST THE NATURE OF THE WORLD THESE DAYS, ALL THIS DESTRUCTION AND VIOLENCE.
BUT SOMETIMES IT SEEMS LIKE SO MUCH OF IT IS DIRECTLY ON MY DOORSTEP--I CAN'T HELP BUT WONDER IF I'M DOING SOMETHING TO ATTRACT IT.
AM I SOMEHOW RESPONSIBLE FOR ALL THIS?
I PROMISE YOU THAT'S NOT THE CASE, LADY.
YOU'RE TRYING TO DO SOMETHING TRULY GOOD AND SELFLESS. JUST LIKE ALWAYS. THAT TAKES A LOT OF COURAGE.
UT, MAY--PROMISE ME THAT IF SOMEONE LIKE ARTIN LI EVER SHOWS UP ERE AGAIN, YOU CALL THE POLICE.
I GET YOU WANNA SAVE EVERYONE, BUT YOU CAN'T BE THAT TRUSTING.
OH, PETER, YOU KNOW BETTER THAN THAT.
I HAVE TO BE THAT TRUSTING. AND SO DO YOU.
IF WE DON'T HAVE HOPE THAT PEOPLE CAN BECOME SOMETHING BETTER--

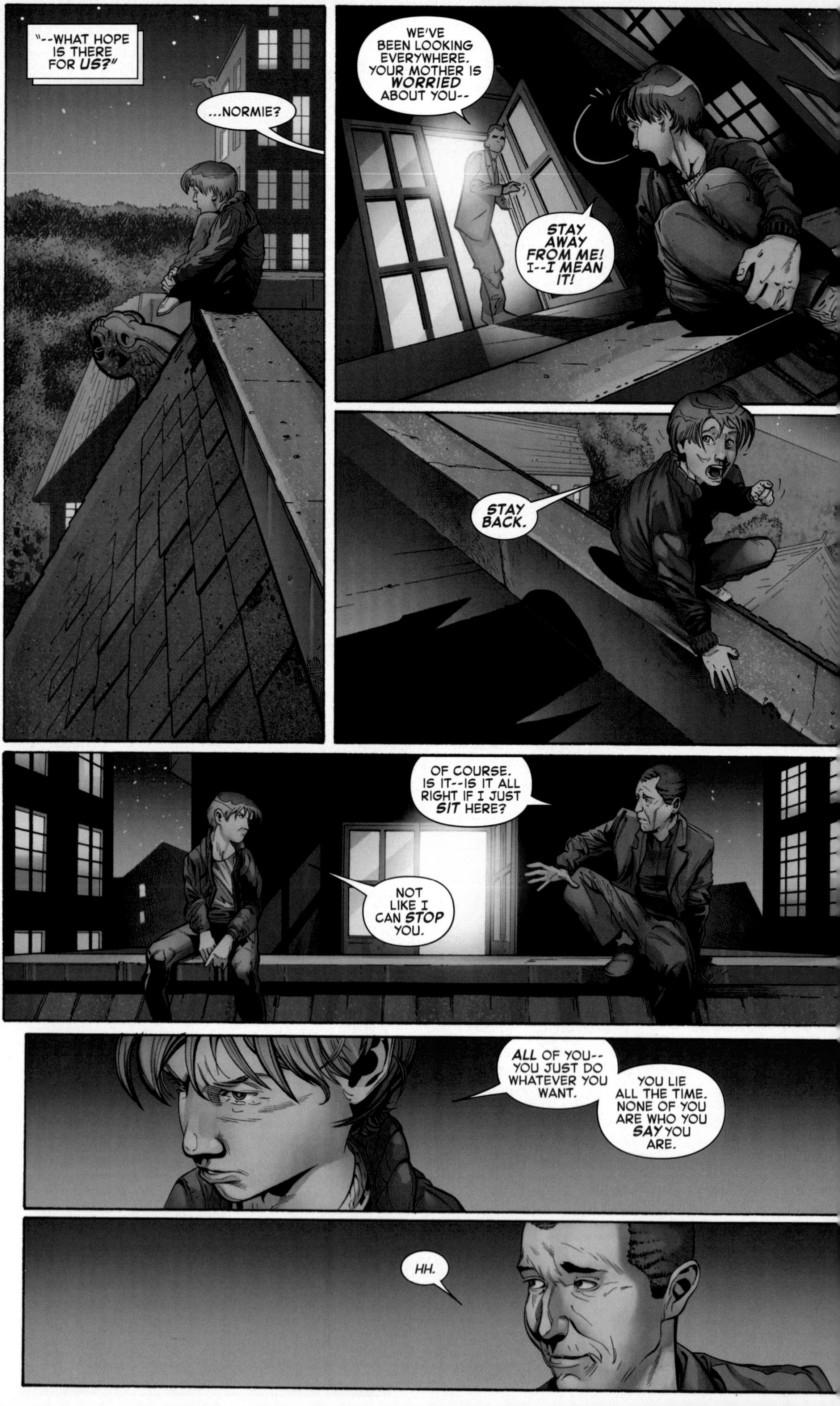
"--WHAT HOPE IS THERE FOR US?"
...NORMIE?
WE'VE BEEN LOOKING EVERYWHERE. YOUR MOTHER IS WORRIED ABOUT YOU--
STAY AWAY FROM ME! I--I MEAN IT!
STAY BACK.
OF COURSE. IS IT--IS IT ALL RIGHT IF I JUST SIT HERE?
NOT LIKE I CAN STOP YOU.
ALL OF YOU--YOU JUST DO WHATEVER YOU WANT.
YOU LIE ALL THE TIME. NONE OF YOU ARE WHO YOU SAY YOU ARE.
HH.

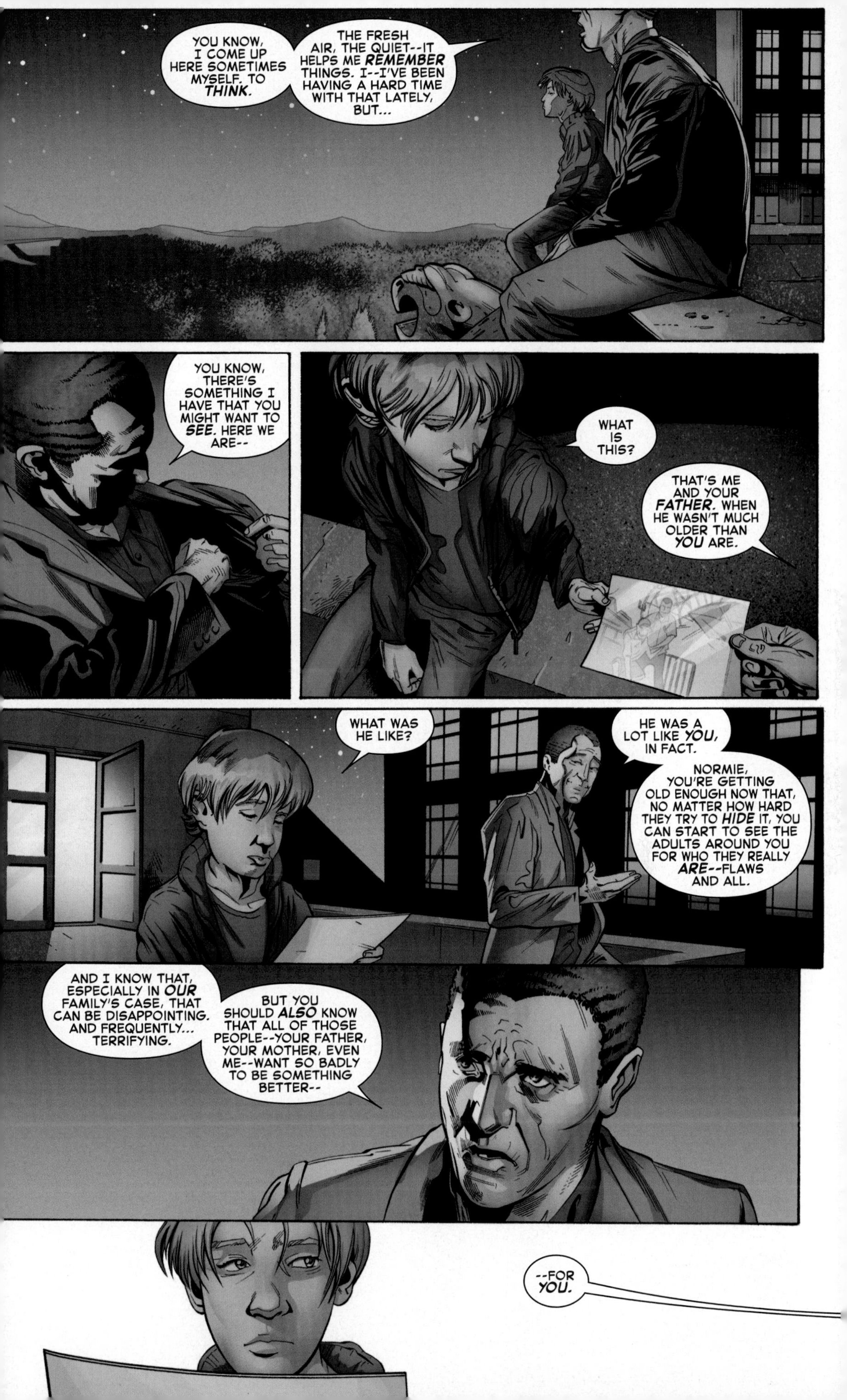
YOU KNOW, I COME UP HERE SOMETIMES MYSELF. TO THINK.
THE FRESH AIR, THE QUIET--IT HELPS ME REMEMBER THINGS. I--I'VE BEEN HAVING A HARD TIME WITH THAT LATELY, BUT...
YOU KNOW, THERE'S SOMETHING I HAVE THAT YOU MIGHT WANT TO SEE. HERE WE ARE--
WHAT IS THIS?
THAT'S ME AND YOUR FATHER. WHEN HE WASN'T MUCH OLDER THAN YOU ARE.
WHAT WAS HE LIKE?
HE WAS A LOT LIKE YOU, IN FACT.
NORMIE, YOU'RE GETTING OLD ENOUGH NOW THAT, NO MATTER HOW HARD THEY TRY TO HIDE IT, YOU CAN START TO SEE THE ADULTS AROUND YOU FOR WHO THEY REALLY ARE--FLAWS AND ALL.
AND I KNOW THAT, ESPECIALLY IN OUR FAMILY'S CASE, THAT CAN BE DISAPPOINTING. AND FREQUENTLY... TERRIFYING.
BUT YOU SHOULD ALSO KNOW THAT ALL OF THOSE PEOPLE--YOUR FATHER, YOUR MOTHER, EVEN ME--WANT SO BADLY TO BE SOMETHING BETTER--
--FOR YOU.

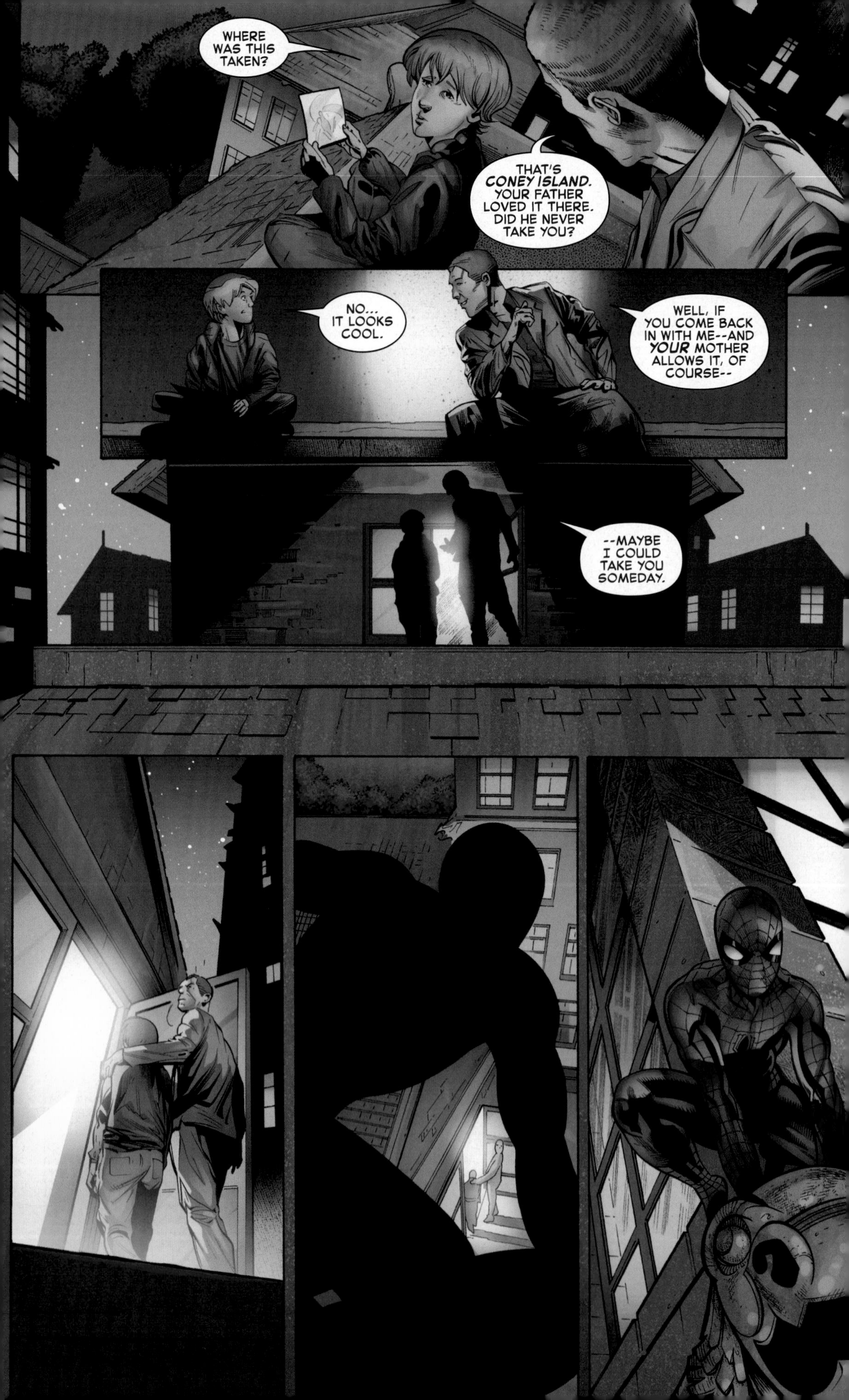
WHERE WAS THIS TAKEN?
THAT'S CONEY ISLAND. YOUR FATHER LOVED IT THERE. DID HE NEVER TAKE YOU?
NO... IT LOOKS COOL.
WELL, IF YOU COME BACK IN WITH ME--AND YOUR MOTHER ALLOWS IT, OF COURSE--
--MAYBE I COULD TAKE YOU SOMEDAY.

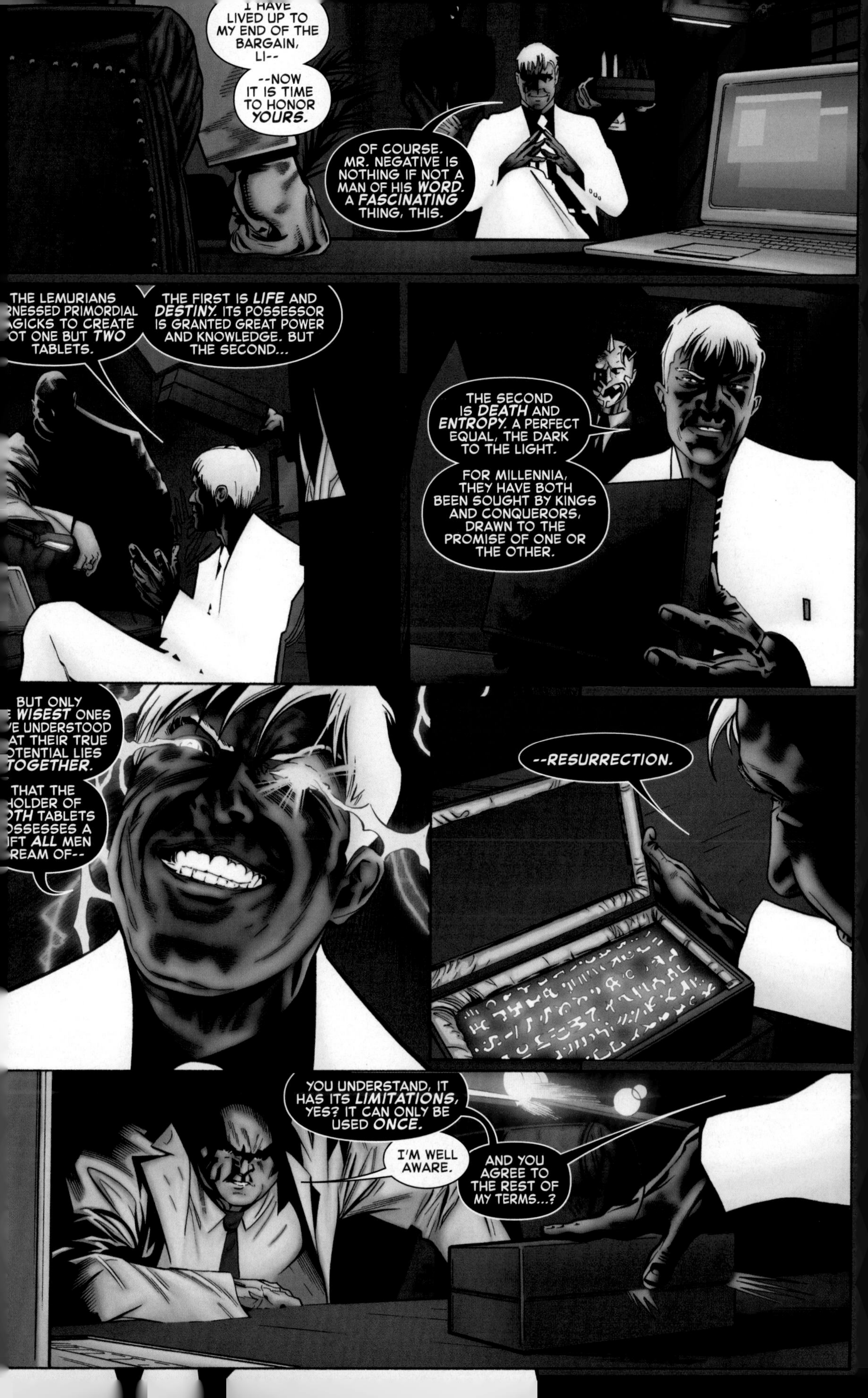
I HAVE LIVED UP TO MY END OF THE BARGAIN, LI--
--NOW IT IS TIME TO HONOR YOURS.
OF COURSE. MR. NEGATIVE IS NOTHING IF NOT A MAN OF HIS WORD. A FASCINATING THING, THIS.
THE LEMURIANS RNESSED PRIMORDIAL AGICKS TO CREATE OT ONE BUT TWO TABLETS.
THE FIRST IS LIFE AND DESTINY. ITS POSSESSOR IS GRANTED GREAT POWER AND KNOWLEDGE. BUT THE SECOND...
THE SECOND IS DEATH AND ENTROPY. A PERFECT EQUAL, THE DARK TO THE LIGHT.
FOR MILLENNIA, THEY HAVE BOTH BEEN SOUGHT BY KINGS AND CONQUERORS, DRAWN TO THE PROMISE OF ONE OR THE OTHER.
BUT ONLY E WISEST ONES VE UNDERSTOOD AT THEIR TRUE OTENTIAL LIES TOGETHER.
THAT THE HOLDER OF OTH TABLETS OSSESSES A IFT ALL MEN REAM OF--
--RESURRECTION.
YOU UNDERSTAND, IT HAS ITS LIMITATIONS, YES? IT CAN ONLY BE USED ONCE.
I'M WELL AWARE.
AND YOU AGREE TO THE REST OF MY TERMS...?

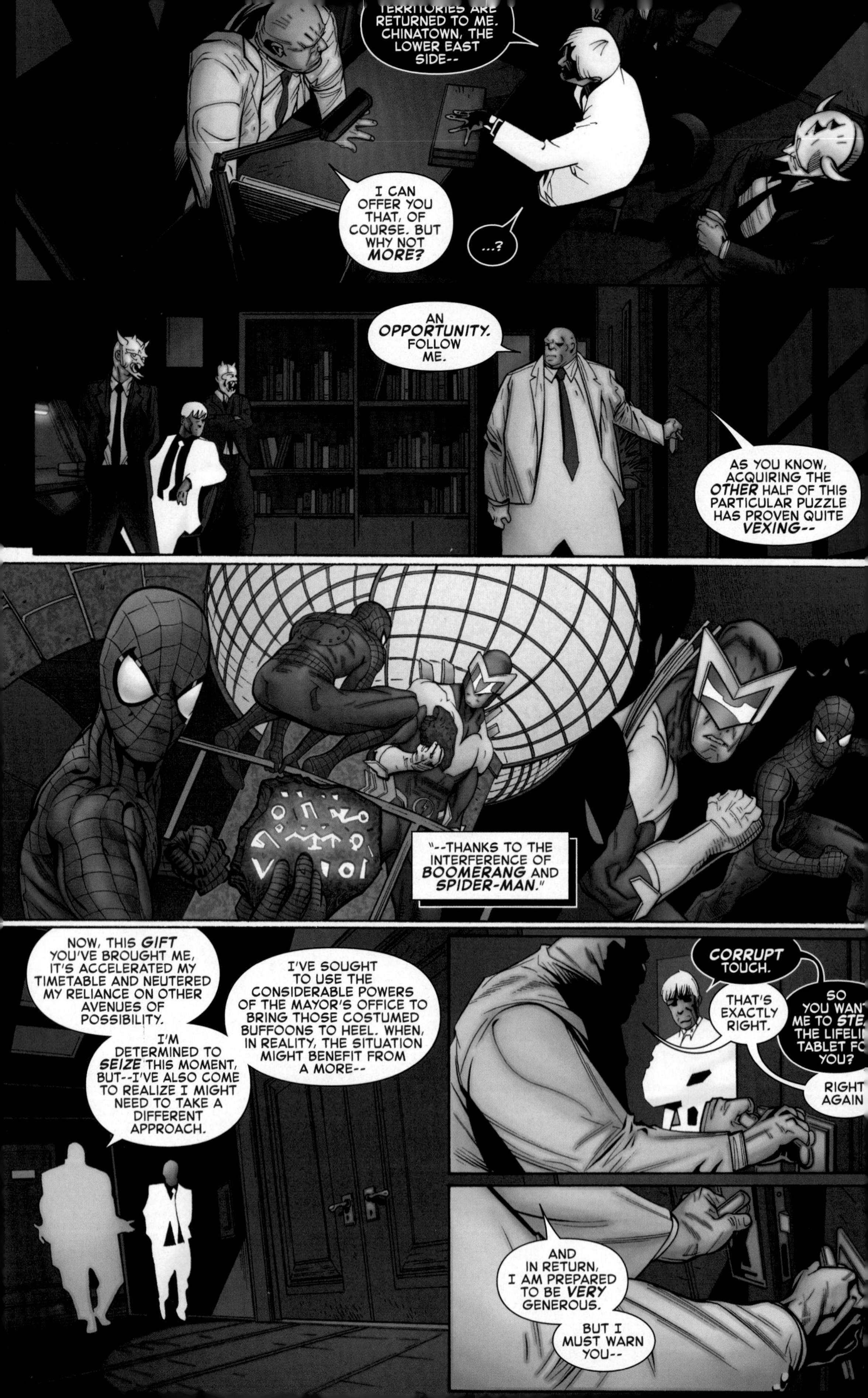
TERRITORIES ARE RETURNED TO ME. CHINATOWN, THE LOWER EAST SIDE--
I CAN OFFER YOU THAT, OF COURSE. BUT WHY NOT MORE?
...?
AN OPPORTUNITY. FOLLOW ME.
AS YOU KNOW, ACQUIRING THE OTHER HALF OF THIS PARTICULAR PUZZLE HAS PROVEN QUITE VEXING--
"--THANKS TO THE INTERFERENCE OF BOOMERANG AND SPIDER-MAN."
NOW, THIS GIFT YOU'VE BROUGHT ME, IT'S ACCELERATED MY TIMETABLE AND NEUTERED MY RELIANCE ON OTHER AVENUES OF POSSIBILITY.
I'M DETERMINED TO SEIZE THIS MOMENT, BUT--I'VE ALSO COME TO REALIZE I MIGHT NEED TO TAKE A DIFFERENT APPROACH.
I'VE SOUGHT TO USE THE CONSIDERABLE POWERS OF THE MAYOR'S OFFICE TO BRING THOSE COSTUMED BUFFOONS TO HEEL. WHEN, IN REALITY, THE SITUATION MIGHT BENEFIT FROM A MORE--
CORRUPT TOUCH.
THAT'S EXACTLY RIGHT.
RIGHT AGAIN
AND IN RETURN, I AM PREPARED TO BE VERY GENEROUS.
BUT I MUST WARN YOU--

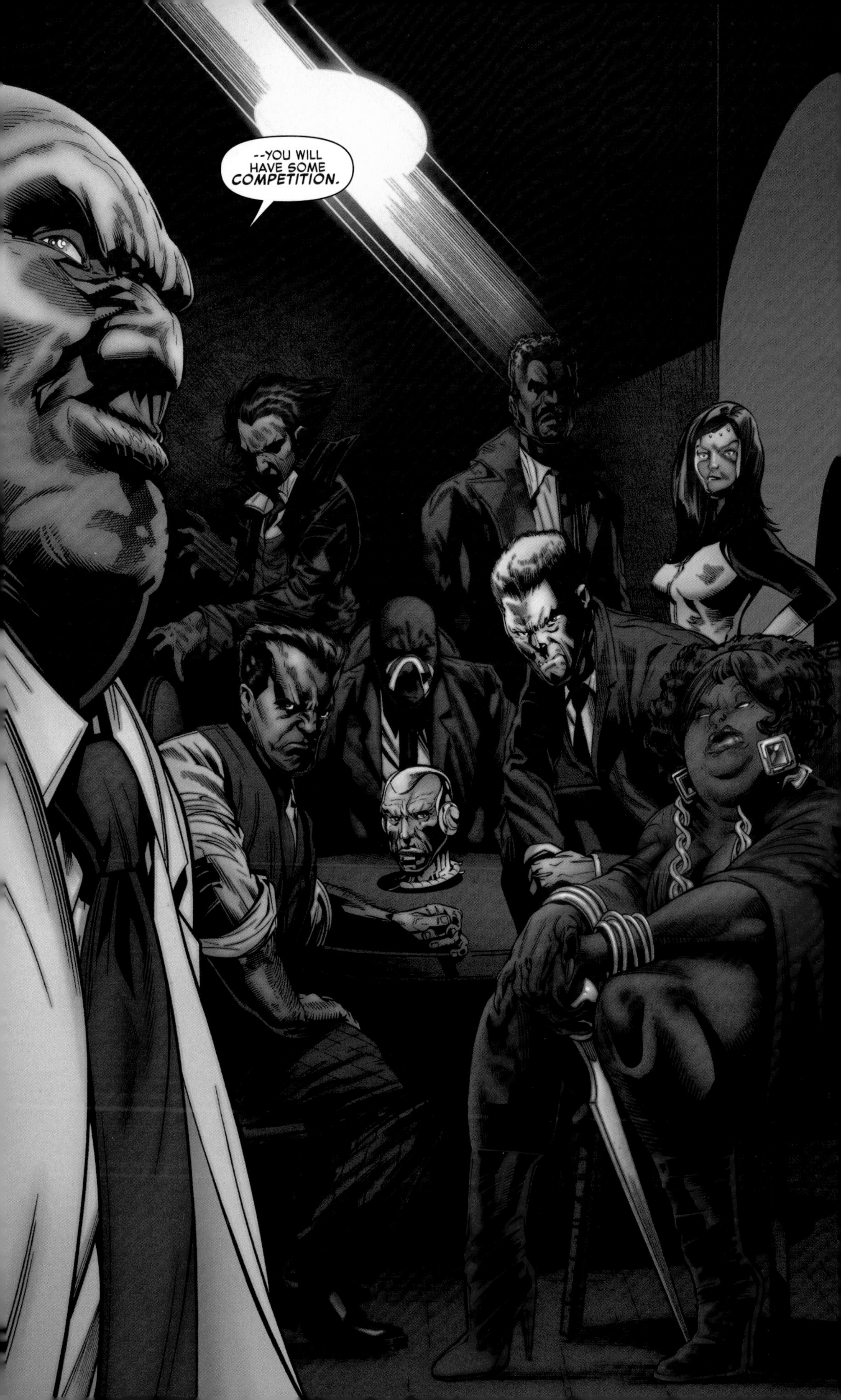
--YOU WILL HAVE SOME COMPETITION.

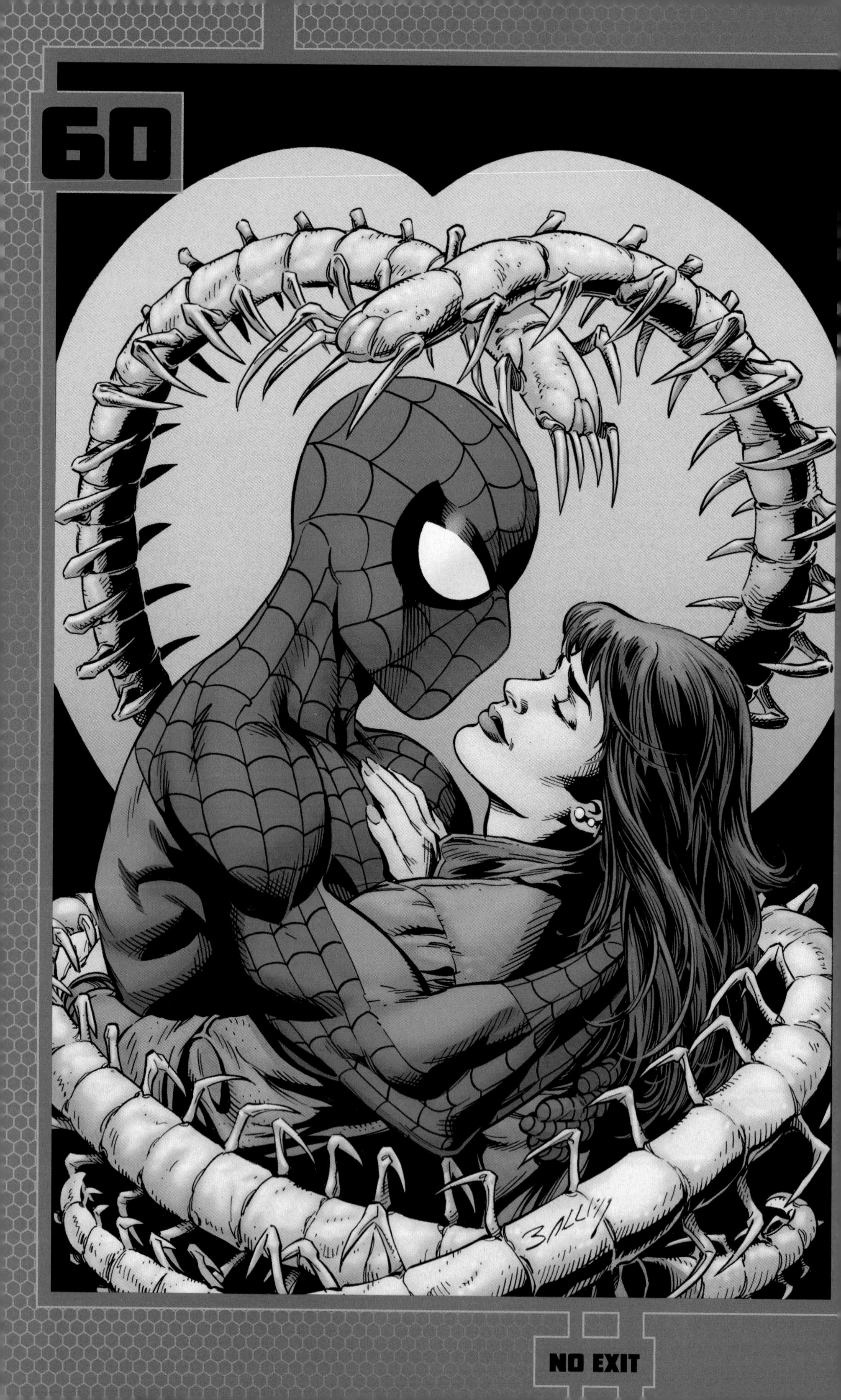
60
NO EXIT

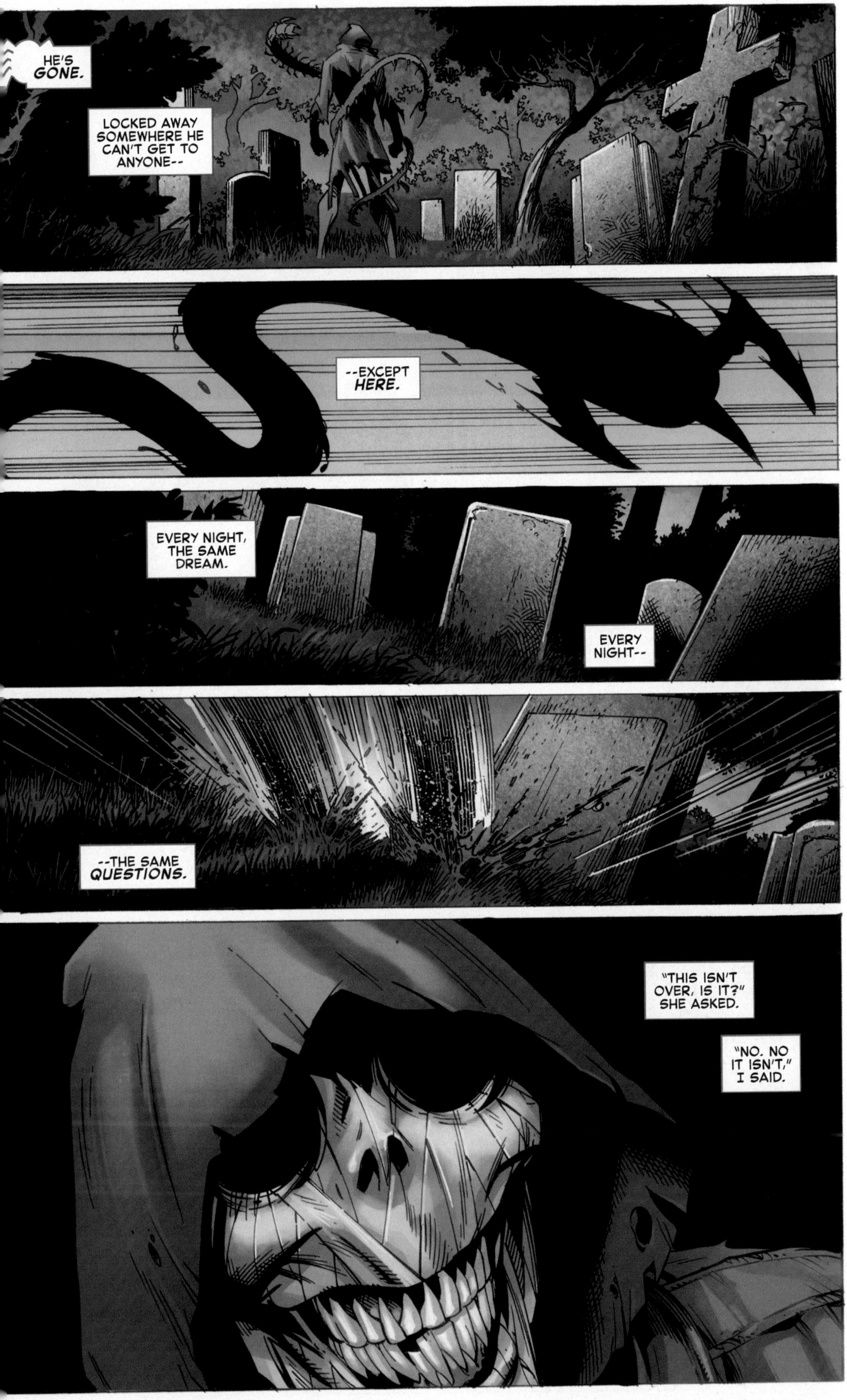
HE'S GONE.
LOCKED AWAY SOMEWHERE HE CAN'T GET TO ANYONE--
--EXCEPT HERE.
EVERY NIGHT, THE SAME DREAM.
EVERY NIGHT--
--THE SAME QUESTIONS.
"THIS ISN'T OVER, IS IT?" SHE ASKED.
"NO. NO IT ISN'T," I SAID.

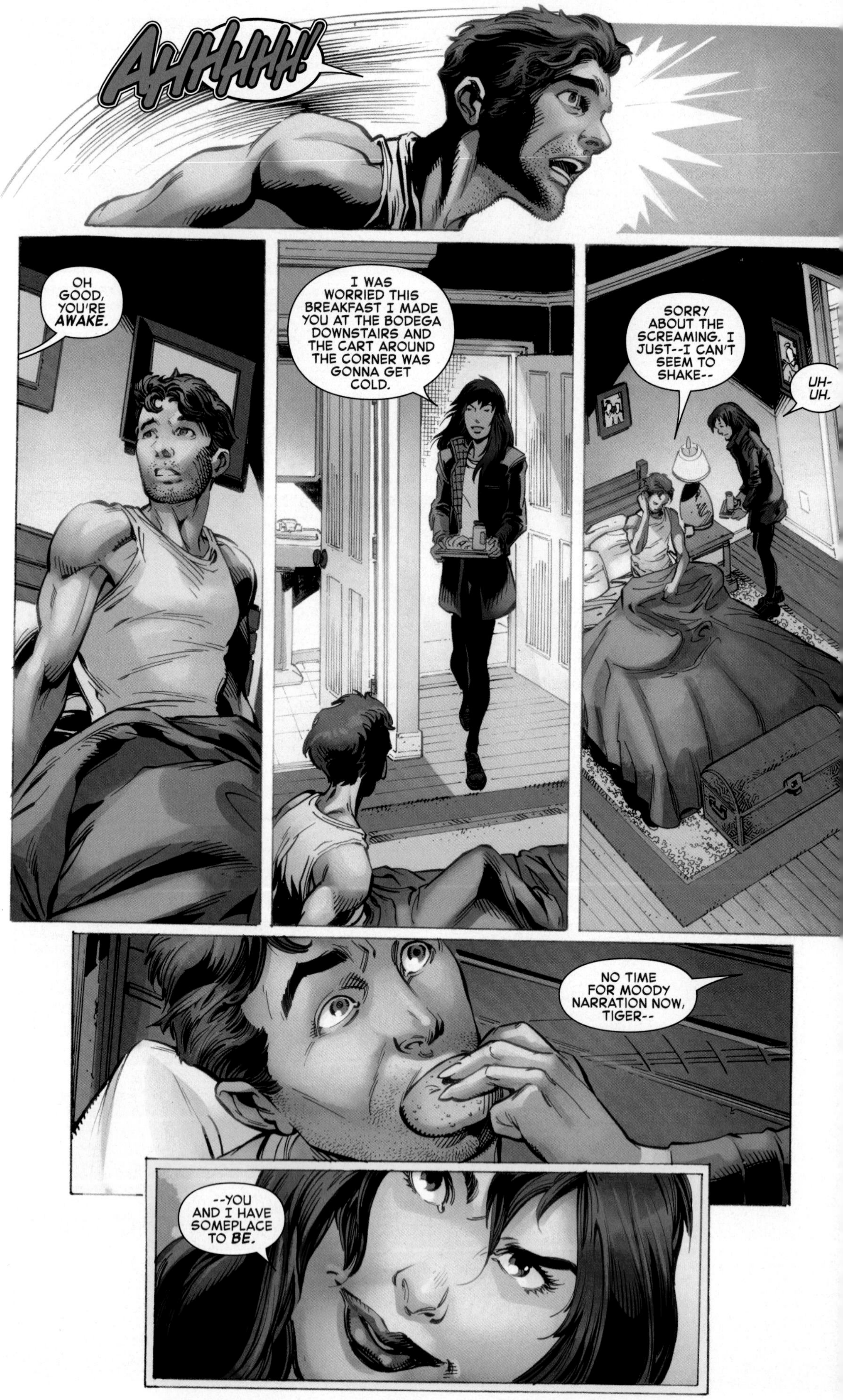
AHHHHHH!
OH GOOD, YOU'RE *AWAKE.*
I WAS WORRIED THIS BREAKFAST I MADE YOU AT THE BODEGA DOWNSTAIRS AND THE CART AROUND THE CORNER WAS GONNA GET COLD.
SORRY ABOUT THE SCREAMING. I JUST--I CAN'T SEEM TO SHAKE--
UH-UH.
NO TIME FOR MOODY NARRATION NOW, TIGER--
--YOU AND I HAVE SOMEPLACE TO *BE.*

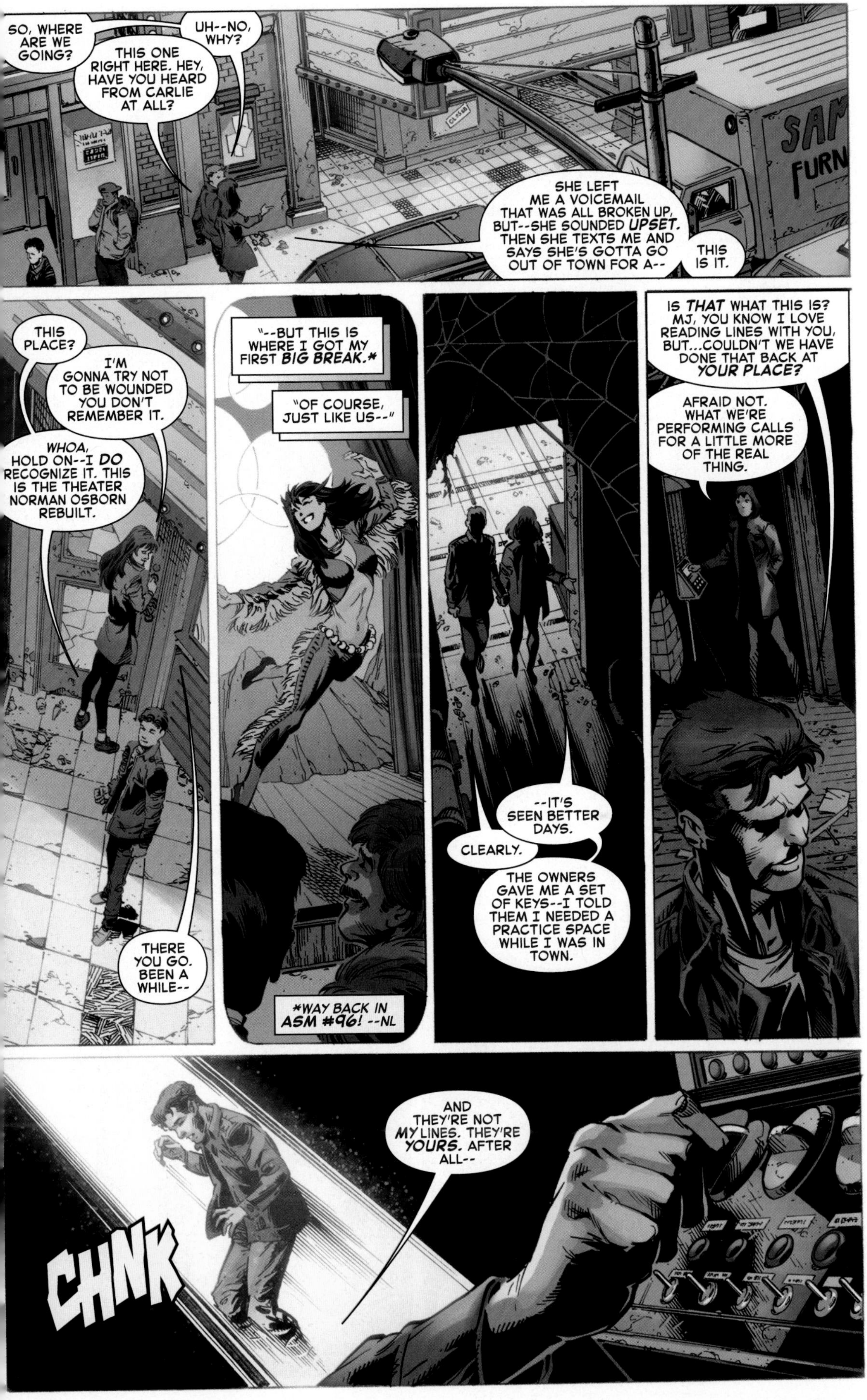

SO, WHERE ARE WE GOING?
THIS ONE RIGHT HERE. HEY, HAVE YOU HEARD FROM CARLIE AT ALL?
UH--NO, WHY?
SHE LEFT ME A VOICEMAIL THAT WAS ALL BROKEN UP, BUT--SHE SOUNDED UPSET. THEN SHE TEXTS ME AND SAYS SHE'S GOTTA GO OUT OF TOWN FOR A--
THIS IS IT.
THIS PLACE?
I'M GONNA TRY NOT TO BE WOUNDED YOU DON'T REMEMBER IT.
WHOA, HOLD ON--I DO RECOGNIZE IT. THIS IS THE THEATER NORMAN OSBORN REBUILT.
THERE YOU GO. BEEN A WHILE--
"--BUT THIS IS WHERE I GOT MY FIRST BIG BREAK.*
"OF COURSE, JUST LIKE US--"
*WAY BACK IN ASM #96! --NL
--IT'S SEEN BETTER DAYS.
CLEARLY.
THE OWNERS GAVE ME A SET OF KEYS--I TOLD THEM I NEEDED A PRACTICE SPACE WHILE I WAS IN TOWN.
IS THAT WHAT THIS IS? MJ, YOU KNOW I LOVE READING LINES WITH YOU, BUT...COULDN'T WE HAVE DONE THAT BACK AT YOUR PLACE?
AFRAID NOT. WHAT WE'RE PERFORMING CALLS FOR A LITTLE MORE OF THE REAL THING.
AND THEY'RE NOT MY LINES. THEY'RE YOURS. AFTER ALL--
CHNK

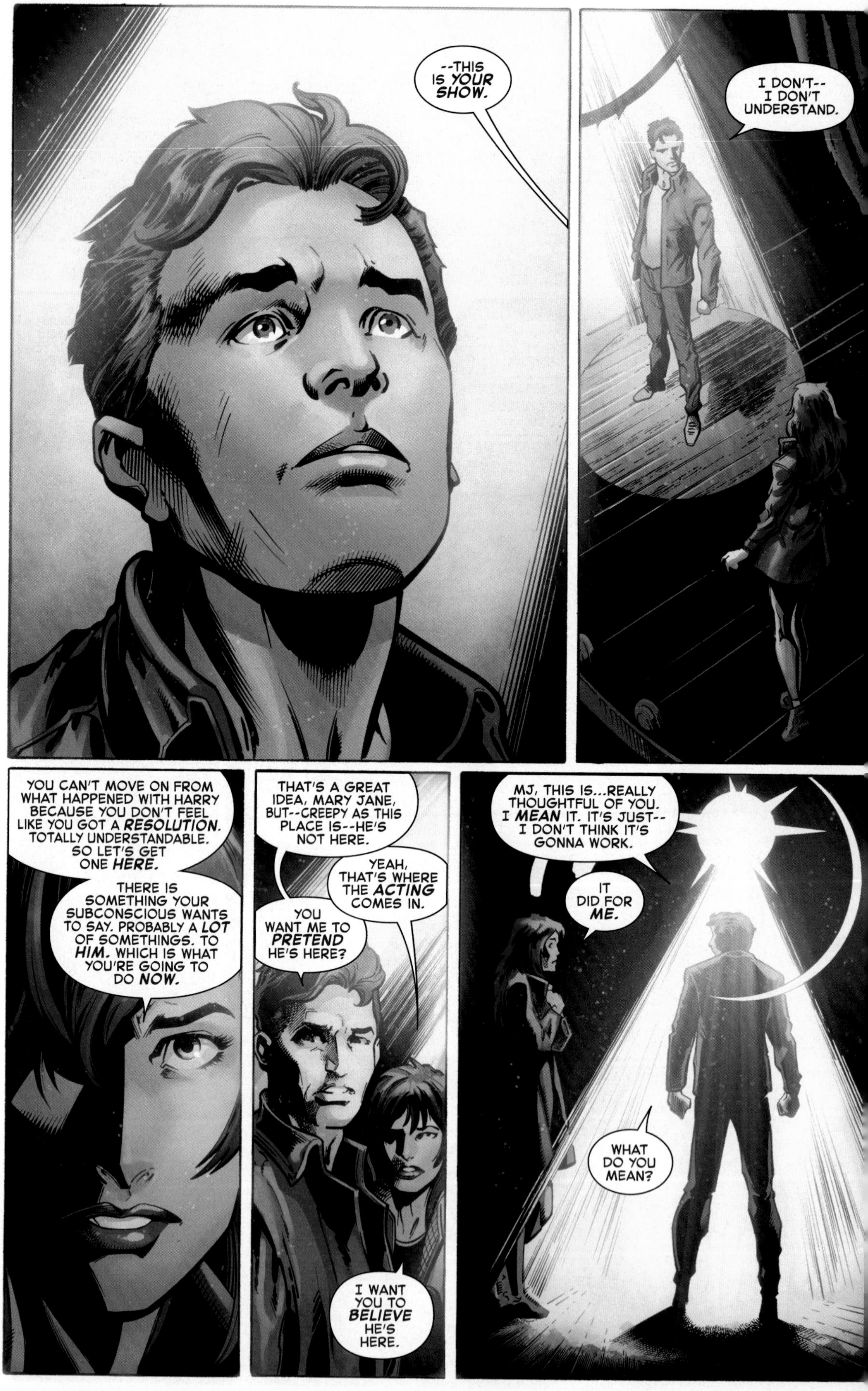
--THIS IS YOUR SHOW.
I DON'T-- I DON'T UNDERSTAND.
YOU CAN'T MOVE ON FROM WHAT HAPPENED WITH HARRY BECAUSE YOU DON'T FEEL LIKE YOU GOT A RESOLUTION. TOTALLY UNDERSTANDABLE. SO LET'S GET ONE HERE.
THERE IS SOMETHING YOUR SUBCONSCIOUS WANTS TO SAY. PROBABLY A LOT OF SOMETHINGS. TO HIM. WHICH IS WHAT YOU'RE GOING TO DO NOW.
THAT'S A GREAT IDEA, MARY JANE, BUT--CREEPY AS THIS PLACE IS--HE'S NOT HERE.
YEAH, THAT'S WHERE THE ACTING COMES IN.
YOU WANT ME TO PRETEND HE'S HERE?
I WANT YOU TO BELIEVE HE'S HERE.
MJ, THIS IS...REALLY THOUGHTFUL OF YOU. I MEAN IT. IT'S JUST-- I DON'T THINK IT'S GONNA WORK.
IT DID FOR ME.
WHAT DO YOU MEAN?

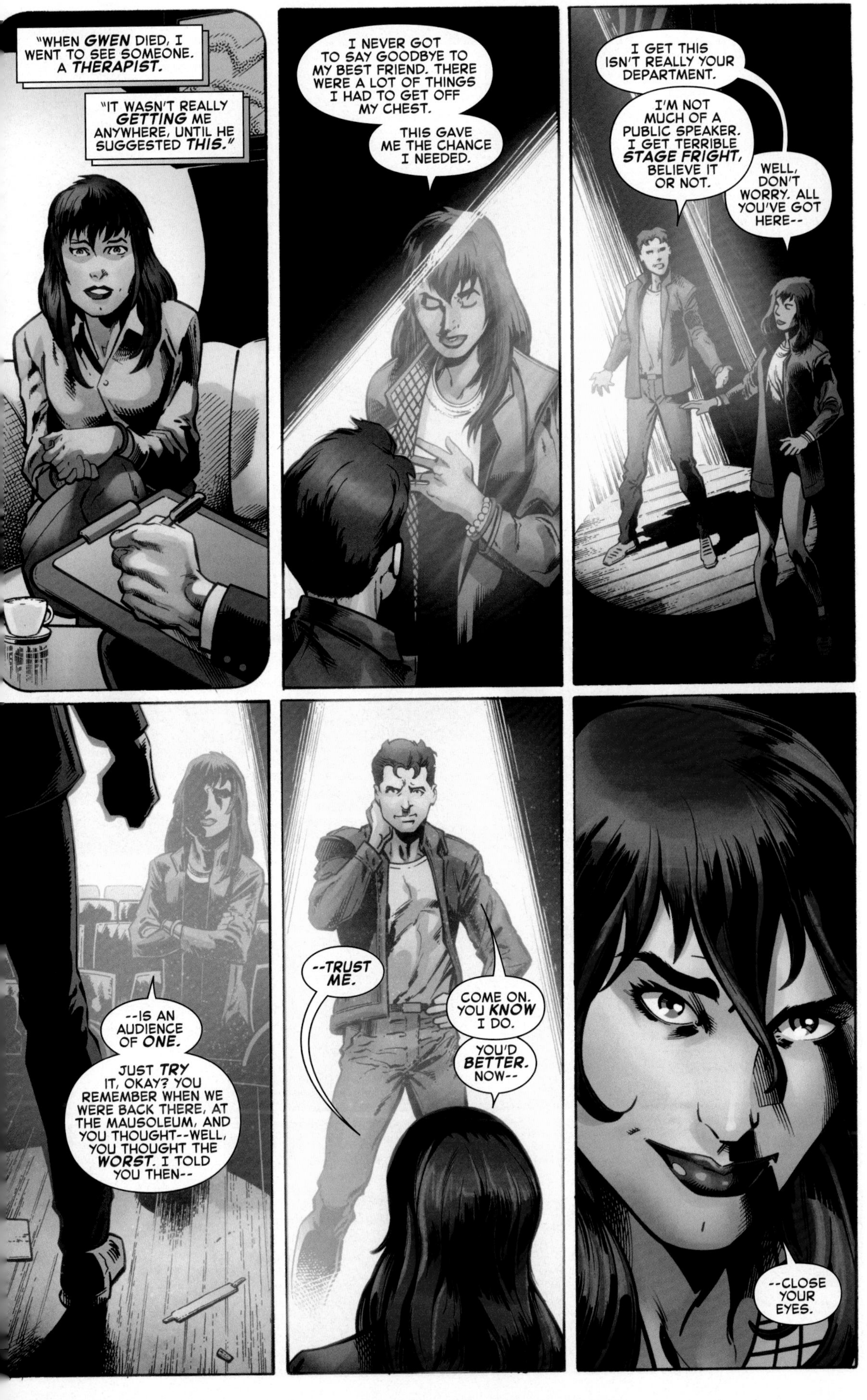
"WHEN GWEN DIED, I WENT TO SEE SOMEONE. A THERAPIST.
"IT WASN'T REALLY GETTING ME ANYWHERE, UNTIL HE SUGGESTED THIS."
I NEVER GOT TO SAY GOODBYE TO MY BEST FRIEND. THERE WERE A LOT OF THINGS I HAD TO GET OFF MY CHEST.
THIS GAVE ME THE CHANCE I NEEDED.
I GET THIS ISN'T REALLY YOUR DEPARTMENT.
I'M NOT MUCH OF A PUBLIC SPEAKER. I GET TERRIBLE STAGE FRIGHT, BELIEVE IT OR NOT.
WELL, DON'T WORRY. ALL YOU'VE GOT HERE--
--IS AN AUDIENCE OF ONE.
JUST TRY IT, OKAY? YOU REMEMBER WHEN WE WERE BACK THERE, AT THE MAUSOLEUM, AND YOU THOUGHT--WELL, YOU THOUGHT THE WORST. I TOLD YOU THEN--
--TRUST ME.
COME ON. YOU KNOW I DO.
YOU'D BETTER. NOW--
--CLOSE YOUR EYES.

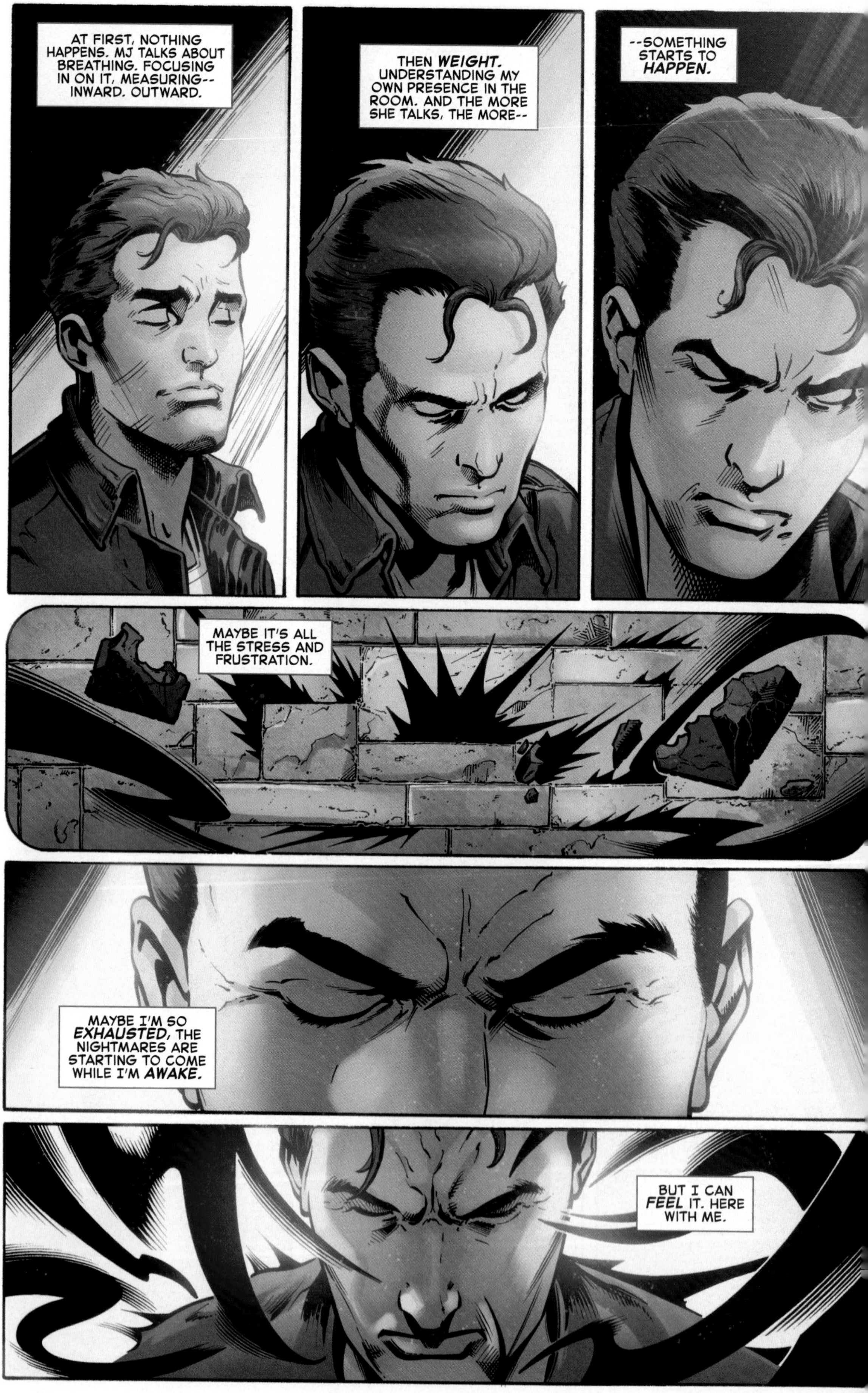
AT FIRST, NOTHING HAPPENS. MJ TALKS ABOUT BREATHING. FOCUSING IN ON IT, MEASURING-- INWARD. OUTWARD.
THEN WEIGHT. UNDERSTANDING MY OWN PRESENCE IN THE ROOM. AND THE MORE SHE TALKS, THE MORE--
--SOMETHING STARTS TO HAPPEN.
MAYBE IT'S ALL THE STRESS AND FRUSTRATION.
MAYBE I'M SO EXHAUSTED, THE NIGHTMARES ARE STARTING TO COME WHILE I'M AWAKE.
BUT I CAN FEEL IT. HERE WITH ME.

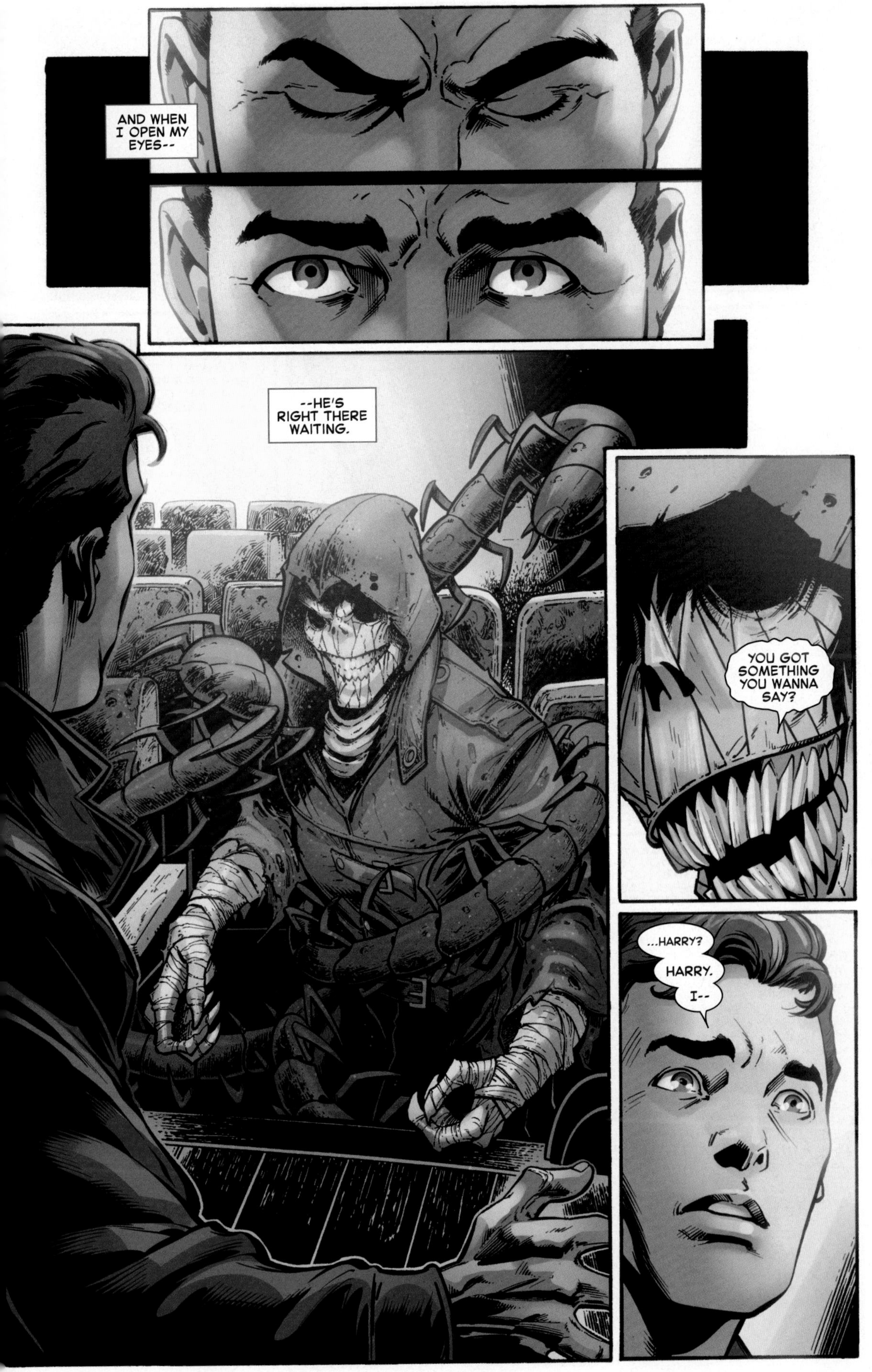
AND WHEN I OPEN MY EYES--
--HE'S RIGHT THERE WAITING.
YOU GOT SOMETHING YOU WANNA SAY?
...HARRY?
HARRY.
I--

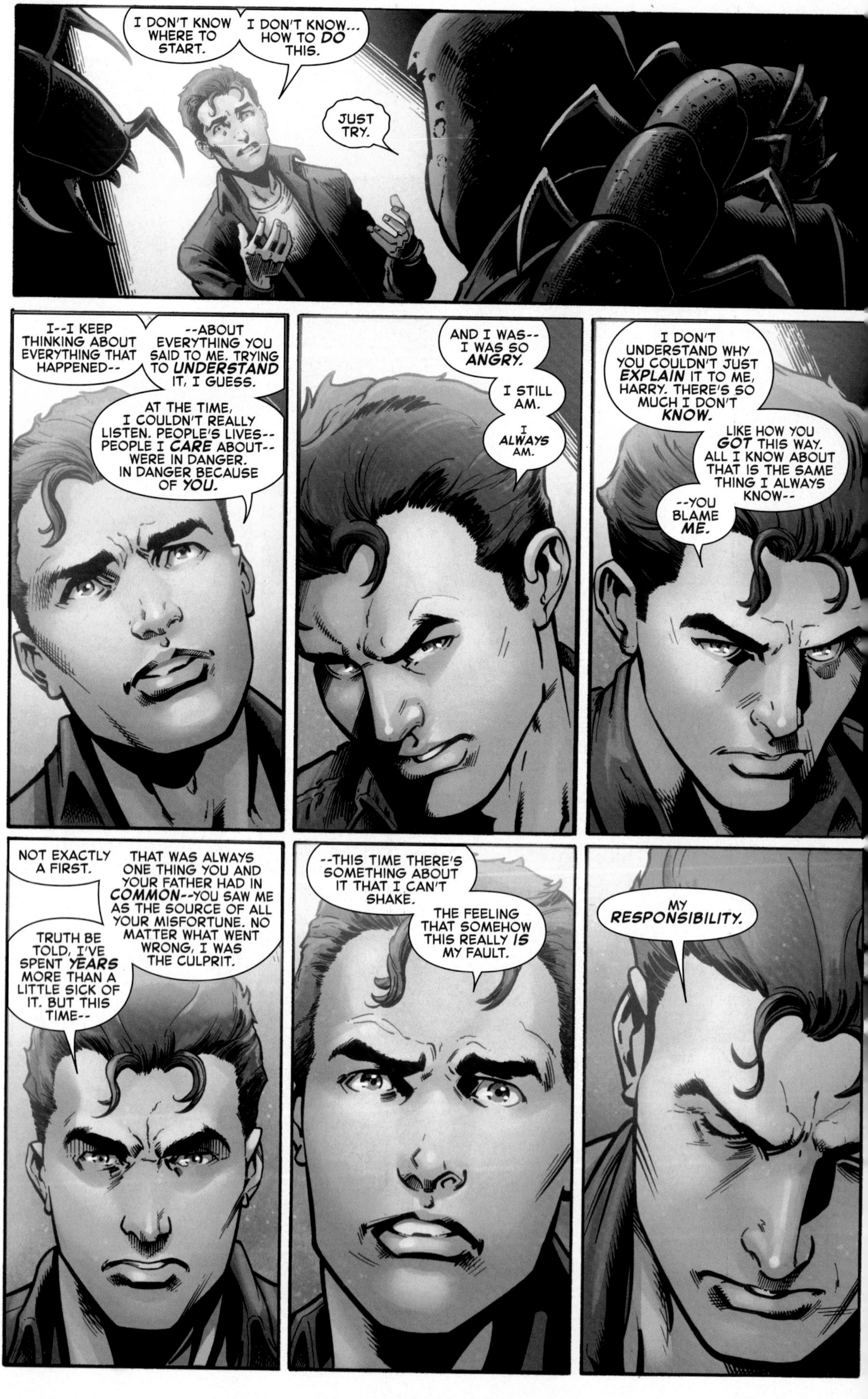
I DON'T KNOW WHERE TO START.
I DON'T KNOW... HOW TO DO THIS.
JUST TRY.
I--I KEEP THINKING ABOUT EVERYTHING THAT HAPPENED--
--ABOUT EVERYTHING YOU SAID TO ME. TRYING TO UNDERSTAND IT, I GUESS.
AT THE TIME, I COULDN'T REALLY LISTEN. PEOPLE'S LIVES--PEOPLE I CARE ABOUT--WERE IN DANGER. IN DANGER BECAUSE OF YOU.
AND I WAS--I WAS SO ANGRY.
I STILL AM.
I ALWAYS AM.
I DON'T UNDERSTAND WHY YOU COULDN'T JUST EXPLAIN IT TO ME, HARRY. THERE'S SO MUCH I DON'T KNOW.
LIKE HOW YOU GOT THIS WAY. ALL I KNOW ABOUT THAT IS THE SAME THING I ALWAYS KNOW--
--YOU BLAME ME.
NOT EXACTLY A FIRST.
THAT WAS ALWAYS ONE THING YOU AND YOUR FATHER HAD IN COMMON--YOU SAW ME AS THE SOURCE OF ALL YOUR MISFORTUNE. NO MATTER WHAT WENT WRONG, I WAS THE CULPRIT.
TRUTH BE TOLD, I'VE SPENT YEARS MORE THAN A LITTLE SICK OF IT. BUT THIS TIME--
--THIS TIME THERE'S SOMETHING ABOUT IT THAT I CAN'T SHAKE.
THE FEELING THAT SOMEHOW THIS REALLY IS MY FAULT.
MY RESPONSIBILITY.

WHAT YOU TRIED TO SHOW ME--HOW EVERYTHING I DO TO TRY TO MAKE THINGS BETTER ENDS UP MAKING THINGS WORSE--

--IT'S NOTHING I DON'T ALREADY *KNOW*, HARRY.

I'VE BEEN PUTTING THAT SUIT ON AND TRYING TO DO THIS SINCE I WAS A *KID*. TRYING TO ATONE FOR THIS STUPID, SELFISH *CHOICE* I MADE--A CHOICE THAT ENDED UP TAKING THE MAN WHO RAISED ME.

I DIDN'T MEAN FOR THAT TO HAPPEN, I COULDN'T HAVE *KNOWN*--

--BUT HOW IS THAT DIFFERENT FROM SO MANY OF THE ONES THAT *FOLLOWED*?

I KNOW I'M TRYING TO DO SOMETHING GOOD. I KNOW I'M TRYING TO *SAVE PEOPLE*. AND I GET THAT I *HAVE*. I'VE DONE GOOD THINGS. SPIDER-MAN HAS SAVED *LIVES*.

BUT IF THE PEOPLE I LOVE KEEP PAYING THE *PRICE* FOR THAT...IS THAT ANY LESS SELFISH THAN WHAT STARTED ALL THIS OFF? IS MY NEED TO TRY MAKING SOMETHING RIGHT JUST MAKING MORE THINGS GO *WRONG*?

WHAT IF THAT KID WHO PUT THE MASK ON SO THAT HE COULD BE SOMEONE ELSE--SOMEONE *BETTER*, SOMEONE WHO *DIDN'T* GET HIS UNCLE KILLED--IS THE ONE TO BLAME?

MAYBE NONE OF US CHANGE AS MUCH AS WE *THINK* WE DO. MAYBE I'M JUST TRYING TO RUN FROM GUILT AND TAKING EVERYONE ALONG WITH ME.

SOMETIMES I FEEL LIKE I'M TRAPPED IN THIS CYCLE OF PUNISHMENT FOR ALL OF IT. LOCKED IN PLACE, NEVER MOVING FORWARD.

LIKE THIS WILL *ALWAYS* BE MY LIFE.

YOU SAID YOU WANTED TO *SHOW* ME HELL, HARRY--

--WELL, MAYBE I'M *LIVING* IN IT RIGHT NOW.

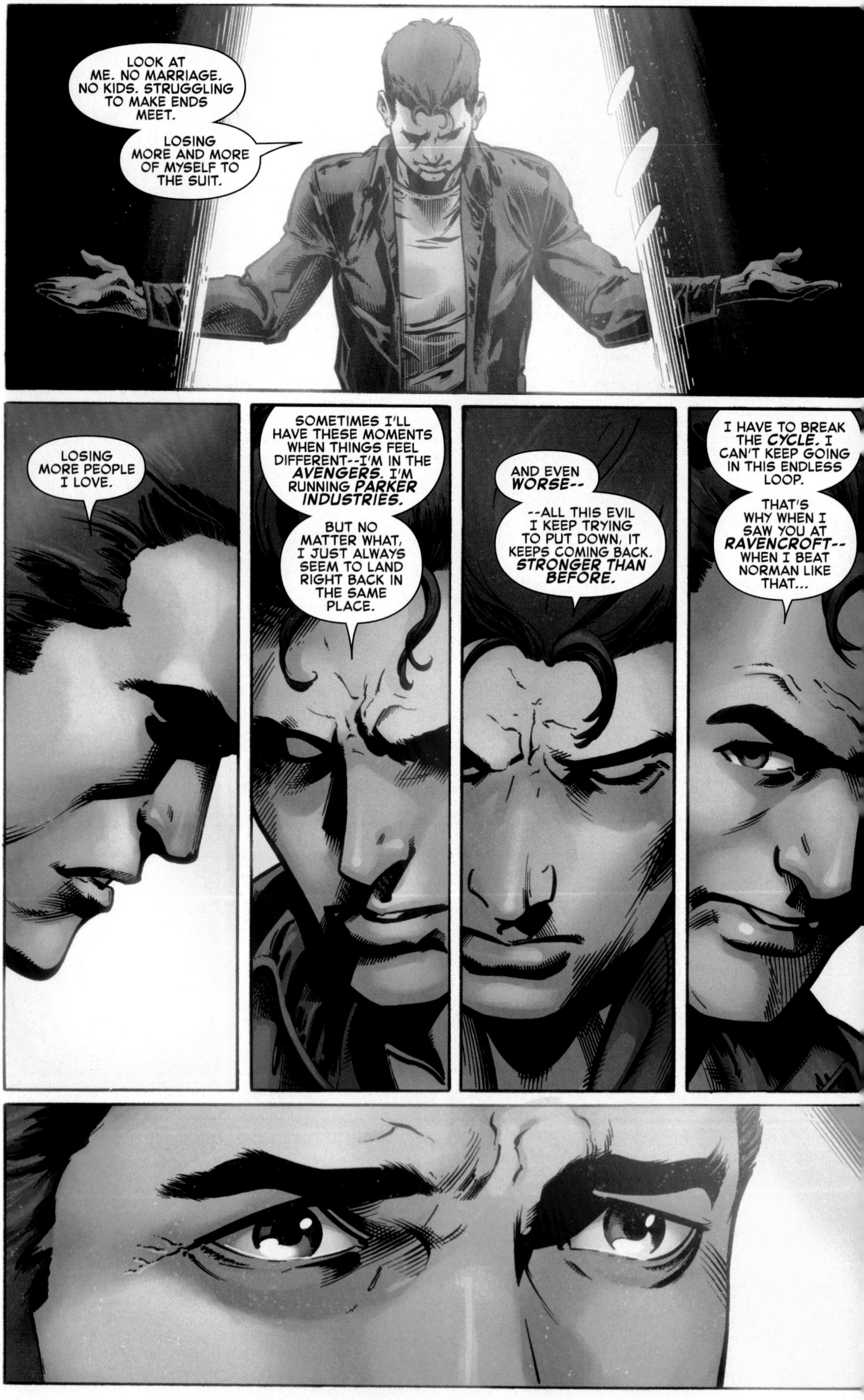
LOOK AT ME. NO MARRIAGE. NO KIDS. STRUGGLING TO MAKE ENDS MEET.
LOSING MORE AND MORE OF MYSELF TO THE SUIT.
LOSING MORE PEOPLE I LOVE.
SOMETIMES I'LL HAVE THESE MOMENTS WHEN THINGS FEEL DIFFERENT--I'M IN THE AVENGERS. I'M RUNNING PARKER INDUSTRIES.
BUT NO MATTER WHAT, I JUST ALWAYS SEEM TO LAND RIGHT BACK IN THE SAME PLACE.
AND EVEN WORSE--
--ALL THIS EVIL I KEEP TRYING TO PUT DOWN, IT KEEPS COMING BACK. STRONGER THAN BEFORE.
I HAVE TO BREAK THE CYCLE. I CAN'T KEEP GOING IN THIS ENDLESS LOOP.
THAT'S WHY WHEN I SAW YOU AT RAVENCROFT--WHEN I BEAT NORMAN LIKE THAT...

I SAID I WAS DONE. WITH *BOTH* OF YOU.

BUT I KNOW THAT WAS A *LIE.*

FOR GOD'S SAKE, YOU'RE MY *BEST FRIEND,* HAR. WHEN YOU KEPT KILLING ME OVER AND OVER, YOU KNOW WHAT I *SAW?* ALL OF US TOGETHER--THE WAY IT *WAS.*

IT HURT WORSE THAN *ANYTHING* YOU DID TO ME.

I KEEP TRYING TO GO BACK. I WOULD GIVE *ANYTHING* TO GO BACK. TO FIX THINGS.

AND WHILE I'M BACK THERE, THINKING ABOUT WHAT I'D DO DIFFERENTLY, EVERYTHING IN FRONT OF ME JUST KEEPS GETTING WORSE.

I HAVE TO *STOP.*

JUST TELL ME HOW TO FIX IT, HARRY. TELL ME WHAT TO *DO.*

I'LL CONFESS TO ANYTHING, *DO* ANYTHING--

--JUST TELL ME WHAT TO DO.

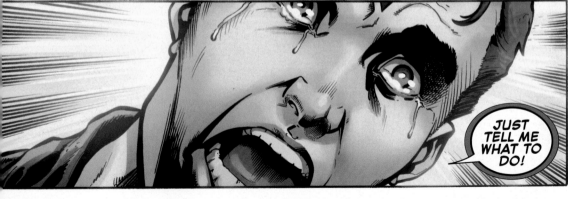

*JUST TELL ME WHAT TO DO!*

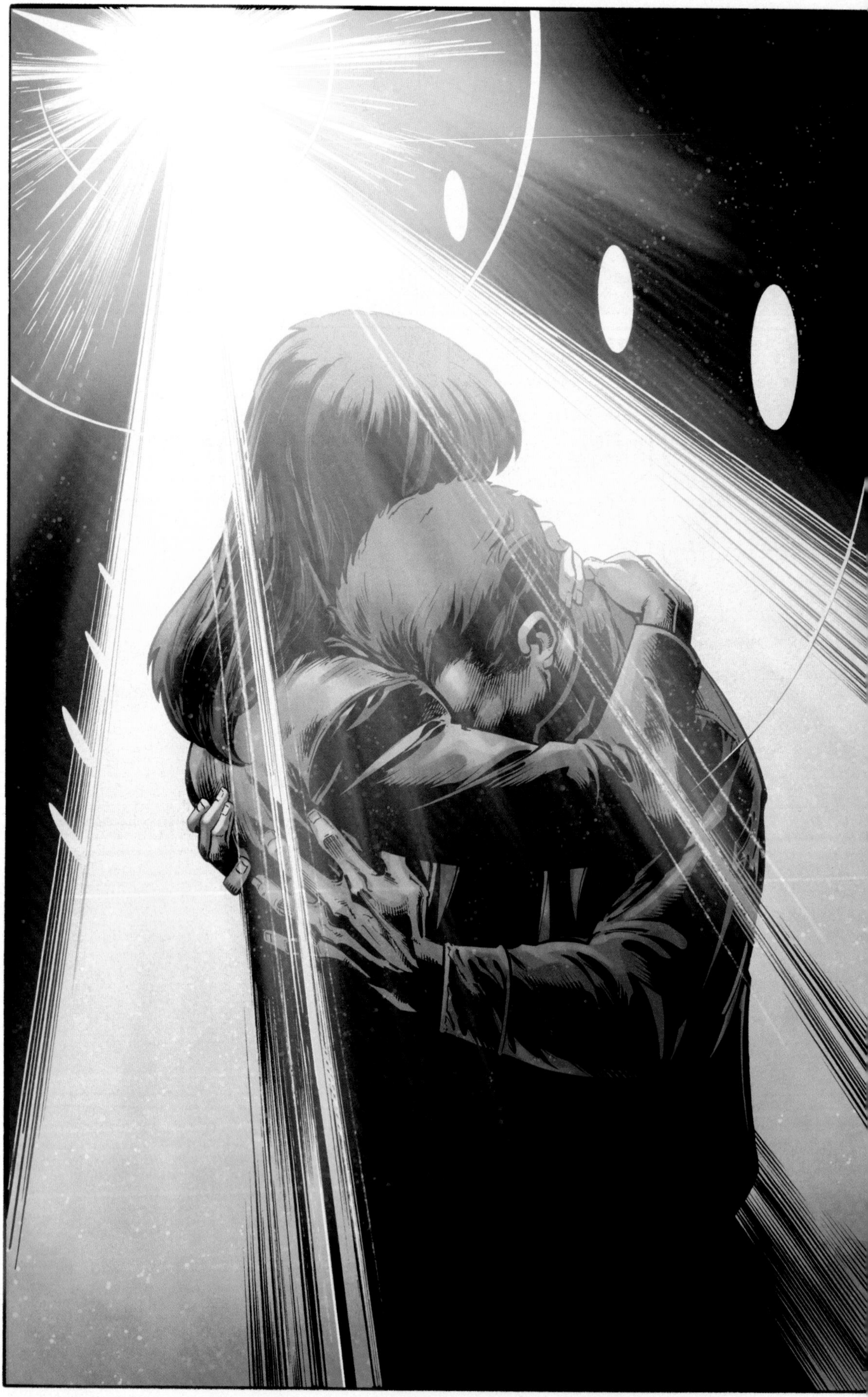

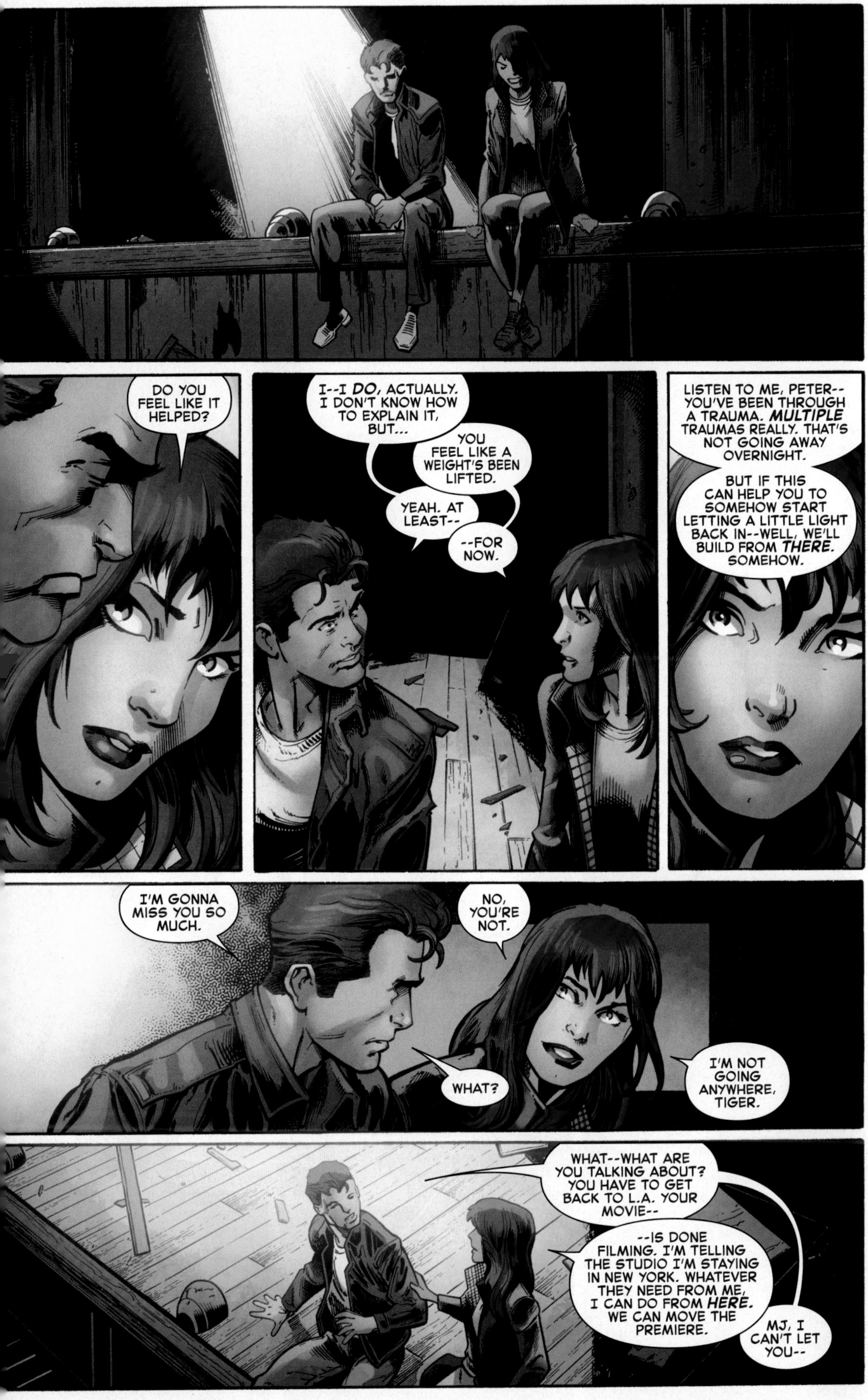
DO YOU FEEL LIKE IT HELPED?
I--I DO, ACTUALLY. I DON'T KNOW HOW TO EXPLAIN IT, BUT...
YOU FEEL LIKE A WEIGHT'S BEEN LIFTED.
YEAH. AT LEAST--
--FOR NOW.
LISTEN TO ME, PETER--YOU'VE BEEN THROUGH A TRAUMA. MULTIPLE TRAUMAS REALLY. THAT'S NOT GOING AWAY OVERNIGHT.
BUT IF THIS CAN HELP YOU TO SOMEHOW START LETTING A LITTLE LIGHT BACK IN--WELL, WE'LL BUILD FROM THERE. SOMEHOW.
I'M GONNA MISS YOU SO MUCH.
NO, YOU'RE NOT.
WHAT?
I'M NOT GOING ANYWHERE, TIGER.
WHAT--WHAT ARE YOU TALKING ABOUT? YOU HAVE TO GET BACK TO L.A. YOUR MOVIE--
--IS DONE FILMING. I'M TELLING THE STUDIO I'M STAYING IN NEW YORK. WHATEVER THEY NEED FROM ME, I CAN DO FROM HERE. WE CAN MOVE THE PREMIERE.
MJ, I CAN'T LET YOU--

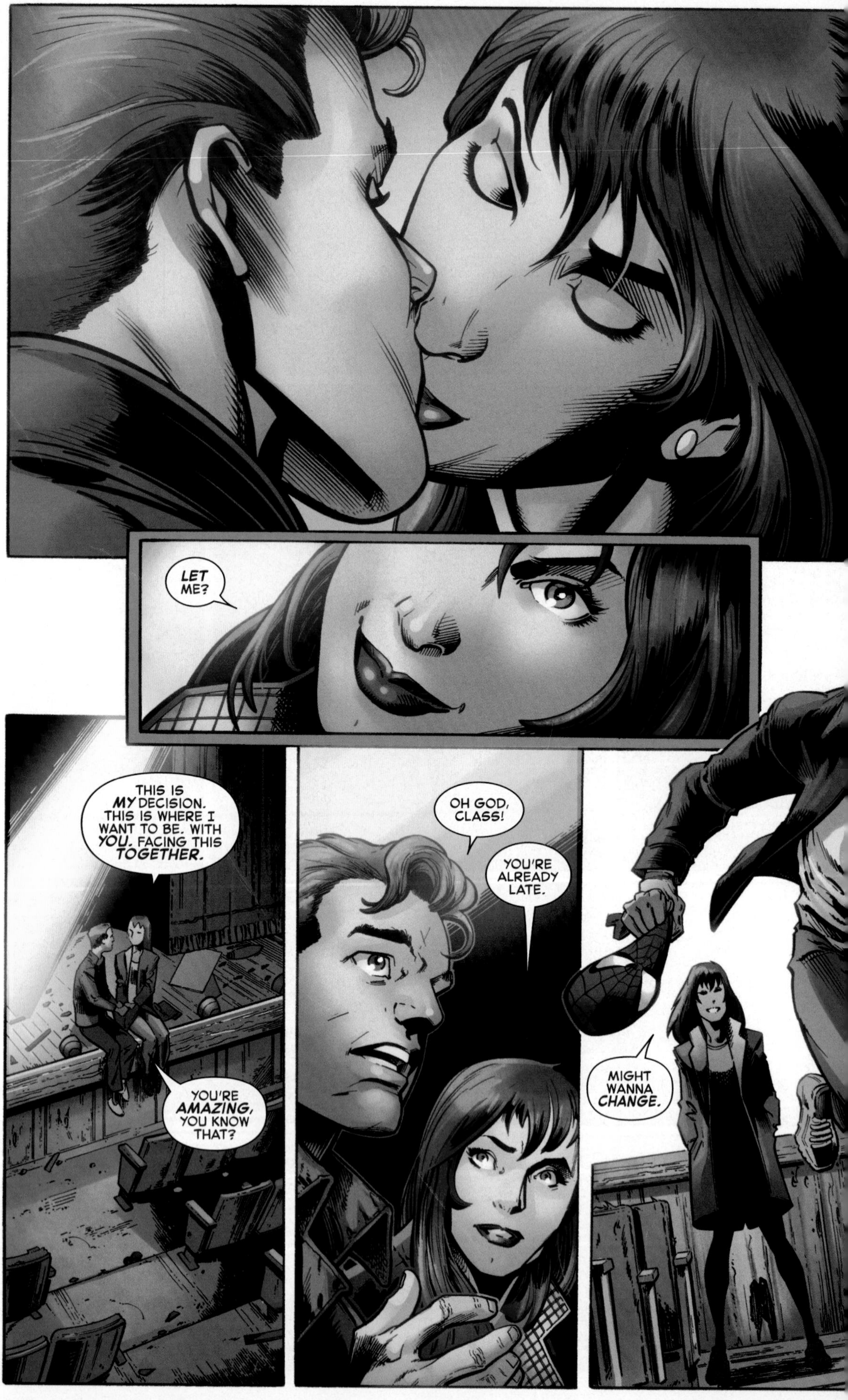
LET ME?
THIS IS MY DECISION. THIS IS WHERE I WANT TO BE. WITH YOU. FACING THIS TOGETHER.
YOU'RE AMAZING, YOU KNOW THAT?
OH GOD, CLASS!
YOU'RE ALREADY LATE.
MIGHT WANNA CHANGE.

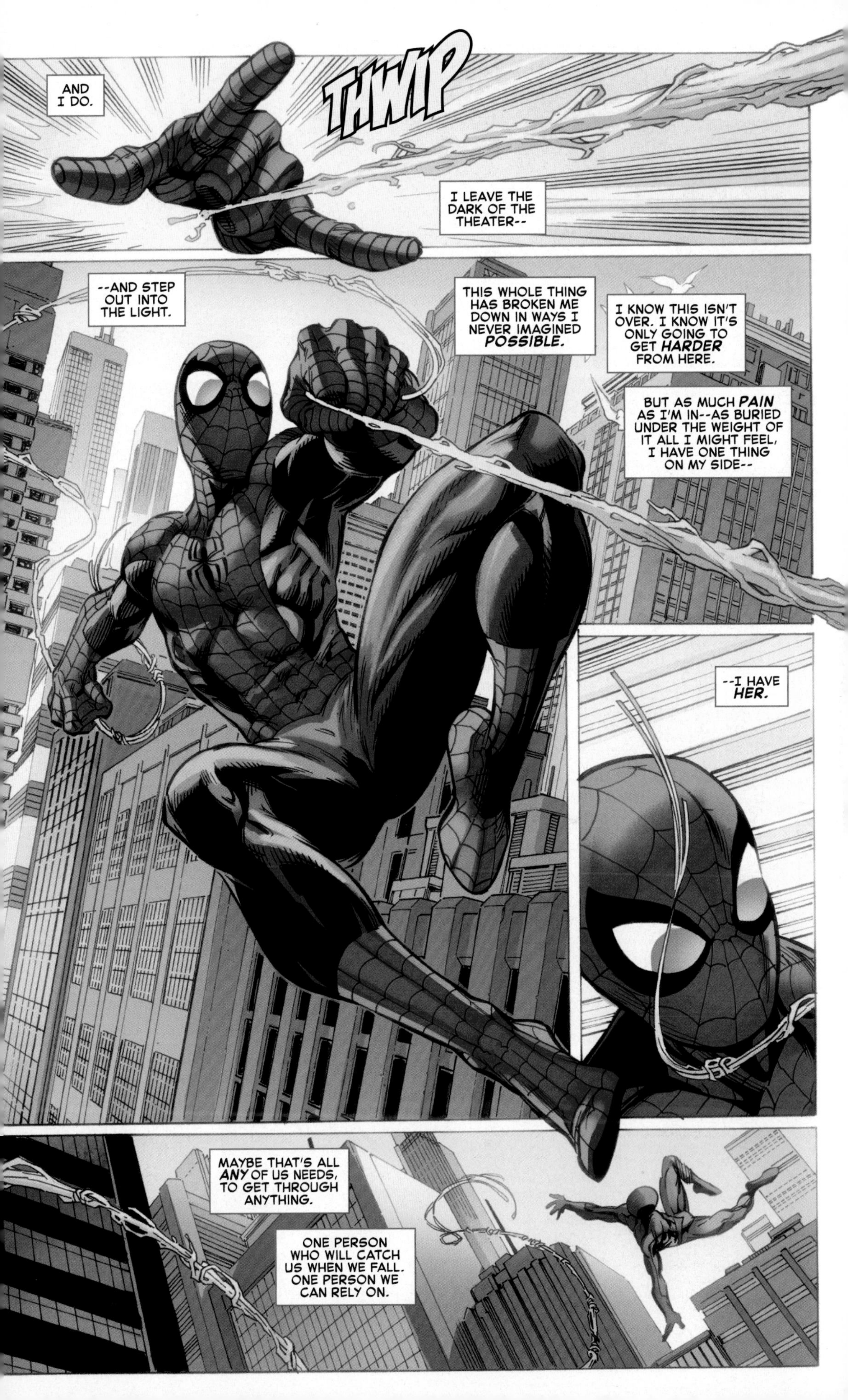

AND I DO.
THWIP
I LEAVE THE DARK OF THE THEATER--
--AND STEP OUT INTO THE LIGHT.
THIS WHOLE THING HAS BROKEN ME DOWN IN WAYS I NEVER IMAGINED POSSIBLE.
I KNOW THIS ISN'T OVER. I KNOW IT'S ONLY GOING TO GET HARDER FROM HERE.
BUT AS MUCH PAIN AS I'M IN--AS BURIED UNDER THE WEIGHT OF IT ALL I MIGHT FEEL, I HAVE ONE THING ON MY SIDE--
--I HAVE HER.
MAYBE THAT'S ALL ANY OF US NEEDS, TO GET THROUGH ANYTHING.
ONE PERSON WHO WILL CATCH US WHEN WE FALL. ONE PERSON WE CAN RELY ON.

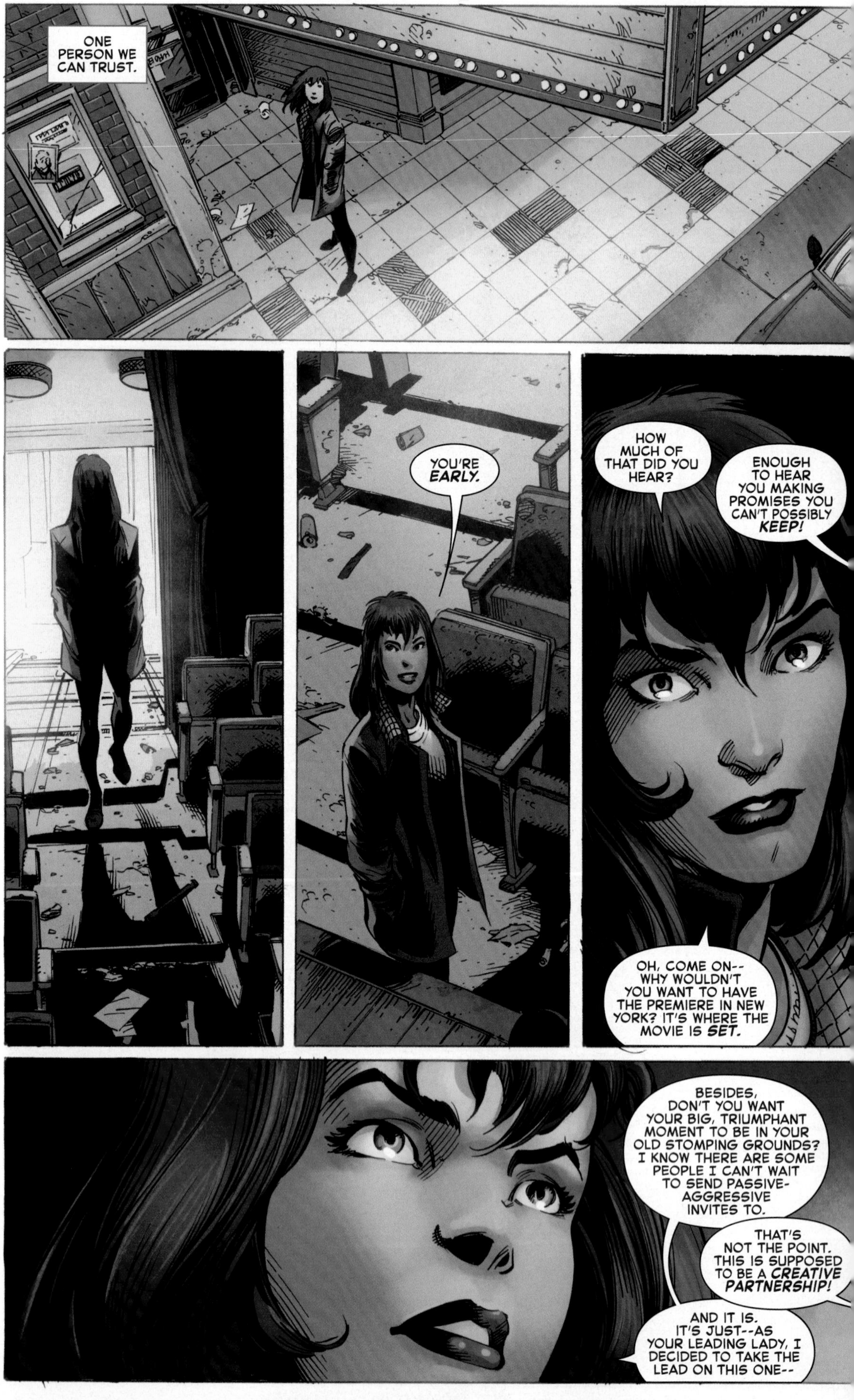
ONE PERSON WE CAN TRUST.
YOU'RE *EARLY.*
HOW MUCH OF THAT DID YOU HEAR?
ENOUGH TO HEAR YOU MAKING PROMISES YOU CAN'T POSSIBLY *KEEP!*
OH, COME ON-- WHY WOULDN'T YOU WANT TO HAVE THE PREMIERE IN NEW YORK? IT'S WHERE THE MOVIE IS *SET.*
BESIDES, DON'T YOU WANT YOUR BIG, TRIUMPHANT MOMENT TO BE IN YOUR OLD STOMPING GROUNDS? I KNOW THERE ARE SOME PEOPLE I CAN'T WAIT TO SEND PASSIVE-AGGRESSIVE INVITES TO.
THAT'S NOT THE POINT. THIS IS SUPPOSED TO BE A *CREATIVE PARTNERSHIP!*
AND IT IS. IT'S JUST--AS YOUR LEADING LADY, I DECIDED TO TAKE THE LEAD ON THIS ONE--

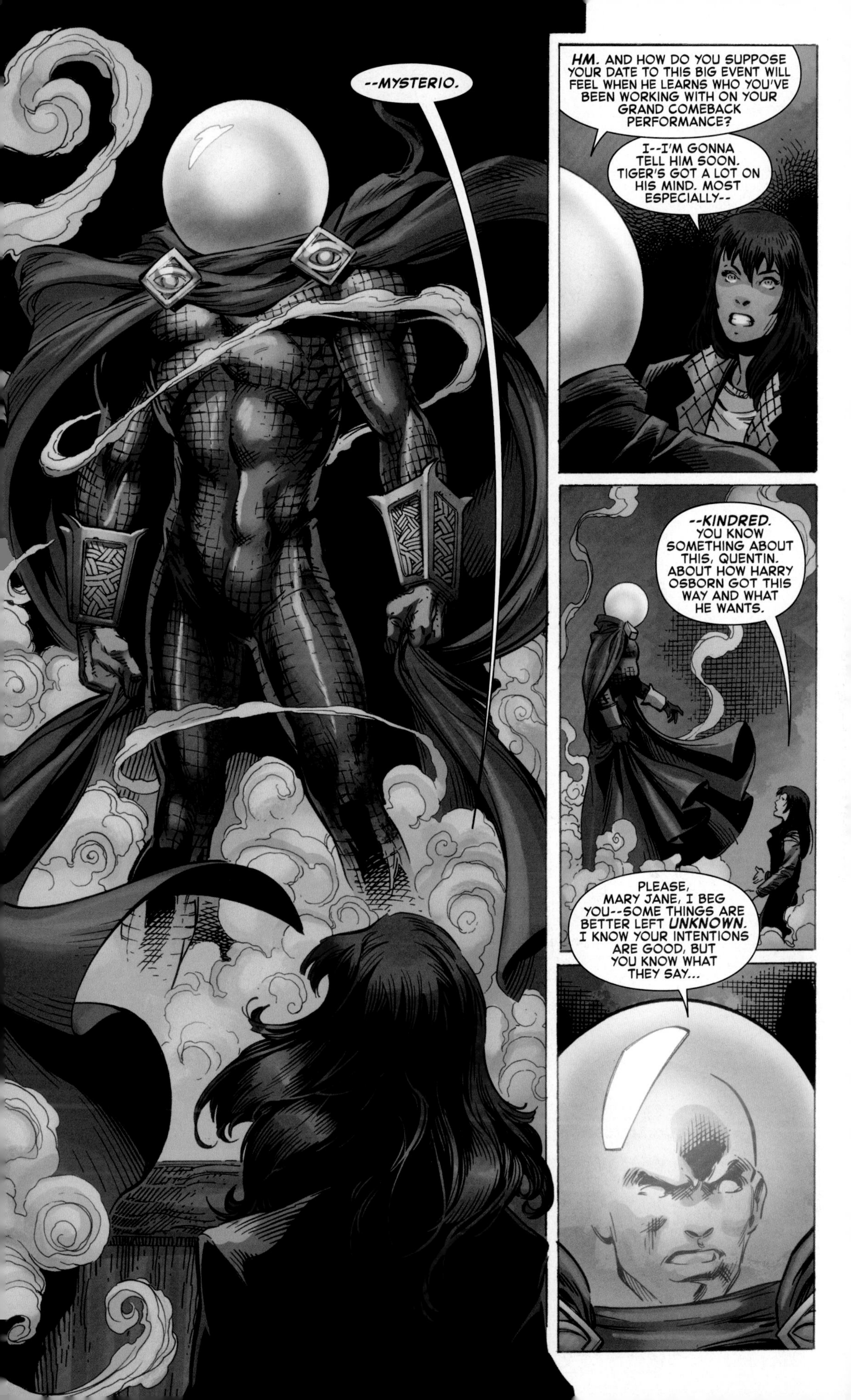
--MYSTERIO.
HM. AND HOW DO YOU SUPPOSE YOUR DATE TO THIS BIG EVENT WILL FEEL WHEN HE LEARNS WHO YOU'VE BEEN WORKING WITH ON YOUR GRAND COMEBACK PERFORMANCE?
I--I'M GONNA TELL HIM SOON. TIGER'S GOT A LOT ON HIS MIND. MOST ESPECIALLY--
--KINDRED. YOU KNOW SOMETHING ABOUT THIS, QUENTIN. ABOUT HOW HARRY OSBORN GOT THIS WAY AND WHAT HE WANTS.
PLEASE, MARY JANE, I BEG YOU--SOME THINGS ARE BETTER LEFT UNKNOWN. I KNOW YOUR INTENTIONS ARE GOOD, BUT YOU KNOW WHAT THEY SAY...

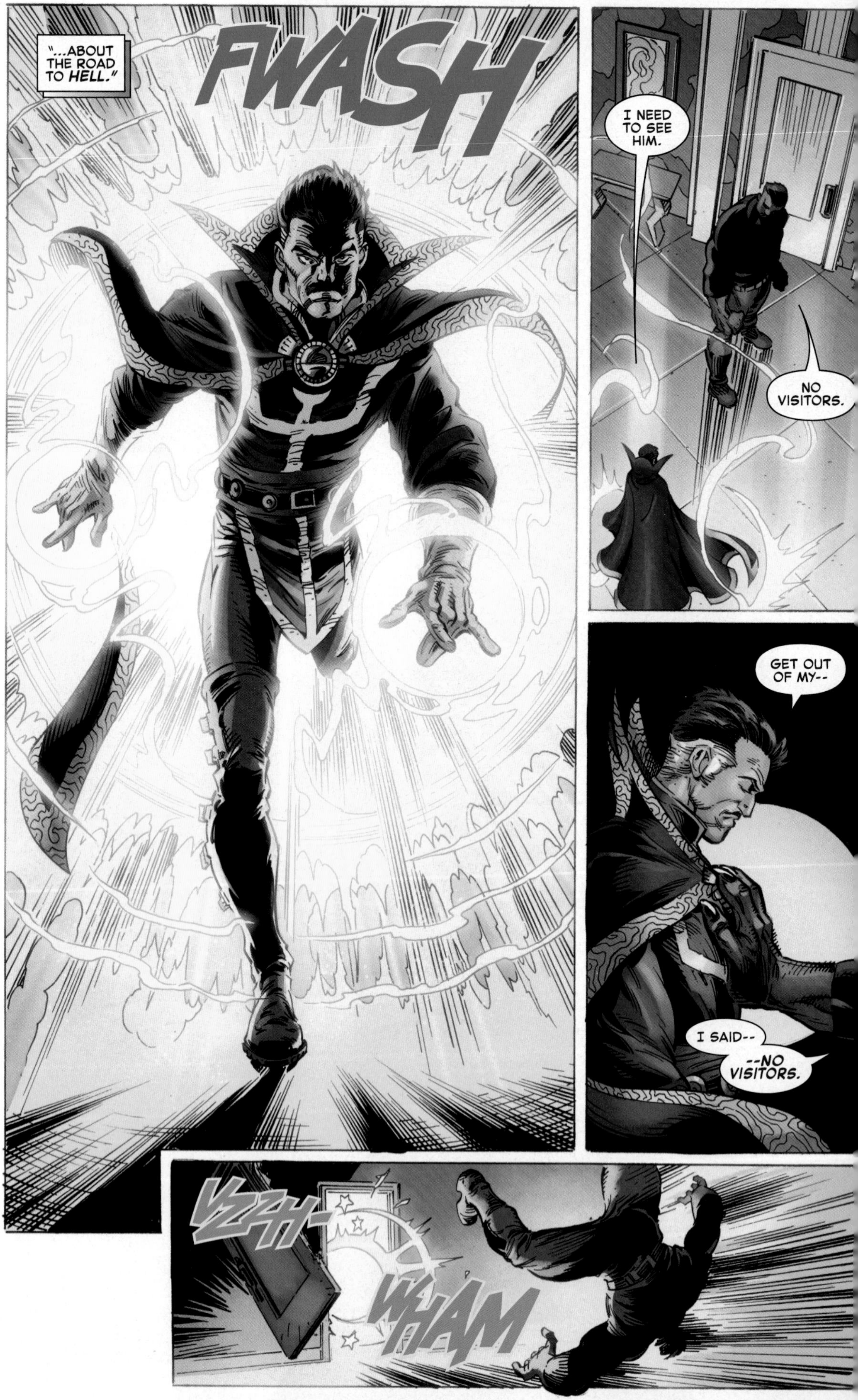
"...ABOUT THE ROAD TO HELL."
FWASH
I NEED TO SEE HIM.
NO VISITORS.
GET OUT OF MY--
I SAID--
--NO VISITORS.
VZZH-
WHAM

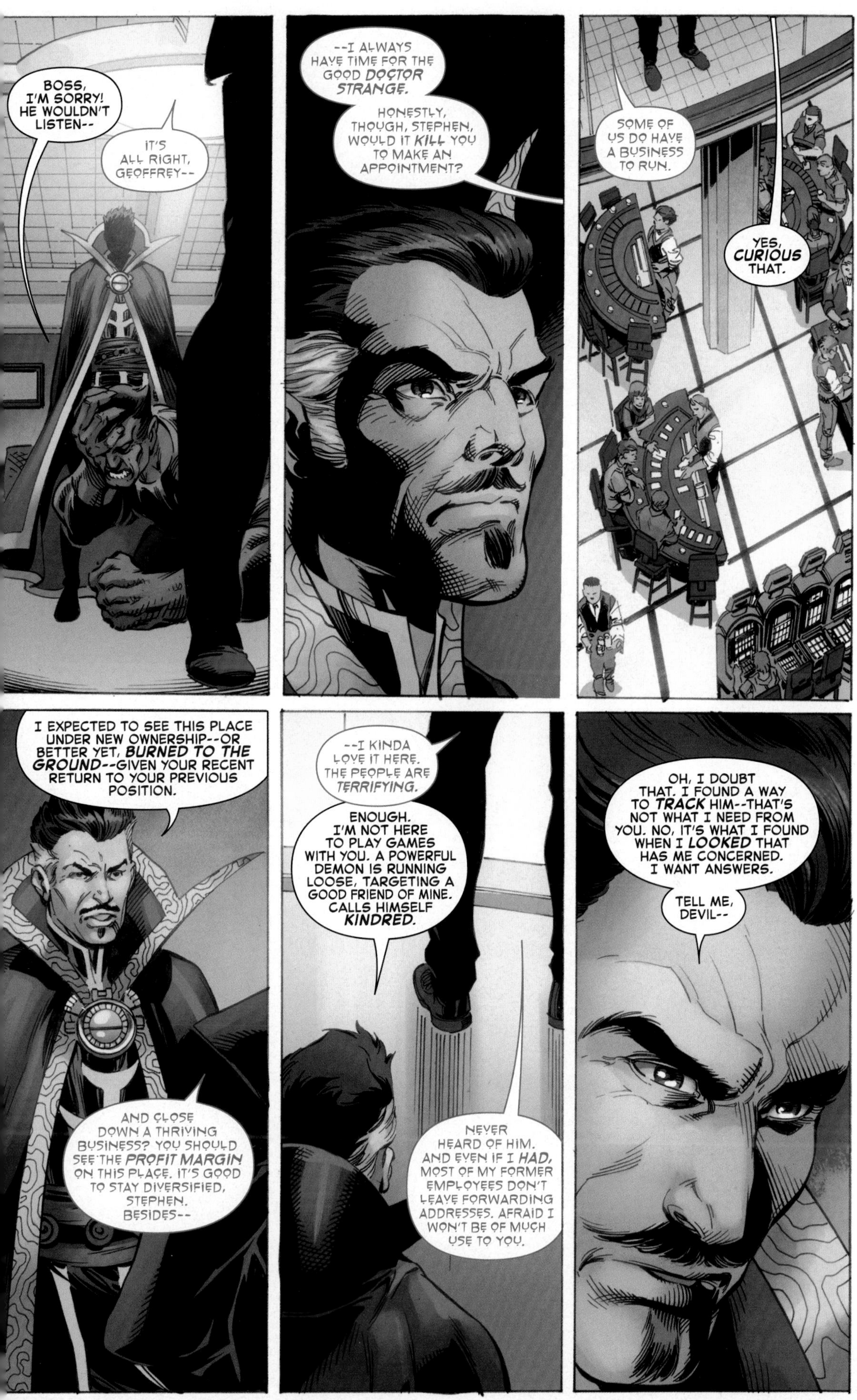
BOSS, I'M SORRY! HE WOULDN'T LISTEN--
IT'S ALL RIGHT, GEOFFREY--
--I ALWAYS HAVE TIME FOR THE GOOD DOCTOR STRANGE.
HONESTLY, THOUGH, STEPHEN, WOULD IT KILL YOU TO MAKE AN APPOINTMENT?
SOME OF US DO HAVE A BUSINESS TO RUN.
YES, CURIOUS THAT.
I EXPECTED TO SEE THIS PLACE UNDER NEW OWNERSHIP--OR BETTER YET, BURNED TO THE GROUND--GIVEN YOUR RECENT RETURN TO YOUR PREVIOUS POSITION.
AND CLOSE DOWN A THRIVING BUSINESS? YOU SHOULD SEE THE PROFIT MARGIN ON THIS PLACE. IT'S GOOD TO STAY DIVERSIFIED, STEPHEN. BESIDES--
--I KINDA LOVE IT HERE. THE PEOPLE ARE TERRIFYING.
ENOUGH. I'M NOT HERE TO PLAY GAMES WITH YOU. A POWERFUL DEMON IS RUNNING LOOSE, TARGETING A GOOD FRIEND OF MINE. CALLS HIMSELF KINDRED.
NEVER HEARD OF HIM. AND EVEN IF I HAD, MOST OF MY FORMER EMPLOYEES DON'T LEAVE FORWARDING ADDRESSES. AFRAID I WON'T BE OF MUCH USE TO YOU.
OH, I DOUBT THAT. I FOUND A WAY TO TRACK HIM--THAT'S NOT WHAT I NEED FROM YOU. NO, IT'S WHAT I FOUND WHEN I LOOKED THAT HAS ME CONCERNED. I WANT ANSWERS.
TELL ME, DEVIL--

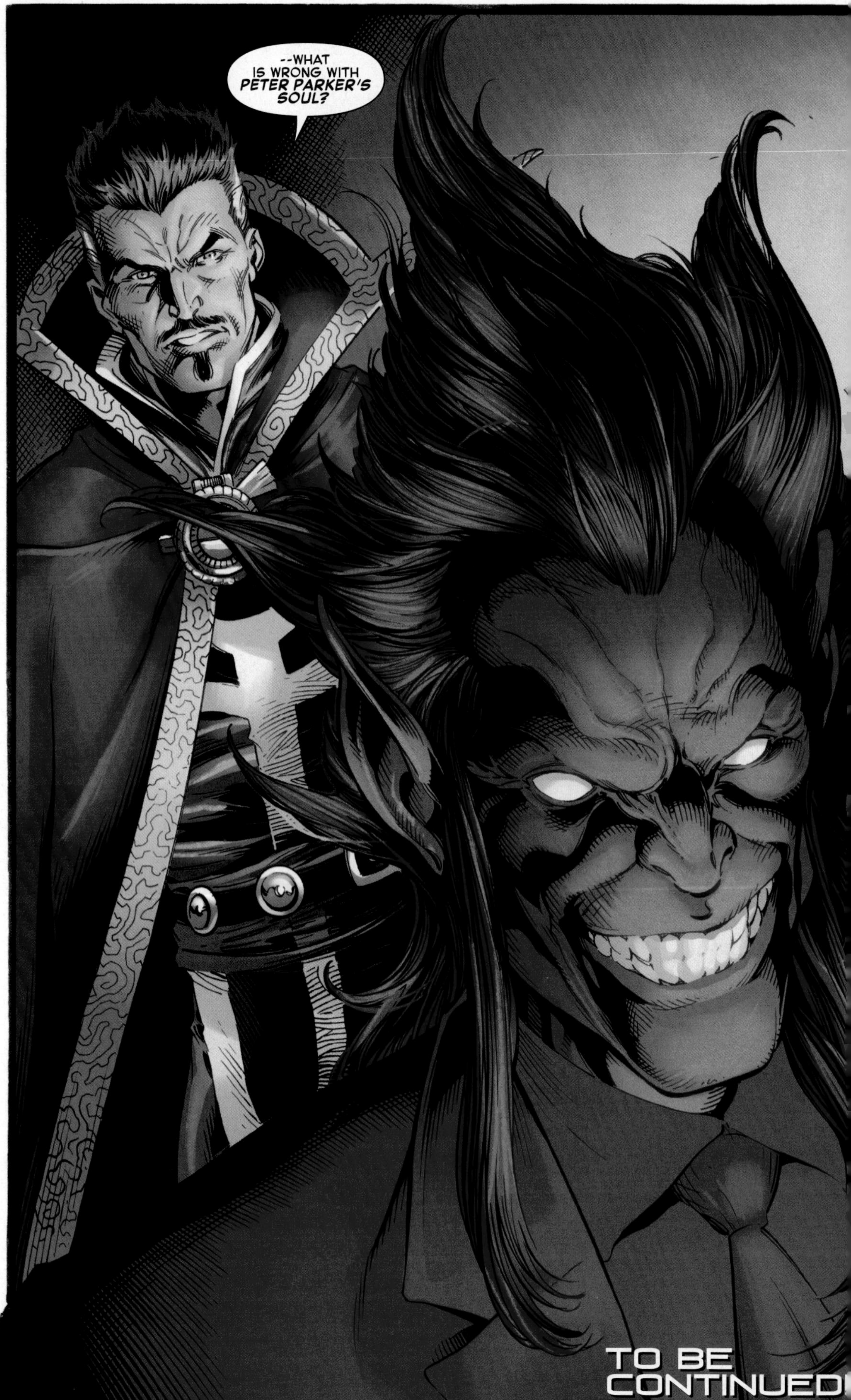
--WHAT IS WRONG WITH PETER PARKER'S SOUL?
TO BE CONTINUED

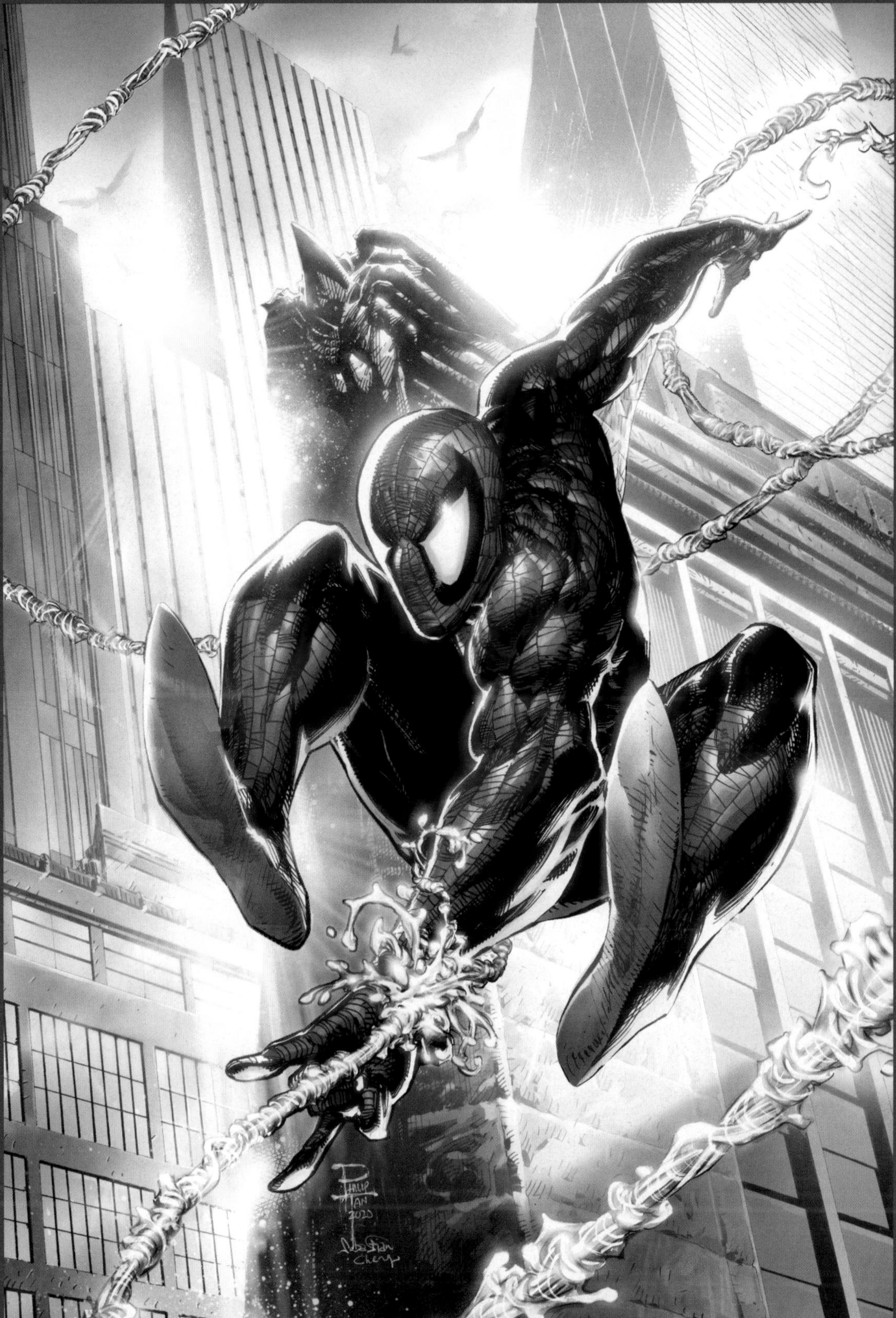

#56 VARIANT BY PHILIP TAN & SEBASTIAN CHENG

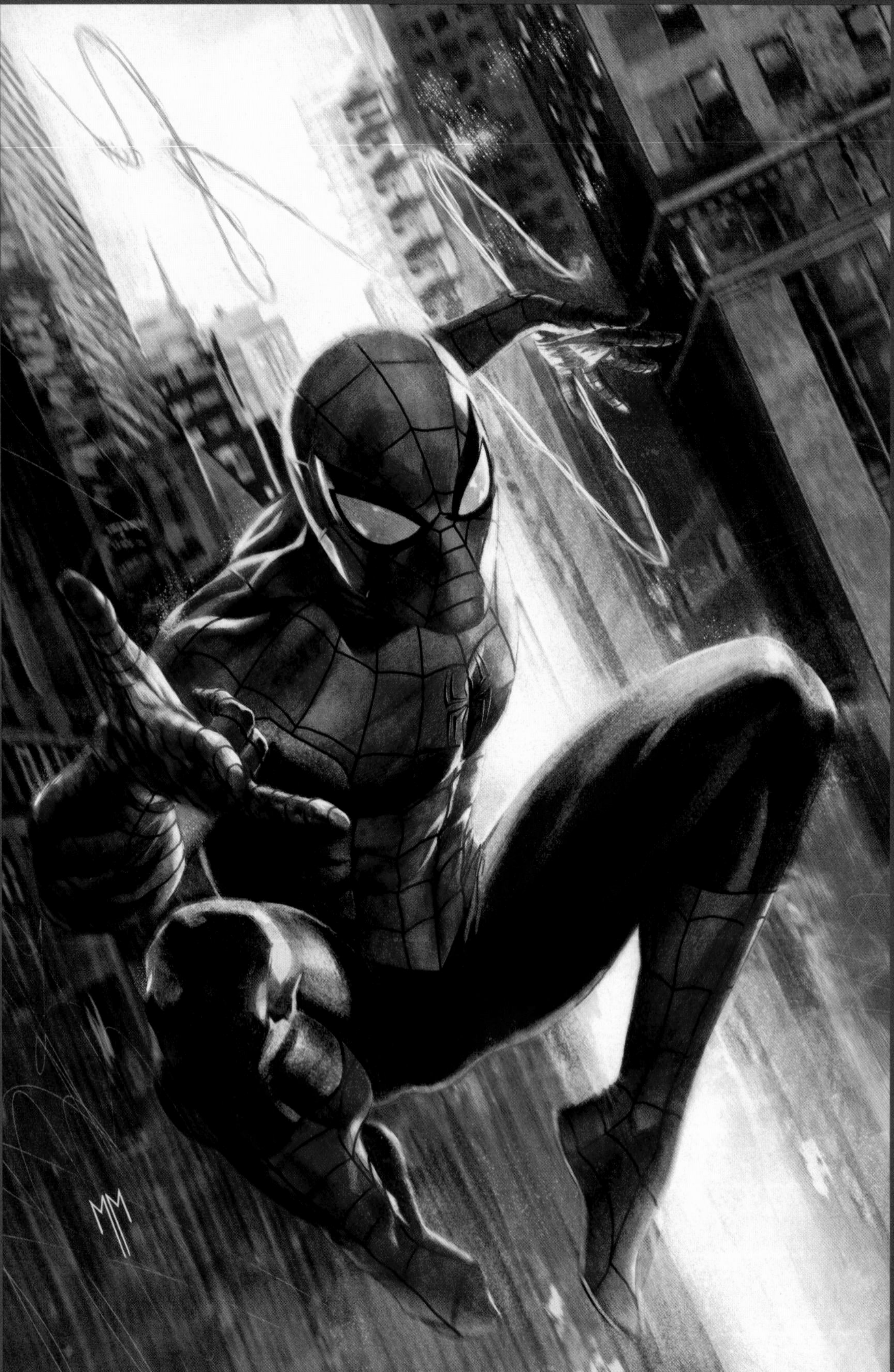
MM

#57 VARIANT BY MARCO MASTRAZZO

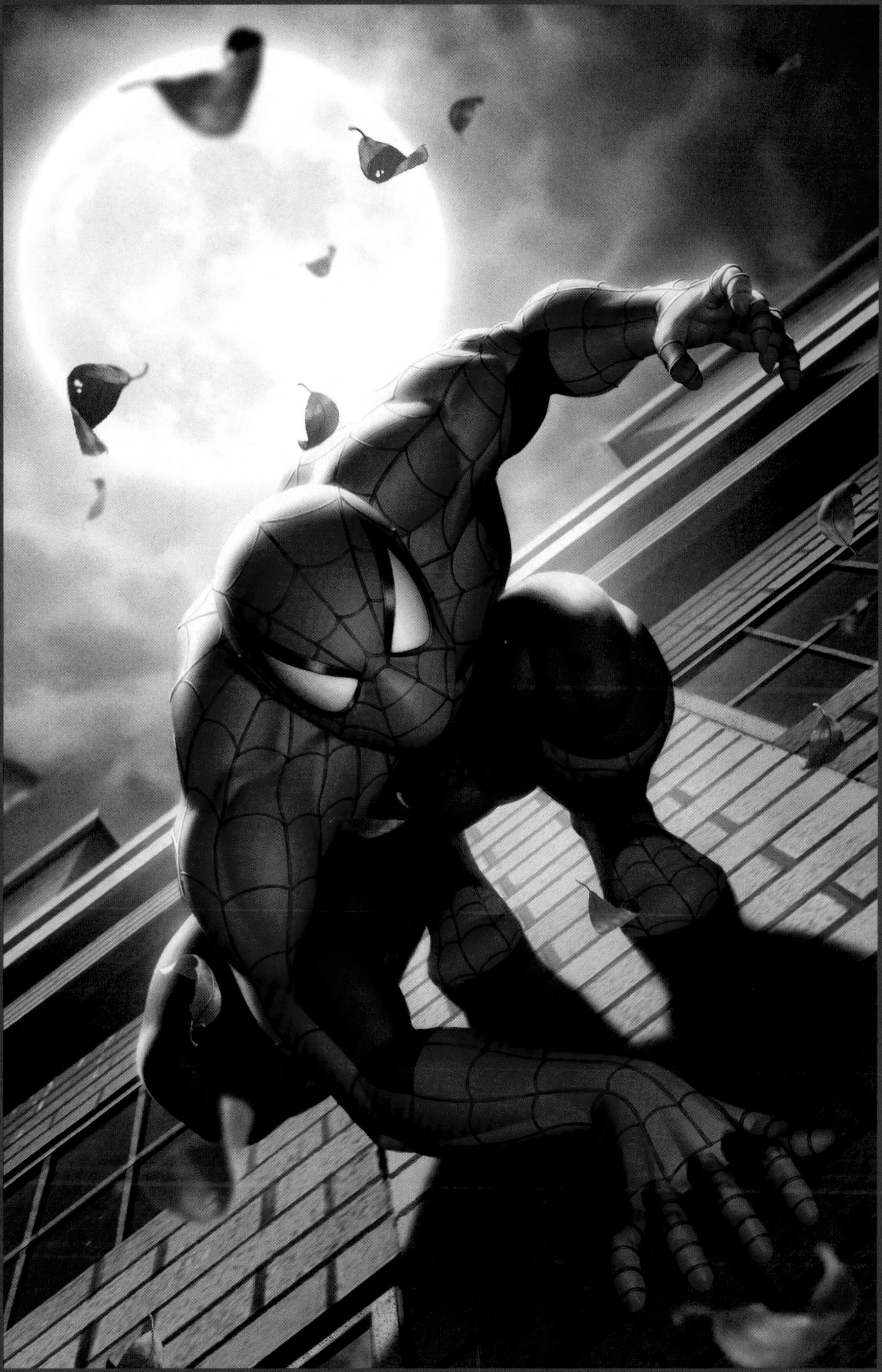

#58 VARIANT BY JUNGGEUN YOON

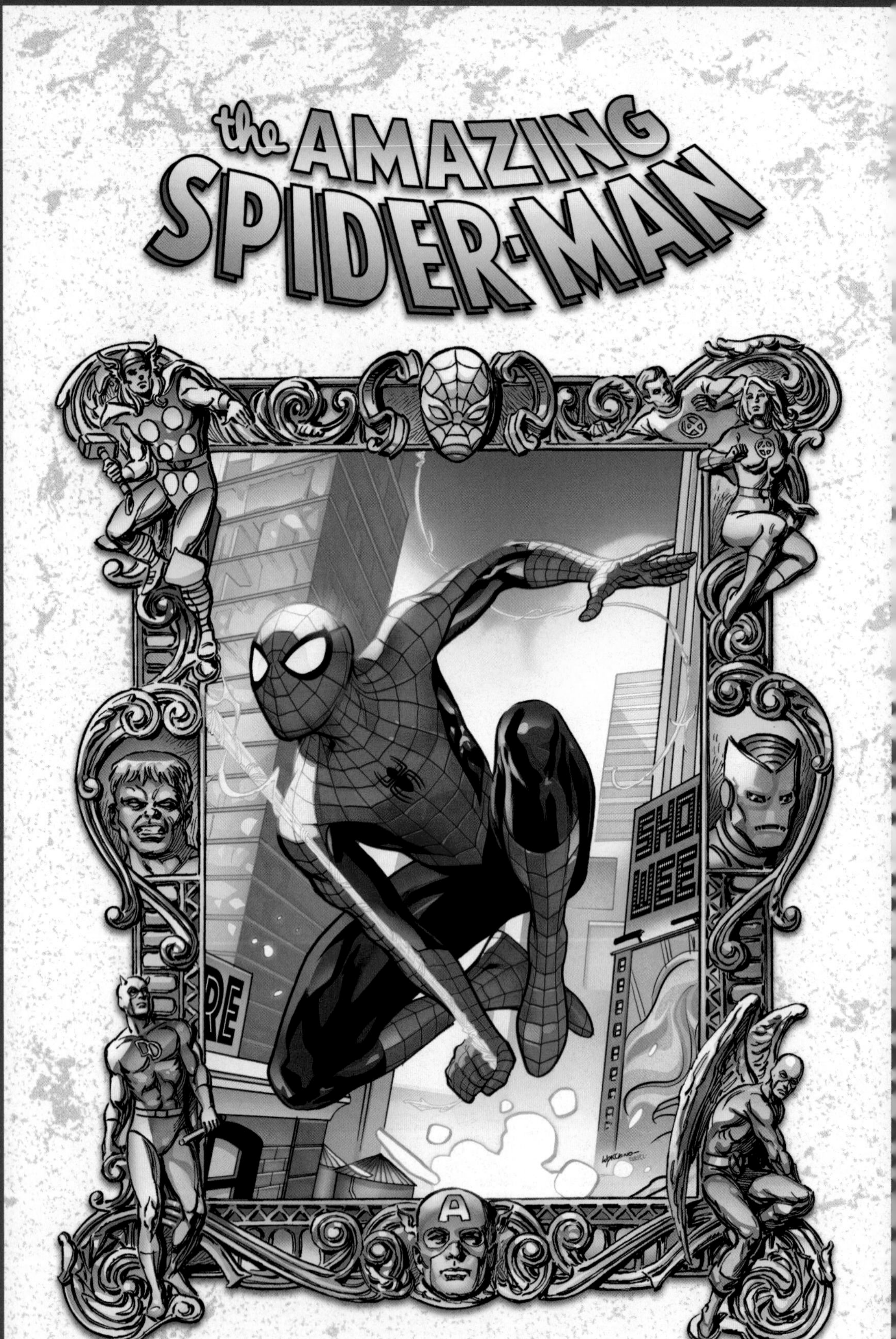
the AMAZING
SPIDER-MAN

#59 MARVEL MASTERWORKS VARIANT BY EMA LUPACCHINO & DAVID CURIEL

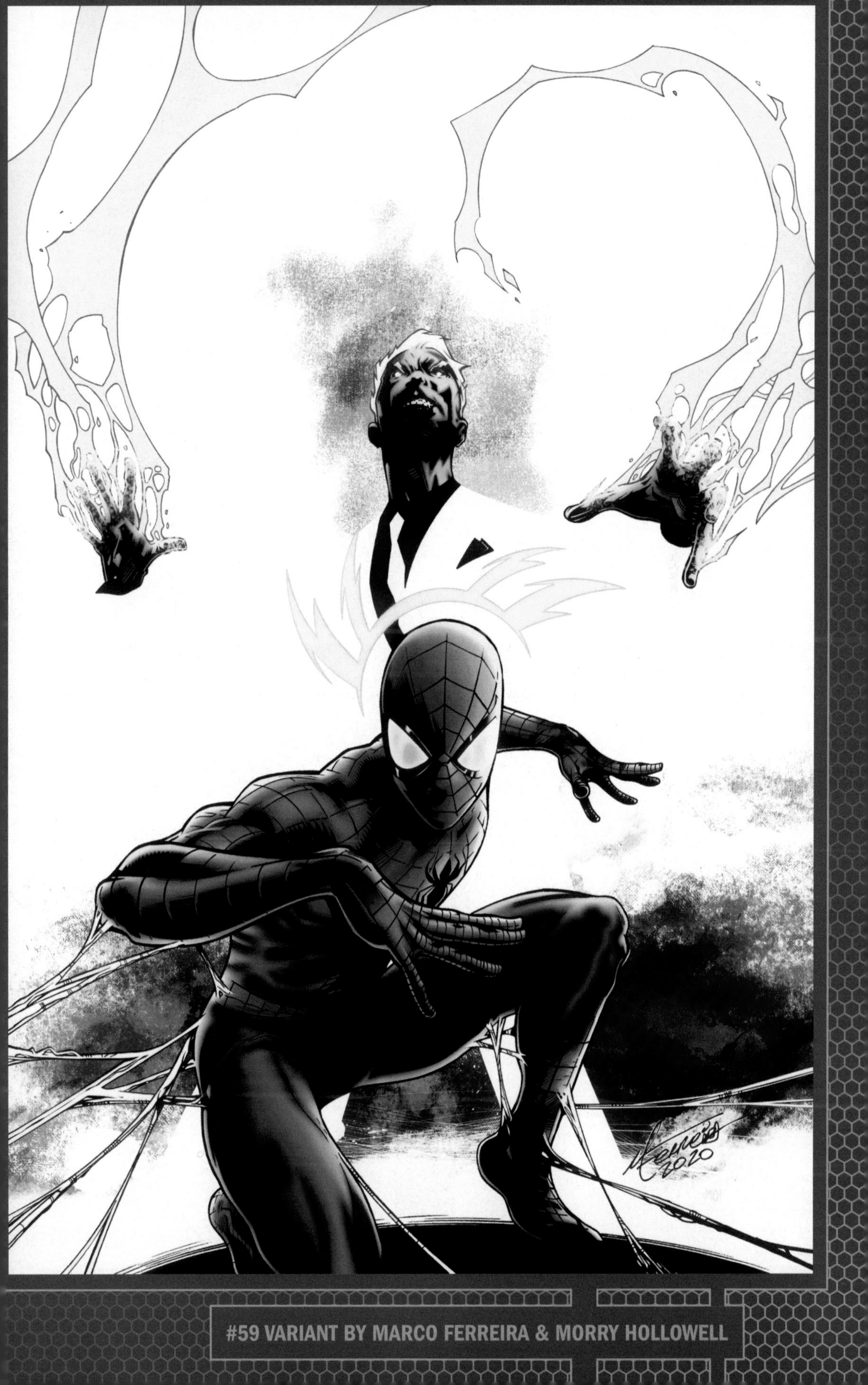

#59 VARIANT BY MARCO FERREIRA & MORRY HOLLOWELL

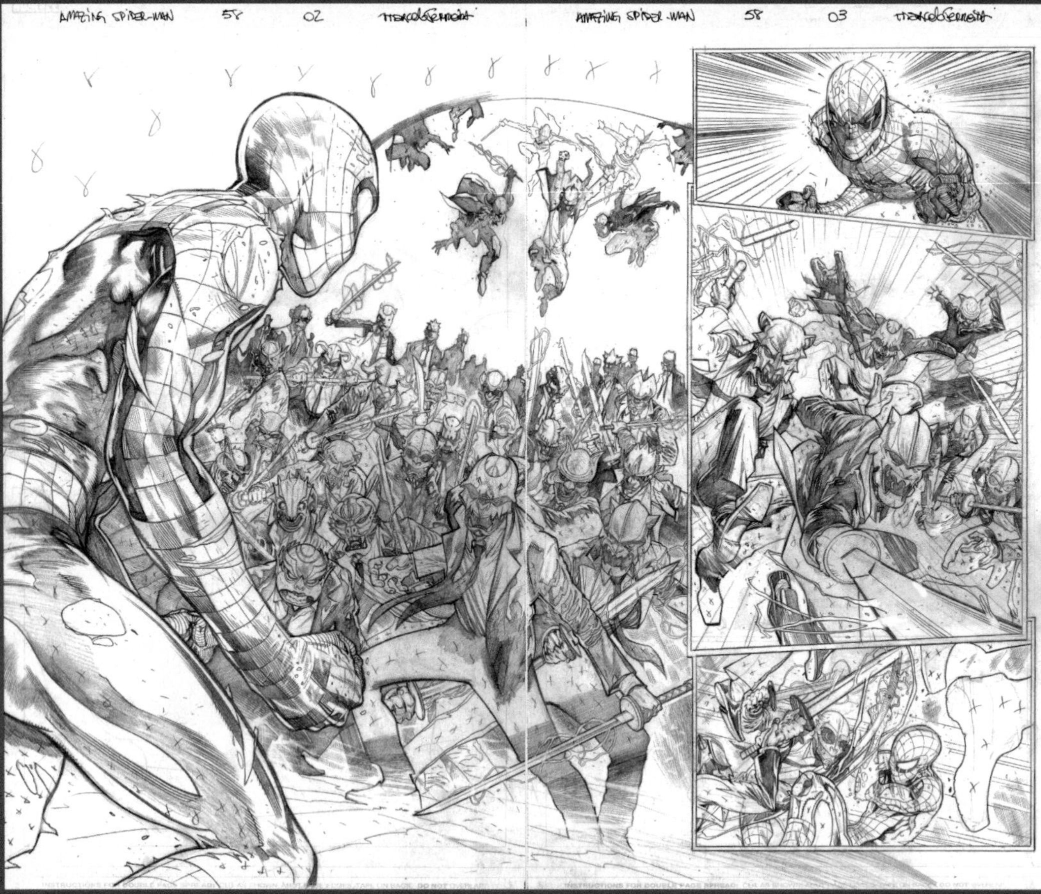
AMAZING SPIDER-MAN 58 02
AMAZING SPIDER-MAN 58 03

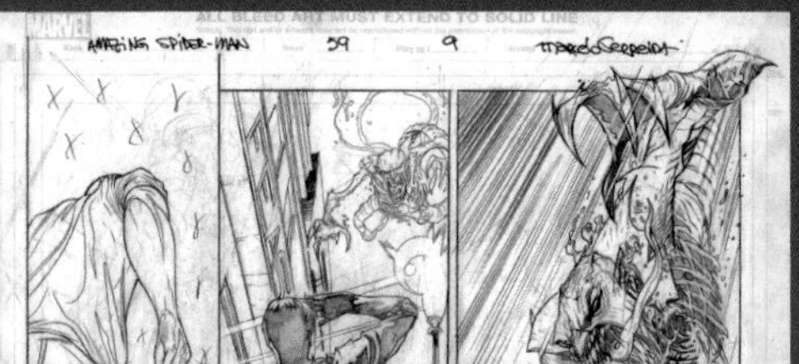
AMAZING SPIDER-MAN 59 9

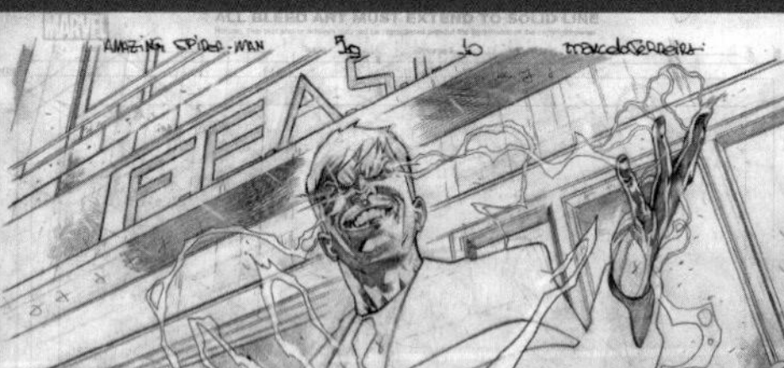

#58, PAGES 2-3 & #59, PAGES 9-10 PENCILS BY MARCELO FERREIRA

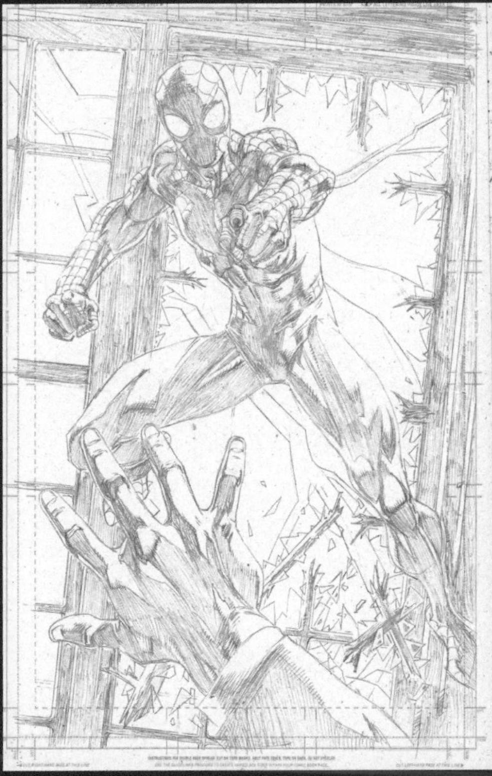

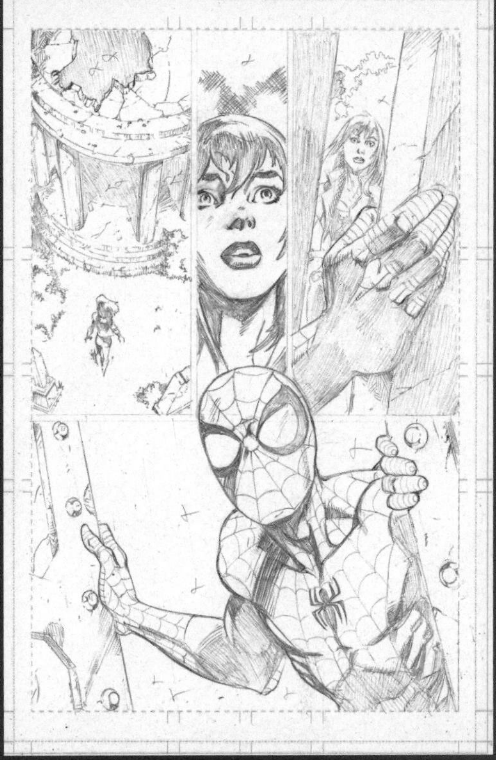

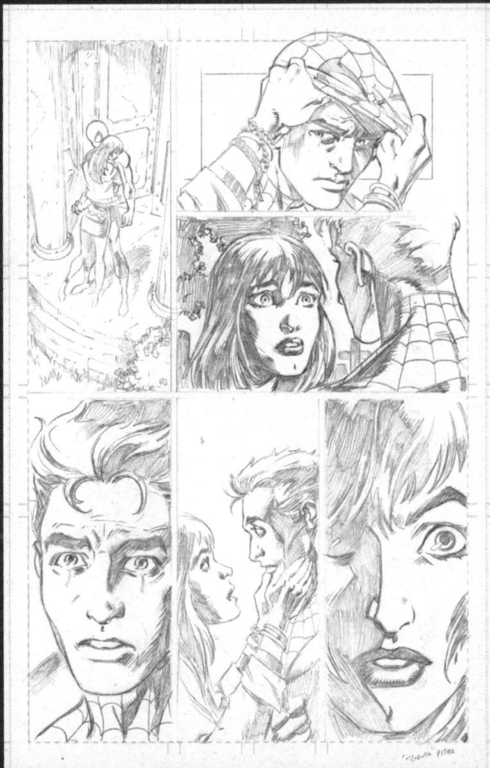

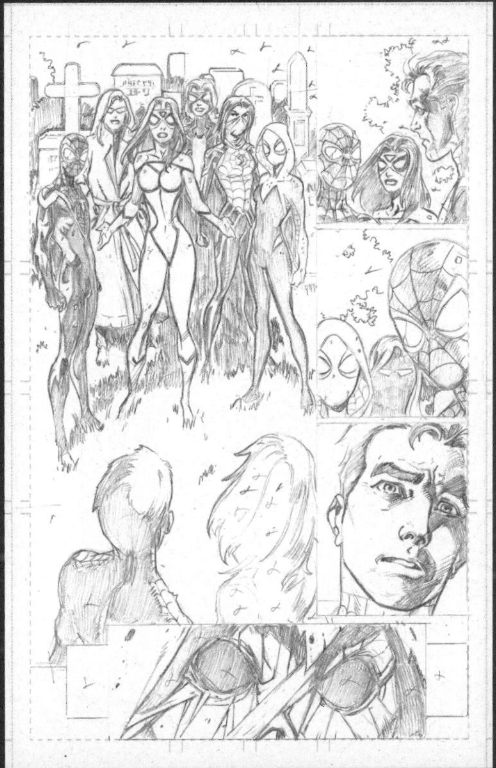

#56, PAGE 30 & #57, PAGES 2-4 PENCILS BY MARK BAGLEY

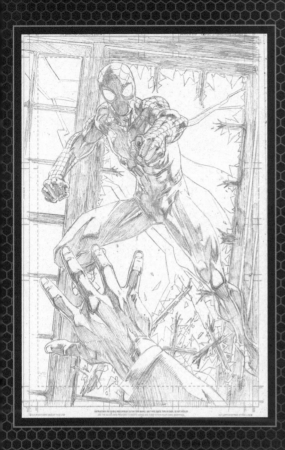

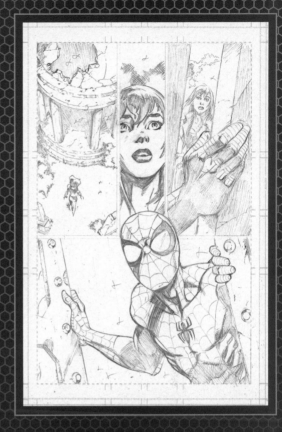

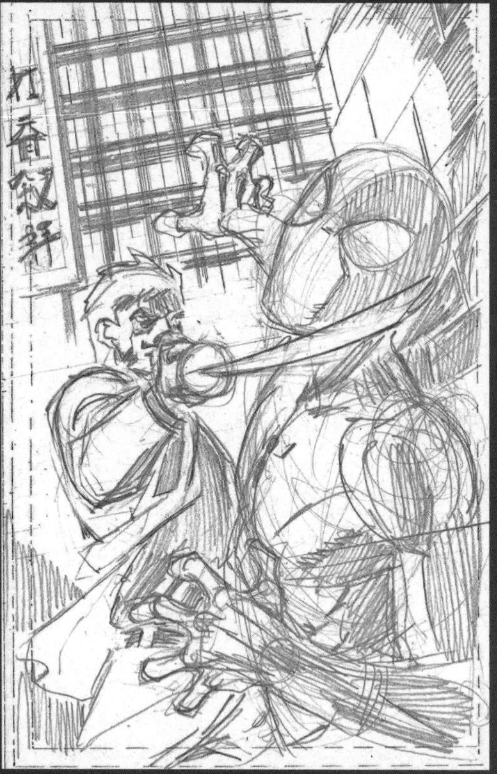
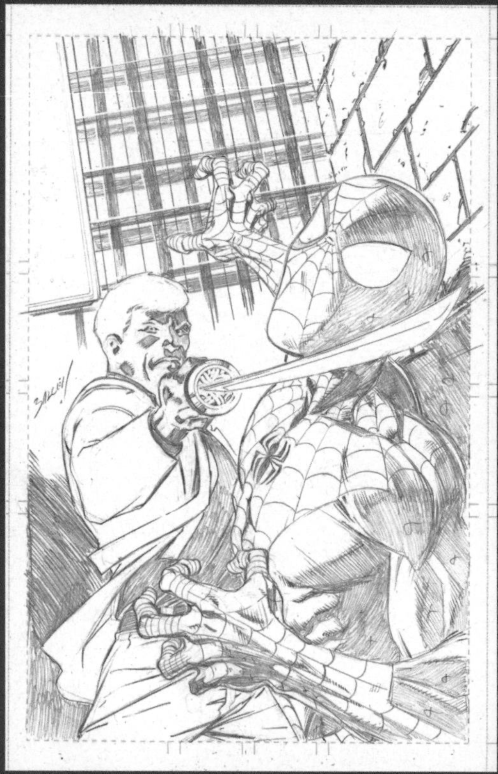
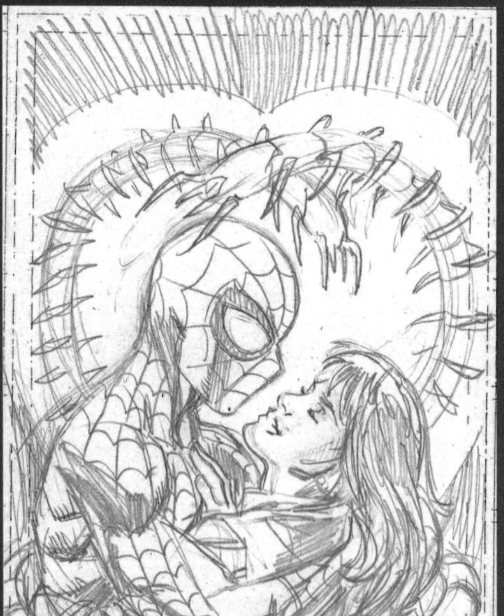
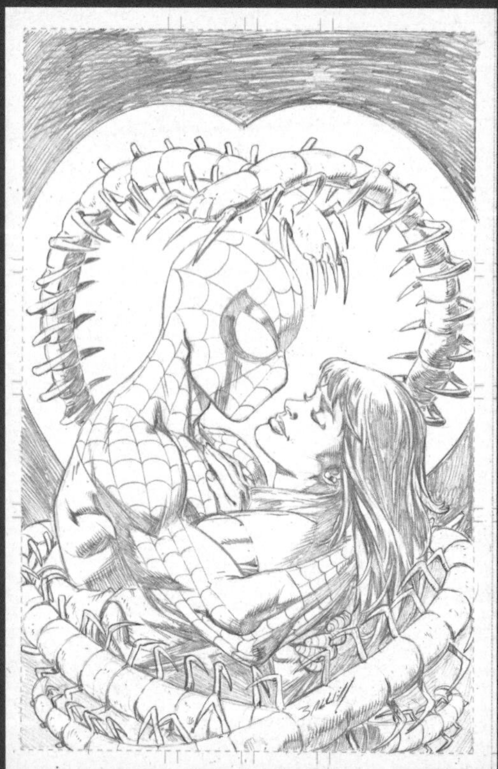

#59-60, COVER SKETCHES & PENCILS BY MARK BAGLEY

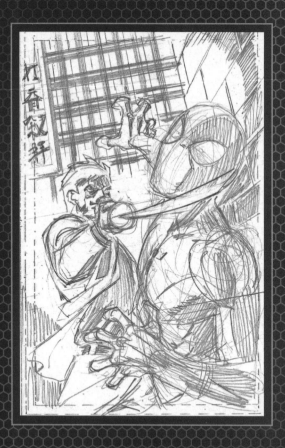

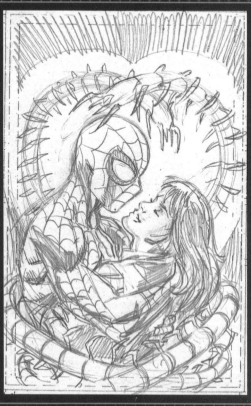